25.95

THE ELEMENTS OF MUSIC:
CONCEPTS AND APPLICATIONS
Volume One

THE ELEMENTS OF MUSIC:
CONCEPTS AND APPLICATIONS
Volume One

RALPH TUREK

The University of Akron

Consulting Editor in Music
ALLAN W. SCHINDLER
Eastman School of Music

ALFRED A. KNOPF

New York • 1988

THIS IS A BORZOI BOOK

PUBLISHED BY ALFRED A. KNOPF, INC.

First Edition

98765432

Copyright © 1988 by Alfred A. Knopf, Inc.

Library of Congress Cataloging-in-Publication Data

Turek, Ralph.
    The elements of music.

    Discography: p.
    Includes index.
    1. Music—Theory, Elementary.   I. Title.
MT7.T9   1988   781   87-21374
ISBN 0-394-33972-X (v. 1)

Manufactured in the United States of America

Why Study Music Theory?

What is it that separates the truly great musical performers from all others? Chances are, it is not their technical prowess *in and of itself,* but rather, the insight they bring to a piece of music. How many times have you read a review of a concert in which the music critic discussed the conductor's baton technique? The critic quite rightly assumes a professional level of competence in this respect and dwells, instead, on that which truly distinguishes this conductor from all others—his or her interpretation of the music.

Interpretation is actually a form of musical analysis—partly at an intuitive level. Since you have probably spent many years learning to play your instrument or to sing, you no doubt already possess a degree of interpretative ability. When you prepare a work for performance, you add a *crescendo* here, a more forceful attack there, a slight pause at the end of a certain phrase, and so on. These things you do initially because your teacher has told you to do so. In time, as you mature musically, you begin to sense the places where such nuances are required—you add them because they "sound right." The purpose of music theory is to make you more fully aware of the factors that govern your interpretation, and to deepen your awareness, understanding, and appreciation of the elements that make up a piece of music. By knowing how these elements interact to create musical style and effect, you, as a performer or teacher, will be better able to bring a piece of music to life and to communicate its essence to others.

On Using This Book

Following are some suggestions for using this book. To paraphrase an old adage: "One example is worth a thousand words." Because I believe this to be true, and because the focal point of this text is the music itself, you will find numerous musical examples. It is important that, as you read this text, you look carefully at the musical examples—better yet, play them at the keyboard (no matter how slowly) and *listen* to recordings of the larger excerpts. It is only through the examples that you will come to understand how the various musical devices and techniques are actually applied.

Questions for class discussion appear throughout the text. In doing your assigned readings, you should ponder these questions and be prepared to discuss them in class.

BEADGCF

At the end of many of the chapters in Volume One, you will find Comprehension Tests. You should take them on your own. After you have completed a test, you should consult the indicated answer page in the back of the book. In this way, you can evaluate your comprehension of the material. In some cases—particularly the part-writing problems—more than one possible solution exists. Due to space limitations, only one sample solution can be given. Do not be concerned if yours is slightly different, but rather, use the sample solution as a basis for comparison.

At the beginning of each chapter, you will find a list of the important terms introduced. These terms are contained, in alphabetical order, in a Glossary at the end of the book, where they are defined. You should make it a practice to try formulating your own definition of each term and then to check it against the definition in the Glossary.

As with any undertaking—perhaps more so than with most—the benefits that you derive from this study will be proportional to the amount of effort you put into it. The insights you gain from your study of music theory will time and again prove relevant to your personal musical goals. In the world of professional music, there is no substitute for solid musicianship. This text is designed to assist in providing you with this foundation.

—Ralph Turek
The University of Akron

The Elements of Music: Concepts and Applications is a two-volume text with workbooks, designed for use in theory and musicianship courses at the freshman and sophomore levels of college instruction. The title is descriptive of both the method and organization of the text. The elements of music are the subject matter, and in these volumes, they are grouped into four categories—formal structure, melodic/rhythmic structure, harmonic/tonal structure, and texture/articulation/dynamics. The musical analyses throughout the text focus on the interaction of these elements and provide a larger context within which to view specific concepts as they are presented.

Volume One consists of several units, although they are not specifically identified as such. Chapters One through Three deal with rudiments. Chapters Four through Six focus on harmony, melody, and their interaction. Chapters Seven and Eight introduce principles of voice leading and harmonization. Chapter Nine deals with the creation of musical form through the interaction of *all* the musical elements. In the remainder of Volume One and in Volume Two, the material is presented in a way that couples a comprehensive look at music with a detailed focus on specific devices and techniques. As the chapters of Volume One progress, more attention is focused on the analysis of longer excerpts, so that by the time that binary and ternary forms and variations are considered (Chapters Thirteen, Fourteen, and Fifteen), they are approached *through* the analysis of complete movements.

Following is a more detailed description of some of Volume One's important features.

1. A complete, yet succinct review of rudiments is provided, including detailed guidelines on notational practices—a skill too often assumed in college-level musicianship courses (Chapters One, Two, and Three).
2. A generally chronological approach is followed, with occasional deviations in the interest of pedagogical effectiveness. One such departure is the introduction of Harmony (Chapter Four) before Melody (Chapter Five). Although the latter appeared earlier chronologically, it is awkward—almost futile—to discuss melodic practices of the Baroque and Classical periods (which are the focus of Volume One) without a basic understanding of the harmonic implications present in the phrase and period, as well as the way in which harmony helps to determine the melodic material.
3. A logical and thorough examination of melody (Chapter Five), beginning with the smallest units (figure and motive) and working toward

the largest (the period), is followed by methods of phrase extension and compression and other techniques of melodic development. This is followed by a set of guidelines for melodic analysis, along with the application of those guidelines to the analysis of a substantial excerpt.

4. A clear and understandable discussion of larger scale melodic-harmonic relationships within a melodic line (Chapter Six) includes the concepts of structural melody, melodic prolongation, step progression, large-scale arpeggiation, and a simplified but effective technique for reductive analysis. Embellishing (nonchord) tones are presented within this context so that students acquire an early familiarity with the complete hierarchy of melodic relationships, from surface to structure.

5. A concise and uncomplicated presentation of voice leading is given (Chapter Seven), in which the myriad of specific "rules" or "guidelines" set forth in many approaches is distilled into a few elemental principles. These principles generally apply with little, if any, qualification to all the harmonic elements subsequently introduced in Volume One. One of the most frequently appearing statements in this volume is: "No new voice-leading principles are involved."

6. A clear and concise presentation of functional harmonic principles includes the classification of harmonic motion into three types—progression, retrogression, and repetition—and discussion of their interaction in a musical passage (Chapter Eight).

7. An early introduction to the process by which musical form is created includes an examination of the interaction of all the musical elements. Some often overlooked aspects are considered, including dramatic shape and musical intensification. The chapter (Nine) concludes with a comprehensive analysis that serves as a model for subsequent analyses in Volume One and Volume Two.

8. Diatonic seventh chords are presented in two basic groups—dominant-functioning (Chapter Ten) and nondominant (Chapter Eleven). By this approach, the functional similarity and the common voice leading inherent in the V^7, $vii^{\emptyset 7}$ and vii^{o7} chords are recognized and stressed. Also emphasized is the fact that *all* the diatonic seventh chords, while varying in frequency, are treated in practically identical ways in matters of voice leading.

9. Modulation (Chapter Twelve) is presented before tonicization (Chapter Thirteen). Although these two topics can be taught successfully in the reverse order, I believe that it is somewhat easier for students to understand tonicization as an extremely brief modulation than to recognize modulation as an extended tonicization. In other words, once students understand that an extended change of tonal center can occur in a piece, it is easy for them to grasp the concept of a very brief, momentary allusion to a new tonal center. The modulatory process is described as it was most commonly employed in the Baroque and Classical eras—specifically, to closely related keys through a pivot chord or chromatic tone. A distinction between modulation and tonal shift is made. Students are not burdened in Volume One with modulation to remote keys, through pivot tone and enharmonic spelling. These are more difficult procedures, characteristic of the nineteenth century, and they are properly reserved for Volume Two.

10. The presentation of a musical form—binary—in conjunction with an important technique in the creation of many binary forms—tonicization (secondary function)—is unique and, I believe, effective. The approach is based on a complete movement from the literature and accomplishes several goals.

   a. It renders the presentation of the technique (tonicization) less abstract and more immediately relevant.
   b. It places the technique within a larger musical context.
   c. It provides an opportunity to apply the comprehensive analytical approach outlined in Chapter Nine.

   Some instructors may, nevertheless, wish to present tonicization and binary form separately. This is entirely possible, since the two topics, while part of a single chapter, are nevertheless self-contained. I recommend, however, that instructors present tonicization (Part B of the chapter) first, followed by melody harmonization (Part C) and finally, simple binary form (Part A).

11. Rounded binary and ternary forms are presented in a single chapter (Chapter Fourteen) to emphasize and clarify their similarities and differences. (The differences between simple binary and rounded binary forms are more obvious to students than the sometimes subtle distinction between rounded binary and ternary forms.) These forms are approached through the comprehensive analysis of complete movements from the eighteenth and nineteenth centuries.

12. Baroque variation techniques are discussed through analysis of two basic types—continuous and sectional variations. The theme of the Handel variations is itself a rounded binary form, thus providing a reinforcement of a recently learned concept.

With the exception of Chapter One, each chapter is organized into two or three parts. The practice material and assignments at the end of the chapters are grouped to correspond to these divisions so that it is not necessary to complete an entire chapter before proceeding with drill work and assignments.

The exercises are of three basic types:

1. Analytical and part-writing drills that focus on theoretical problems in isolation, divorced, as it were, from their musical context
2. Analytical problems dealing with larger musical examples, taken from the literature
3. Exercises involving the application of theoretical concepts through actual composition

The last type of exercise is the most challenging and, at the same time, the most creative. Instructors are free to choose the types of exercise they prefer, although it is recommended that all three types be undertaken.

It is my firm belief that aural and keyboard skills are essential parts of a musician's training and that these skills are best developed concurrently with analytical and compositional skills. Although this text does not pretend to serve the purposes of an ear-training or keyboard harmony course, an effort has been made to provide at least some exercises relating to both skills. Also, the student is frequently exhorted to play at the keyboard or sing the written exercises after he or she has completed them. Material for harmonic/melodic dictation and further keyboard harmony exercises are contained in the accompanying Instructor's Manual. This manual also provides insight into my approach, practical suggestions for the presentation of the material, supplementary material that can be photocopied for handout in class, tests, suggestions for the use of additional examples, and answers to most of the assignment questions.

Several other instructional aids merit mention. Comprehension Tests included at the end of most of the chapters provide an opportunity for students to test their comprehension. Answers are provided in the back of the book so that students may immediately check their work. These tests may also be used as a classroom activity. A list of terms appears at the beginning of each chapter. These terms are defined in a Glossary at the end of the book. Because I feel that an effective method of teaching is through asking questions, discussions throughout the text are punctuated by questions for class discussion (set off from the body of the text by a box). This feature, which becomes more frequent in the later chapters of Volume One and is carried forward in Volume Two, provides a format for class interaction and affords the instructor a means of evaluating the level of class understanding at various points within a chapter. Instructors may use these questions as they like or they may disregard them. Their omission will not interrupt the flow of the text. Where the given musical examples are to be found in more complete form in an existing anthology, a notation to this effect is made. Instructors may wish to play the larger excerpt or to use additional parts of the excerpt for class discussion. A cassette tape accompanies each volume of this text. It contains most of the longer musical examples found in the text, except for those that are easily playable at the keyboard. It is hoped that this feature will save time for instructors and be of assistance to students. The value of *hearing* all of the musical examples cannot be overstressed.

As was already mentioned, the approach of the two volumes is *generally* chronological, and historical perspective is provided for most of the topics. The style periods covered in the two volumes are the Baroque, Classical, nineteenth century, and twentieth century. (An introduction to jazz and popular styles is contained in an appendix to Volume Two and can be presented during the sophomore year.)

It is probably not much of an exaggeration to say that there are nearly as many philosophies on the teaching of theory as there are instructors. For those who prefer a course of more limited scope, the following chapters may be omitted without detriment to the flow of the text.

Chapter Nine: Form and Dramatic Shape in Music

Chapter Fifteen: Variation Techniques

For those instructors so inclined, Appendix One (The Properties of Sound) and Appendix Four (Instrumentation) can be "fleshed out" and presented as chapters in their own right.

The aim of this text is to strike an appropriate balance between:

- the more comprehensive, "holistic" approach to music and the narrower focus on particular skills and details
- the proportion of text, example, and illustration
- the amount of detail provided and the amount left for the instructor to provide or for the student to discover
- the compositional and analytical approaches to music
- attention to large-scale and more local musical relationships

If, at the end of a two-year course of study using this text, students possess a command of essential compositional/analytical skills (including a strong grounding in four-part writing) and have an understanding of the ways in which the various musical elements interact to create form and style, then the goals of this text will have been realized. It is my hope that students will gain an awareness and appreciation of the relevance of the material presented in these volumes to their personal musical goals and that this awareness will deepen as their musical studies progress.

—Ralph Turek
The University of Akron

ACKNOWLEDGMENTS

I wish to thank my colleagues, Dr. David Bernstein, Mr. Richard Jackoboice, and Dr. Nikola Resonavic for teaching from the text in its rough manuscript form and for their valuable suggestions based on their classroom experiences. I am also grateful for the support of this project given by The University of Akron School of Music and Mr. Richard Shirey, who generously provided for typing and photocopying services. Three other people merit special mention—Renee Anthony Dee and Kathy Nelson, who devoted their valuable time to re-typing portions of the manuscript, and Nancy England, Director of the Music Resource Center, for her help in providing musical sources and other bibliographic information. My thanks also to the reviewers of the manuscript for their contributions: Stephen Douglas Burton, George Mason University, Virginia; Kate Covington, University of Kentucky, Lexington; Robert Davine, University of Denver, Colorado; Richard Devore, Kent State University, Ohio; Lathon Jernigan, University of Northern Iowa, Cedar Falls; Charles N. Kyriakos, University of Missouri, Columbia; Maurice I. Laney, Eastern Michigan University, Ypsilanti; Alice Lanning, University of Oklahoma, Norman; Charles Lord, University of Kentucky, Lexington; Charles Nick, University of Missouri, Columbia; Donald J. Para, Western Michigan University, Kalamazoo; Marian Petersen, University of Missouri, Kansas City; Patrick Riley, Bemidji State University, Minnesota; Charles F. Stokes, Jr., Illinois State University, Normal; James Waters, Kent State University, Ohio; and Stephen Yarbrough, University of South Dakota, Vermillion. Finally, I wish to thank my students who patiently endured a year's study using the manuscript and who were singularly adept at discovering flaws, omissions, and ambiguities.

—Ralph Turek
The University of Akron

CONTENTS

*The two topics may be treated as separate chapters. See To the Instructor, page ix.

THE ELEMENTS OF MUSIC: CONCEPTS AND APPLICATIONS
Volume One

CHAPTER ONE

PITCH AND ITS NOTATION

TERMS TO KNOW

accidental	enharmonic	natural
chromatic alteration	flat	neumes
chromatic scale	grand staff	ottava sign
clef	half step	sharp
double flat	interval	staff
double sharp	ledger lines	whole step
	loco	

PITCH

The *pitch* of a musical tone is a measurement of how high or low it sounds. When we hear a melody, we are hearing a series of pitches. Most musical sounds have a very well-defined pitch. In sounds such as normal human speech, and in the sounds produced by drums and some other percussive instruments, the pitch is not so well defined.

NOTATION

Musical notation is the written language of music. The symbols of this language indicate the precise pitch and the duration (length) of every note. Other musical qualities, such as tempo, loudness, tone quality, or style of playing, also can be indicated through the notation. By notating an idea, a composer gives it permanence and enables performers to recreate it.

The origins of our notational system are found in music manuscripts dating from about the tenth century. Symbols called *neumes* were included above the words to be sung or chanted, as a memory aid for the singers. Some of these neumes, along with their present-day forms, are shown in the following illustration.

Illustration 1.1

Neume	Later shape (ca. 1250)	Present-day form

THE
STAFF
AND
CLEFS

By themselves, note symbols can indicate only the *general* upward and downward movement of a melody. When placed on the lines and spaces of a five-line *staff,* however, these same symbols can indicate precise pitches. A *clef sign,* placed at the left-hand side of the staff, is used to denote the general range of the notes and, more important, a reference pitch. With this point of reference, all of the lines and spaces of a staff can indicate specific pitches.

Letters of the alphabet are used to designate particular pitches. During the period when our notational system was first developing, most melodies contained fewer discrete pitches than today's melodies. Thus, the letters A through G were apparently considered sufficient, and clef signs were used to designate the pitches C, F and G. Early clef signs looked like this:

Illustration 1.2

and eventually evolved into our present-day symbols.

Illustration 1.3

Originally, the clefs could be placed on any line of the staff. In current notational practice, however, only the C clefs are movable. The four clefs that remain in common use are shown below. The black notes represent *middle C*—the C closest to the middle of the piano keyboard.

Illustration 1.4

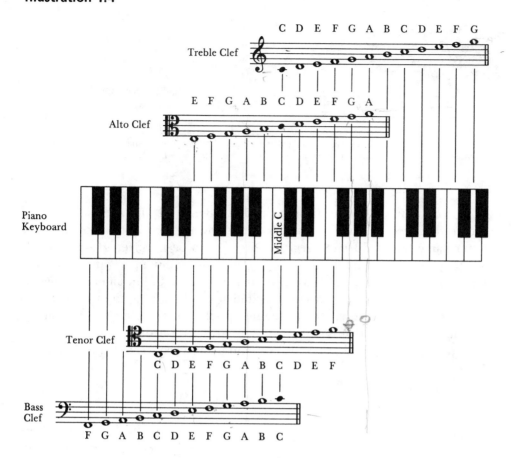

Notice that the treble and bass clefs place middle C lowest and highest respectively on the staff. In fact, middle C must be notated in *either* of these clefs with a *ledger line*. Ledger lines are short horizontal lines representing an upward or downward extension of the staff. They are drawn through the stems of notes too high or too low to be located directly *on* the staff.

Illustration 1.5

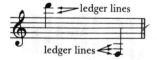

NOTE: Since ledger lines represent an extension of the staff, they should be spaced the same distance apart as the lines of the staff. They should also completely intersect the stem and be slightly longer than the notehead itself.

Together, the treble and bass clefs encompass the widest possible range. In keyboard music, they are used together to form the *grand staff*.

Illustration 1.6

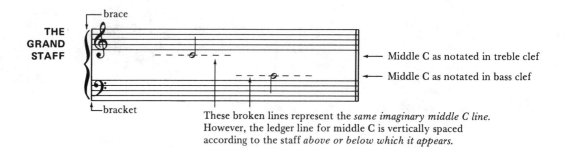

THE GRAND STAFF

brace

Middle C as notated in treble clef
Middle C as notated in bass clef

bracket

These broken lines represent the *same imaginary middle C line*. However, the ledger line for middle C is vertically spaced according to the staff *above or below which it appears.*

OCTAVE DESIGNATION

As you can see from Illustration 1.4, the seven alphabetically named pitches can be duplicated in many high and low registers. Pitches of the same letter name but in different registers are said to be in different *octaves.** If we play the note middle C on the piano and count up eight white keys (counting middle C as *one*), we again reach the note C, but an octave higher. (The word *octave* is derived from an Italian word meaning eight.) The method most commonly used to distinguish pitches of the same letter name in various octaves is shown below. Notice that, even on the grand staff, many ledger lines are required for the lowest and highest registers of the piano.

Illustration 1.7

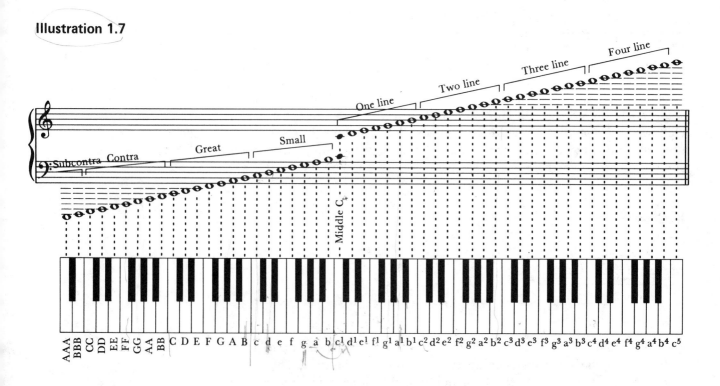

*A more detailed examination of the octave and other acoustical properties of musical sounds can be found in Appendix One.

For ease and speed in music reading, the overuse of ledger lines is avoided when possible. This is one reason for the use of the alto and tenor clefs. The alto clef is used chiefly for the viola. The tenor clef is used on occasion for the cello, bassoon, and trombone, instruments that sometimes play in a register that would require the constant use of ledger lines in *either* treble or bass clef.

Illustration 1.8

a. Melody notated in treble clef requires many ledger lines *below* the staff.

b. Same melody notated in bass clef requires many ledger lines *above* the staff.

c. Same melody notated in tenor clef requires fewer ledger lines and is therefore easier to read.

THE OTTAVA SIGN

Aside from the occasional use of a clef change in music for the cello, bassoon, and trombone, and in keyboard music, a more common means of avoiding excessive ledger lines is the *ottava* sign. When its abbreviation, *8va,* is placed above a note, that note is to be played one octave higher than written. Where a broken line follows the *ottava* sign, the notes should be played an octave higher until the broken line ends. The symbol *8va bassa,* placed below a note, directs the performer to play the note an octave *lower* than written. The term *loco* indicates a return to the pitch in the octave notated.

Illustration 1.9

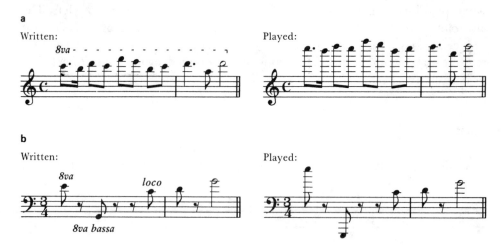

An extension of this practice is the symbol *15ma* (from the Italian *quinde-zima*), meaning that a passage should be played *two* octaves higher than written.

FOR PRACTICE MATERIAL AND ASSIGNMENTS, TURN TO PAGE 9.

The seven letter names—A B C D E F G—are used to name *twelve equally spaced pitches* that divide the octave. The following illustration shows the relationship between the twelve pitches of the octave, the seven letter names, and the white keys of the piano.

Illustration 1.10

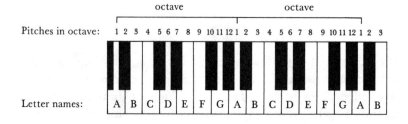

INTERVALS

An *interval* is the distance between two pitches. The smallest interval normally used in our music is the *half step* (also called a *semitone*). The interval between any white key on the piano and an adjacent black key is the half step. Notice, however, that there is no black key between E and F, or between B and C. These are the only two half-step intervals that occur between white keys. Between any two other adjacent white keys, the interval is a *whole step,* which is equal to two half steps.

Illustration 1.11

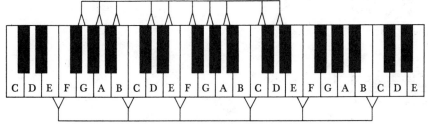

half steps between black and white keys (duplicated in each octave)

half steps between white keys (B-C and E-F)

The black keys share the letter names of the white keys immediately above or below. However, a symbol is added to indicate that the pitch is to be raised or lowered by a half step. This is called *chromatic alteration,* and the symbols used are the:

CHROMATIC ALTERATION

flat	♭	A symbol that, placed before a pitch, indicates that it is to be lowered by a half step.
sharp	♯	A symbol that, placed before a pitch, indicates that it is to be raised by a half step.
double flat	♭♭	A symbol that, placed before a pitch, indicates that it is to be lowered by *two* half steps.
double sharp	✖	A symbol that, placed before a pitch, indicates that it is to be raised by *two* half steps.
natural	♮	A symbol that, placed before a pitch, cancels the effect of a preceding chromatic alteration and restores the original, unaltered pitch.

Notice that the black keys of the piano can be designated using *either* flats or sharps. Different spellings of the same *sounding* pitch are *enharmonic equivalents.*

ENHARMONIC EQUIVALENTS

Illustration 1.12

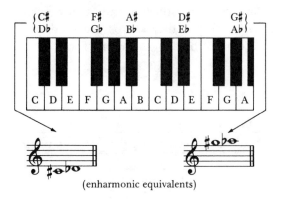

(enharmonic equivalents)

Following are examples of enharmonic equivalents that *do not* involve black keys.

Illustration 1.13

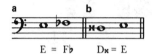

E = F♭   D𝄪 = E

ACCIDENTALS

Flats, sharps, and naturals (also double flats and double sharps) appearing before a pitch to indicate its temporary alteration are termed *accidentals*. By tradition, an accidental affects all following recurrences of the pitch prior to the occurrence of a *bar line* (a vertical line extending from the top to the bottom line of the staff). However, it does *not* affect that pitch *in any other octave*.

Illustration 1.14

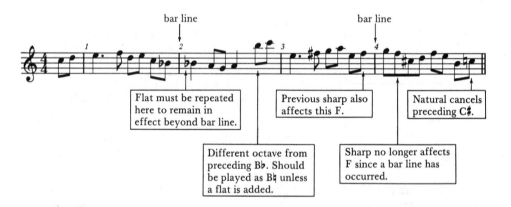

bar line

bar line

Flat must be repeated here to remain in effect beyond bar line.

Previous sharp also affects this F.

Natural cancels preceding C♯.

Different octave from preceding B♭. Should be played as B♮ unless a flat is added.

Sharp no longer affects F since a bar line has occurred.

In general, when a pitch is preceded by a sharp, the next pitch will be higher, and when a pitch is preceded by a flat, the next pitch will be lower, as shown in the preceding illustration.

CHROMATIC SCALE

All twelve pitches of the octave, arranged in either ascending or descending order, constitute a *chromatic scale*. Notice that sharps are used when writing the ascending form and flats are used for the descending form.

Illustration 1.15

sharps used ascending   flats used descending

Half steps can occur between pitches having *adjacent* letter names or between pitches having *the same* letter name.

**ENHARMONIC
INTERVALS**

Illustration 1.16

The intervals of Illustration 1.16a and 1.16b are spelled differently, yet they sound identical. These are called *enharmonic intervals*.

FOR PRACTICE MATERIAL AND ASSIGNMENTS, TURN TO PAGE 12.

PRACTICE MATERIAL AND ASSIGNMENTS FOR PAGES 1-6

A. Before each note, add the clef (treble, bass, alto, or tenor) in which the pitch would be correctly named.

Example:

Given this: ... *Add this:* ⟶ ...

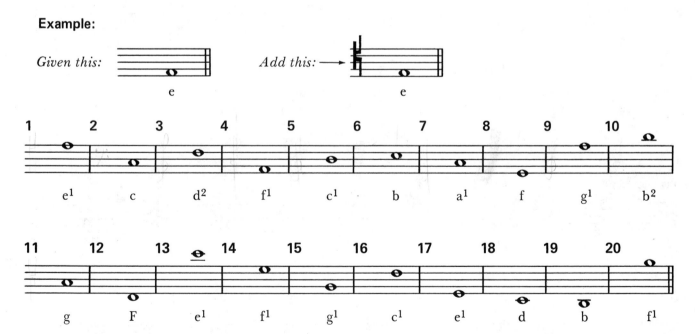

B. In the blanks below the following pitches, write their letter names, with correct octave designation.

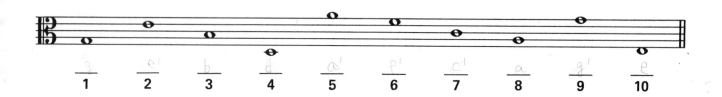

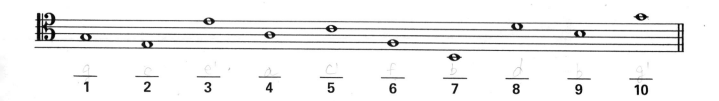

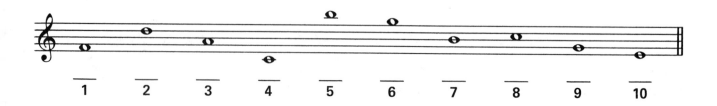

C. Renotate each of the pitches in the clef indicated.

D. Rewrite each of the following melodies in either treble or bass clef as specified. The first note is given.

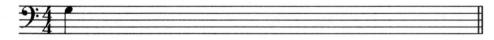

PRACTICE MATERIAL AND ASSIGNMENTS FOR PAGES 6-9

A. Using the diagram of the piano keyboard on page 7 as a reference, indicate whether each of the following is a half step (½) or whole step (1).

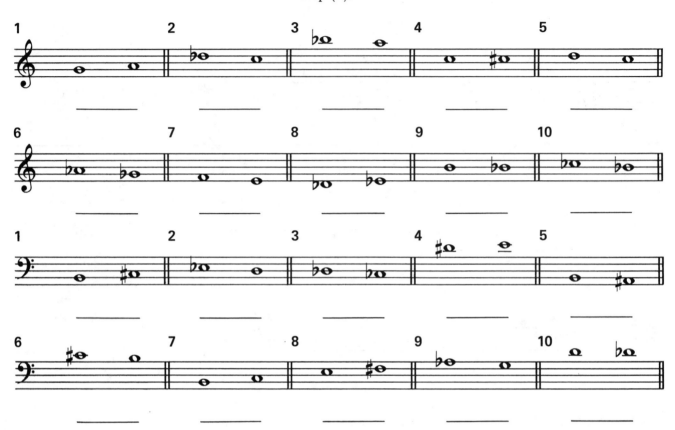

B. Write a half step (½) using an adjacent letter name (and accidental, if necessary) or a whole step (1), as directed.

Example:

½↑

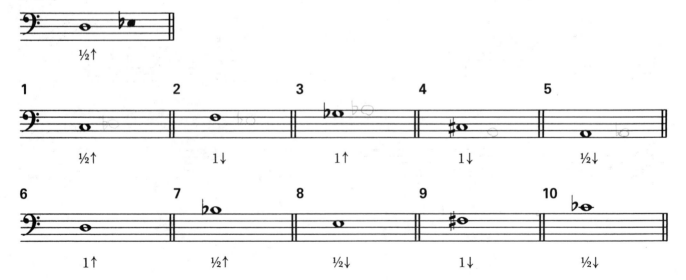

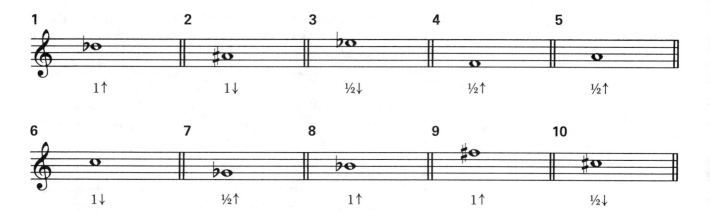

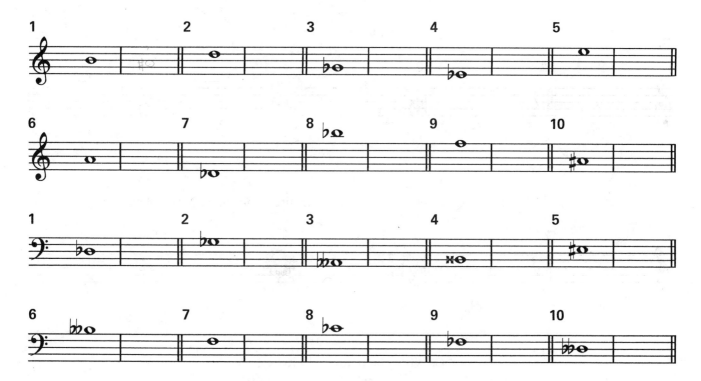

C. Provide one enharmonic spelling for each of the following pitches.

SUGGESTIONS FOR AURAL DRILL

A. Your instructor (or another student) will play a note, which he or she will identify for you, then play this note in several different registers. You are to identify the octave locations of each note that is played (see page 4 for octave designations).

B. Your instructor (or another student) will play ten intervals from Exercise A or from Exercise B on page 12 in random order. You are to identify each interval as a half step (½) or a whole step (1).

C. Your instructor will play a pitch on the piano. You (or the class as a group) are to sing the pitch one half step (½) or one whole step (1) higher or lower, as directed.

D. Your instructor (or another student) will play slowly several times a succession of ten or twelve pitches. You are to identify each melodic interval as a half step (½), a whole step (1), or neither (N).

TEST YOUR COMPREHENSION OF CHAPTER ONE

A. Give the correct letter name and octave designation for the following pitches.

B. Notate the following pitches in the required clefs.

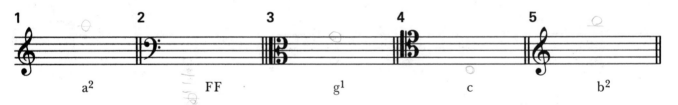

C. Write the requested pitches.

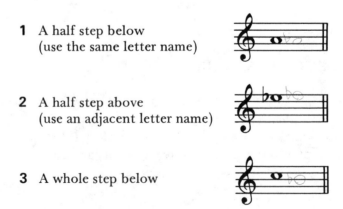

1 A half step below
(use the same letter name)

2 A half step above
(use an adjacent letter name)

3 A whole step below

4 A half step above
(use the same letter name)

5 A half step below
(use an adjacent letter name)

D. Write an enharmonic equivalent for each of the following pitches.

E. Rewrite each interval enharmonically. Where the interval is spelled
with adjacent letter names, rewrite it using the same letter name,
and vice versa. Avoid using double flats or double sharps.

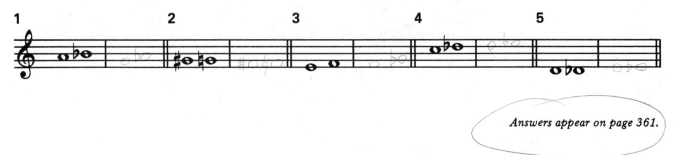

Answers appear on page 361.

CHAPTER TWO
RHYTHM AND OTHER
ASPECTS OF NOTATION

TERMS TO KNOW

accent	breve	meter
agogic accent	compound meter	pulse
articulation	cross rhythm	simple meter
asymmetric meter	duple meter	syncopation
augmentation dot	dynamic accent	tempo
bar line	dynamics	tie
beat	hemiola	tonal accent
borrowed division	measure	triple meter

A. Rhythm

Melodies consist not only of successions of pitches, but also of pitches performed in a particular rhythm. Some notes are long, some are short. The notational symbols used to indicate the pitch of a note also indicate its duration (its length). Additional symbols, called *rests,* are used to indicate the duration of silences.

THE MODERN PROPORTIONAL SYSTEM

Our system of rhythmic notation is a *proportional one,* in which the notational symbols do not designate fixed timings (such as two seconds), but rather, how long each note should be *with respect to all of the other notes.* We can perform a melody rapidly or slowly. The tempo (speed) may change, but the rhythm will still be recognizable, because the proportions of the notes are the same.

The most common durational symbols are included in the table below.

Illustration 2.1

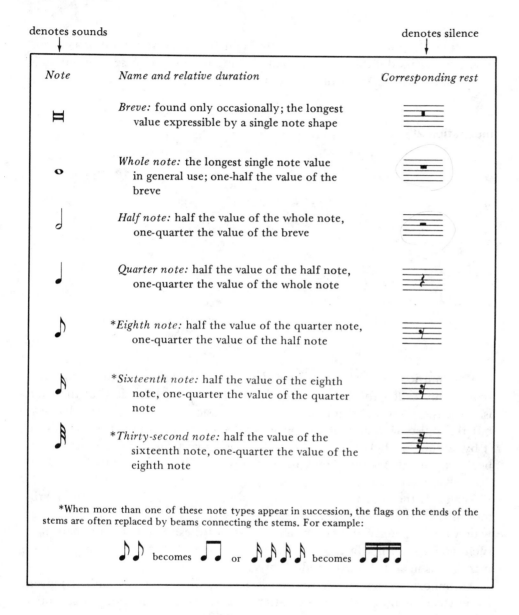

denotes sounds   denotes silence

Note	Name and relative duration	Corresponding rest
	Breve: found only occasionally; the longest value expressible by a single note shape	
	Whole note: the longest single note value in general use; one-half the value of the breve	
	Half note: half the value of the whole note, one-quarter the value of the breve	
	Quarter note: half the value of the half note, one-quarter the value of the whole note	
	Eighth note: half the value of the quarter note, one-quarter the value of the half note	
	Sixteenth note: half the value of the eighth note, one-quarter the value of the quarter note	
	Thirty-second note: half the value of the sixteenth note, one-quarter the value of the eighth note	

*When more than one of these note types appear in succession, the flags on the ends of the stems are often replaced by beams connecting the stems. For example:

Other durations are made possible through the use of the:

1. *Tie:* a curved line connecting adjacent notes of the same pitch, whose effect is to bind the pitches together into a single duration.

Illustration 2.2

Each is performed as a single note with a duration equal to the combined values.

NOTE: Ties connect noteheads (not stems), but do not touch them. Rests are never tied together.

2. *Augmentation dot:* a dot that immediately follows a note or rest, extending its duration by one-half the undotted value. A second dot adds one-half the value of the first dot.

Illustration 2.3

PULSE AND BEAT   Most music moves along at a steady rate according to an underlying *pulse* (commonly called the *beat*). The pulse marks off equal divisions of time and is the basic durational unit in a piece of music. Conductors generally beat out this pulse. However, if the pulse is very slow, the conductor may divide it by adding "in between" beats. If the pulse is very fast, the conductor may beat only every second, third or fourth pulse. Thus, the terms "beat" and "pulse" are *not always* synonymous.

TEMPO   *Tempo* is the speed of the beat. Composers began to include tempo markings in their scores during the eighteenth century, when Italian was the most widely used language among musicians. Most of these Italian tempo markings, such as *allegro* for "fast," are still widely used. A list of common tempo markings is included in Appendix Three.

ACCENT   An important element of rhythm is *accent*, the stress (or emphasis) given to only certain notes. Rhythmic patterns consist of combinations of accented notes and unstressed notes. The most common types of accent are:

Tonal accent: A pitch is stressed because it is noticeably higher or lower than the surrounding pitches.

Agogic accent: A pitch is stressed because of its longer duration than the surrounding pitches.

Dynamic accent: A pitch is stressed because it is played more forcefully than the surrounding pitches.

In the passage below, the tonal and agogic accents create a regular pattern of one strong (accented) beat followed by two weak (unaccented) beats.

Illustration 2.4

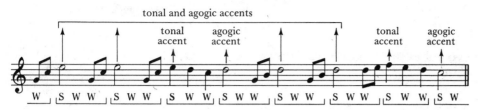

S = Strong
W = Weak

This kind of regular pattern is called a metrical pattern. *Meter* is the grouping of pulses into patterns of two or more beats by means of accents. A *measure* constitutes one complete cycle of the accentual pattern, beginning on an accented beat. Measures are separated from each other by *bar lines*.

METER AND MEASURE

Illustration 2.5

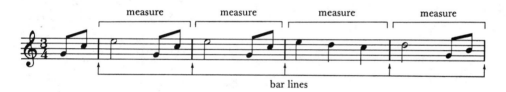

As is evident from the preceding illustration, musical works need not commence with the first strong beat of an accentual pattern. A weak-beat beginning is called an *anacrusis*.

In Illustration 2.5, the sign following the clef is a *meter signature*. A meter signature comprises two numbers that directly supply two important pieces of information.

METER SIGNATURES

1. the number of basic durational units (or their equivalent) that occur within a measure
2. the note value used as the basic durational unit—the pulse (this is not necessarily the *beat*)*

The terms *duple, triple* and *quadruple* refer to meters in which the *pulses are grouped* into measures of two, three, or four beats. The terms *simple* and *compound* refer to meters in which the *beats are divided* into two and three parts respectively.

SIMPLE METERS

A meter with an upper number of 2, 3, or 4 is *simple*. The lower number indicates the note type that represents the pulse, which usually is the beat in simple meters (see the footnote on this page). The upper number indicates how many of those note types, or their equivalent in other values, are contained within a measure.

*While the bottom number *always* designates the value of the *pulse,* the value the conductor chooses to "beat" will depend on factors such as the tempo and style, as pointed out on page 18.

Illustration 2.6

$\frac{2}{4}$ → Signifies that the quarter note = the pulse (which is the beat)

→ Signifies that there are two pulses (hence two quarter notes or the equivalent) in a measure

Meter classification: simple duple

division of beat (pulse) into two parts

$\frac{3}{8}$ → Signifies that the eighth note = the pulse (which is the beat)

→ Signifies that there are three pulses (hence three eighth notes or the equivalent) in a measure

Meter classification: simple triple

division of beat (pulse) into two parts

$\frac{4}{2}$ → Signifies that the half note = the pulse (which is the beat)

→ Signifies that there are four pulses (hence four half notes or the equivalent) in a measure

Meter classification: simple quadruple

division of beat (pulse) into two parts

COMPOUND METERS

Any meter signature with an upper number that is a multiple of three—that is, six, nine, twelve, and so on—is *compound*. The lower number indicates the note type that represents the pulse, but in compound meters, the pulse is *not* the beat. In compound meters, the *beat* comprises *three* pulses. As in simple meters, the upper figure indicates how many of the note types expressed by the lower figure, or their equivalent in other values, are contained within a measure.

Illustration 2.7

$\frac{6}{8}$ → Signifies that the eighth note = the pulse (which is *a third* of a beat)
(♩♩♩ = one beat, and therefore, ♩. = one beat)

→ Signifies that there are six eighth notes or the equivalent (hence two beats) in a measure

Meter classification: compound duple

division of beat into three parts (pulses)

$\frac{9}{4}$ → Signifies that the quarter note = the pulse (which is *a third* of a beat)
(♩♩♩ = one beat, and therefore, ♩. = one beat)

→ Signifies that there are nine quarter notes or the equivalent (hence three beats) in a measure

Meter classification: compound triple

division of beat into three parts (pulses)

The table below summarizes the differences between simple and compound meters.

Illustration 2.8

a Simple meters (pulse = beat)		
	Meter classification	
	Simple duple	*Simple triple*	*Simple quadruple*
Grouping of beats	two beats (pulses) per measure	three beats (pulses) per measure	four beats (pulses) per measure
Division of beat	two parts	two parts	two parts
Subdivision of beat	four and eight parts	four and eight parts	four and eight parts
Example	$\frac{2}{2}$	$\frac{3}{2}$	$\frac{4}{2}$
Other meters	$\frac{2}{2}\ \frac{2}{4}\ \frac{2}{8}\ \frac{2}{16}$	$\frac{3}{2}\ \frac{3}{4}\ \frac{3}{8}\ \frac{3}{16}$	$\frac{4}{2}\ \frac{4}{4}\ \frac{4}{8}\ \frac{4}{16}$

b Compound meters (pulse = 1/3 beat)		
	Meter classification	
	Compound duple	*Compound triple*	*Compound quadruple*
Grouping of beats	two beats per measure	three beats per measure	four beats per measure
Division of beat	three parts (pulses)	three parts (pulses)	three parts (pulses)
Subdivision of beat	six and twelve parts	six and twelve parts	six and twelve parts
Example	$\frac{6}{8}$	$\frac{9}{8}$	$\frac{12}{8}$
Other meters	$\frac{6}{8}\ \frac{6}{4}\ \frac{6}{2}$	$\frac{9}{8}\ \frac{9}{4}\ \frac{9}{2}$	$\frac{12}{8}\ \frac{12}{4}\ \frac{12}{2}$

An *asymmetric meter* is one in which the number of pulses in the measure is not two or three or multiples of these values. Following are two examples.

ASYMMETRIC METERS

Illustration 2.9

Two metric symbols should be mentioned at this point. The symbol **C** is often used to represent $\frac{4}{4}$ meter. The symbol **₵** is used to represent $\frac{2}{2}$ meter (sometimes called *alla breve*).

CONFLICT OF RHYTHM AND METER

BORROWED DIVISIONS

In certain passages, the actual rhythm is at odds with the prevailing meter. Perhaps the simplest example is the *borrowed division* of a note value—for example, a two-part division of the beat in a compound meter or a three-part division of the beat in a simple meter.

Illustration 2.10

a

three-part division of beat (two- or four-part division is the norm)

b

four-part division of beat (three- or six-part division is the norm)

c

three-part division of half note (two-part division—into two quarter notes—is the norm)

d

equivalent of (a three-part division)

Observations: *

1. An Arabic numeral is added to indicate the number of notes in the borrowed division.
2. When note values are not connected by a beam, a bracket can be used with the numeral, for clarity.

SYNCOPATION

Another conflict between rhythm and meter is *syncopation*—the shift in accentuation to a normally unaccented portion of a beat or measure. A very common means of accentuation is through duration. In $\frac{4}{4}$ meter, the first and third beats are normally stronger than the second and fourth beats. This can be illustrated as follows.

$$|1 \quad _2 \quad 3 \quad _4 \quad |$$

Therefore, accentuation through longer duration on the *second* or *fourth* beat creates a type of syncopation.

---

*The placement of the Arabic numerals and the use of brackets in borrowed divisions are among the less uniform aspects of notational practice, as can be seen by examining the musical scores of several publishers.

Illustration 2.11

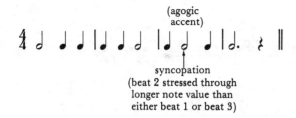

In ¾ meter, the first beat is stronger than either the second or third. Therefore, longer durations on the *second* or *third* beat produce syncopation.

Illustration 2.12

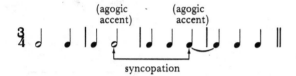

Syncopation can also occur *within a beat*. Since the first part of *any* beat is stronger than any other part, a longer duration that begins at a point other than the downbeat can create a syncopation.

Illustration 2.13

A *cross rhythm* is the simultaneous occurrence of two or more conflicting rhythms. Typically, one of the rhythms involves a borrowed division of the beat.

CROSS RHYTHMS

Illustration 2.14

Following is a typical use of cross rhythms.

Example 2.1   Brahms: *Variations and Fugue on a Theme of Handel* (Var. 2)

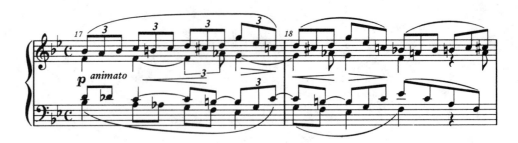

HEMIOLA   *Hemiola* is another technique based on a 3:2 rhythmic ratio. It refers to the division of the quantity six in two different ways—as two groups of three or as three groups of two. This division can occur successively or simultaneously.

Illustration 2.15

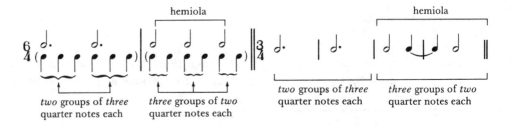

Following is a musical example of hemiola between the melody and bass line.

Example 2.2   Mozart: *Symphony, K. 550* (III) (reduction)

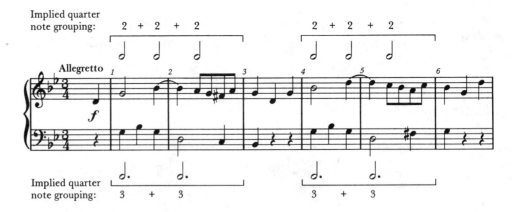

FOR PRACTICE MATERIAL AND ASSIGNMENTS, TURN TO PAGE 32.

B. Notational Guidelines

Music publishers generally adhere to precise notational standards. It is advisable to follow these practices closely in order to give a more professional appearance to your work and to avoid the confusion that may result from nonstandard practices. The guidelines given in this section should be followed carefully in all written musical work. Many of these guidelines are illustrated at different points in the following musical example. The points are numbered for easy reference.

Example 2.3   Schubert: *Moments musicaux, Op. 94, No. 6*

1. Noteheads

   a. All note heads are oval shaped with the long axis on a 45-degree angle with the line or space on which they rest.

   45° axis   horizontal axis   round noteheads

   b. All noteheads on the same beat or fraction thereof are aligned vertically (see 1b).

   c. Where two noteheads a step apart occupy the same stem, the *higher* notehead should always be to the *right* of the stem, and the *lower* notehead should always be to the *left* of the stem (see 1c).

2. Stems

   a. *Upward* stems are adjoined to the *right* of the notehead; *downward* stems are adjoined to the *left* side (see 2a).

   b. Stems extend *downward* for notes *above the middle line* and *upward* for notes *below the middle line.* For notes *on the middle line,* the downward direction is generally preferred unless it creates visual confusion.

   c. When several noteheads are attached to a single stem, the stem direction should be based on the location (above or below the middle line) of the majority of the pitches (see 2c).

   d. Stems should be approximately one octave in length. The stem may be longer if more than one notehead is attached (see 2d and 4d).

3. Ledger Lines

   a. Ledger lines, since they represent an extension of the staff, are spaced the same distance apart as the lines of the staff (see 3a).

   b. When ledger lines are used, the stem extends to the middle line of the staff (see 3b).

4. Dots and Ties (for the use of the dot with rests, see item 6)

   a. A dot may follow any note value, as long as it does not create a value too long for the measure.

   b. A dot may be used at any point in the measure, so long as the beat is not obscured for too long a period. For example:

This:

1 ② ③ 4

(two beats hidden within the note values)

is better written as this:

1 ② 3 4

(one beat hidden within a note value)

or this:

1 2 3 4

(no beats hidden within the note values)

c. When a note falls on a space, the dot following it is placed on the same space. When a note falls on a line, the dot is placed in the space immediately above the line, *regardless of the stem direction.* This also applies to notes appearing on or between ledger lines (see 4c).

d. When a chord appears as a dotted value, the dots are normally affixed in accordance with the guidelines of 4c , except where two dots would require the same space (see 4d).

e. For single noteheads, ties normally connect the noteheads, not the stems, and arc *away from* the note (see 4e).

f. When two tied notes occupy the *same* stem, the ties curve away from each other (see 4f).

5. Flags and Beams

a. For note values smaller than a quarter note, a flag appears to the right side of the stem, *regardless of the stem direction* (see 5a).

b. In instrumental music, beams can be used to replace flags for groups of successive eighth notes or smaller values. The beam is a slightly broader line than that of a note stem. It usually slants upward or downward according to the general direction of the note pattern (see 5b).

c. When several notes are connected by a beam, the note farthest from the middle line usually determines the stem direction for the group.

d. Beams should not cause confusion as to where the beat occurs in the measure.

e. In $\frac{4}{4}$ meter, beams are usually used in such a way that an imaginary bar line could be drawn between the second and third beats. In triple meters, either the second and third or the first and second beats may be beamed together. The choice sometimes depends on the pitch content.

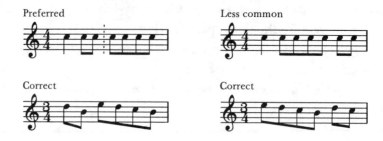

f. In general, more than six notes are not connected by a beam unless they occur within a single beat.

As a general guide: It is always safe to notate your music in such a manner that an imaginary bar line could be placed just before each and every beat in the measure.

6. Rests

a. Rests are never tied.
b. In simple meters, two rest values are preferred to dotted rests, except for values *smaller* than a quarter rest. However, in compound meters, dotted rests are common because they represent the beat or a multiple of it.

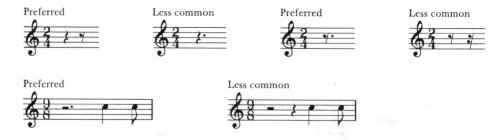

c. Two quarter rests are preferred to a half rest in $\frac{3}{4}$ meter.
d. Whole rests may be used to indicate an empty measure, *regardless of the meter signature.* The rest is placed in the center of the measure.

C. Dynamics and Articulation

In addition to the actual note shapes, a variety of auxiliary symbols is used to indicate the manner in which a musical passage is to be performed. Two important categories are dynamics and articulation.

1. *Dynamics* are markings that indicate relative levels of loudness. Although the ear is sensitive to a very wide range of dynamic levels, the number of symbols used to describe this aspect of music is relatively small.

ppp	*pianississimo*	extremely soft
pp	*pianissimo*	very soft
p	*piano*	soft
mp	*mezzo piano*	moderately soft
mf	*mezzo forte*	moderately loud
f	*forte*	loud
ff	*fortissimo*	very loud
fff	*fortississimo*	extremely loud

These levels have no *absolute* values; they are relative, depending on the size of the performing group and the style of the music.

2. *Articulation markings* indicate the manner in which a musical tone is begun (attacked) or ended (released). Two very common descriptive terms are:

Legato: a smooth, connected style in which one tone leads to another with little or no break in the sound and without strong attacks. Legato may be indicated by a *slur*—a curved line placed above or below the notes: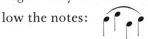

Staccato: a short, detached style in which a perceptible break occurs between pitches. Staccato may be indicated by dots placed above or below the noteheads:

Accent marks are also used to indicate different types of articulation. Two common symbols are:

accent	a forceful attack followed by an immediate lowering of the dynamic level
marcato	similar to the accent but with a more pronounced separation between the tones

In addition to these symbols, a large variety of expressive markings are used to indicate the general manner of performance of a musical passage. These are listed in Appendix Three.

D. The Notated Score Page

Examination of published works will show that there is a preferred position on the notated musical page for every detail. In an orchestral score, woodwinds appear at the top of the page, followed by brass, then other instruments, and finally the string parts, which are normally placed at the bottom of the page. Instruments within each family are arranged from highest sounding at the top to lowest sounding at the bottom of the group. The following diagram shows the arrangement of items on the first page of a musical score (traditionally a right-hand page) for chamber ensemble.

Illustration 2.16

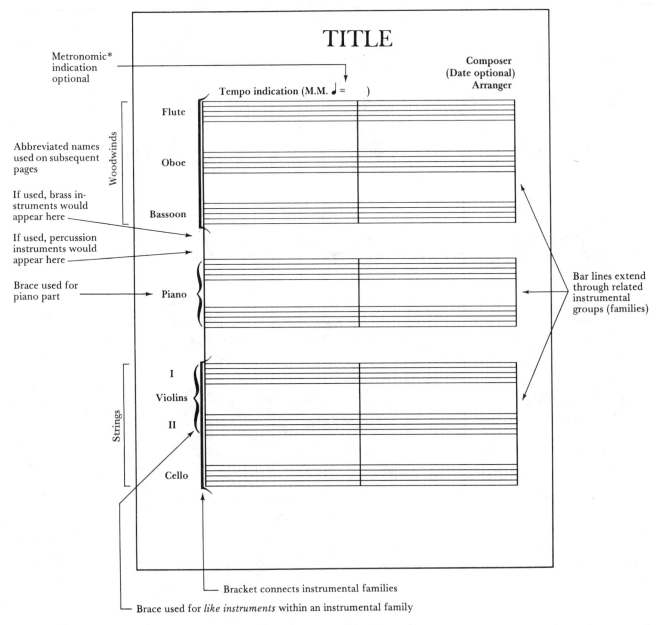

*M.M. stands for the Maelzel Metronome, a mechanical device that gives the precise tempo of a composition by indicating how many times per minute the note value representing the beat will occur.

Following is the opening of a song for voice and piano.

Example 2.4*

„Nun hast du mir den ersten Schmerz gethan."
"Now for the first time thou hast giv'n me pain."
(A. von Chamisso.)

English version by Dr. Th. Baker.

Robert Schumann
Op. 42, № 8.
Composed 1840.

*The entire song is contained in *Schirmer Scores*, by Jocelyn Godwin (Schirmer Books, 1975).

Notice:

1. The placement of dynamic and articulative markings varies with the instrument.

   a. For voice: Markings appear *above* the staff, since the text appears *below* the staff.
   b. For piano: Markings appear *midway between the staves if they apply to both hands* (as at m. 7 and m. 9). If applying to only one hand, they appear directly beneath, and close to, the appropriate staff (as in m. 1 or m. 3).

2. Pedal markings, when they occur, always appear beneath the lower piano staff.
3. Clefs and the flats or sharps that directly follow them (known as *key signatures*) appear *at the beginning of each staff,* but the meter signature appears only at the beginning of the music and at those points in the music where the meter changes.
4. A vertical line connects the left-hand side of all staves that are to be played simultaneously (these constitute a *musical system*). In addition, the two piano staves are connected with a *brace.*
5. Bar lines are continuous through both piano staves but are not connected to those of the voice staff.
6. A clef change occurring at the beginning of a musical system (as at m. 4) is shown by a small clef sign placed at the end of the previous system (as at m. 3).

All of these notational conventions are designed to facilitate accurate performance of the music. That which is easiest to read is easiest to perform.

FOR PRACTICE MATERIAL AND ASSIGNMENTS, TURN TO PAGE 35.

PRACTICE MATERIAL AND ASSIGNMENTS FOR PART A

A. For each single note value, indicate how many of the specified smaller note type would have an equivalent duration.

Example:

$$\text{𝅗𝅥.} = \underset{\text{(How many?)}}{6} \quad ♪$$

1 𝅝 = _____ 𝅘𝅥

2 𝅝. = _____ 𝅘𝅥.

3 𝅗𝅥. = _____ ♪

4 𝅗𝅥.. = _____ 𝅘𝅥𝅮

5 ♪ = _____ 𝅘𝅥𝅯   8 𝅝· = _____ 𝅗𝅥

6 𝅘𝅥𝅮· = _____ 𝅘𝅥𝅯   9 𝅗𝅥· = _____ 𝅘𝅥𝅮·

7 𝅗𝅥·· = _____ 𝅘𝅥𝅰   10 𝅗𝅥· = _____ 𝅘𝅥𝅯

B. Using the fewest notes necessary, along with ties where needed to connect two or more notes, create a single duration lasting for the number of beats specified in each of the given meters. Include bar lines where more than one measure is involved. (Some of these will require an incomplete measure at the end.)

Example:

meter: $\frac{3}{4}$ 𝅗𝅥· | 𝅗𝅥 ♪

duration: 5 1/2 beats

1 meter: $\frac{9}{8}$ _____

duration: 4 2/3 beats

2 meter: $\frac{4}{2}$ _____

duration: 3 1/4 beats

3 meter: $\frac{12}{4}$ _____

duration: 2 1/3 beats

4 meter: $\frac{6}{8}$ _____

duration: 4 1/6 beats

5 meter: $\frac{4}{4}$ _____

duration: 6 3/4 beats

6 meter: $\frac{3}{8}$ _____

duration: 5 1/4 beats

7 meter: $\frac{5}{2}$ _____

duration: 3 1/2 beats

8 meter: $\frac{3}{16}$ _____

duration: 6 1/2 beats

9 meter: $\frac{6}{4}$ _____

duration: 2 1/3 beats

10 meter: $\frac{4}{8}$ _____

duration: 3 1/2 beats

C. Add bar lines to the following rhythmic passages.

D. Select the appropriate meter classification from the list and place it before each of the meter signatures. Then, using no less than four note or rest values, compose two measures (rhythm only) that reflect the proper grouping and division of pulses in each.

simple duple
simple triple
simple quadruple
compound duple
compound triple
compound quadruple
asymmetric

Example:

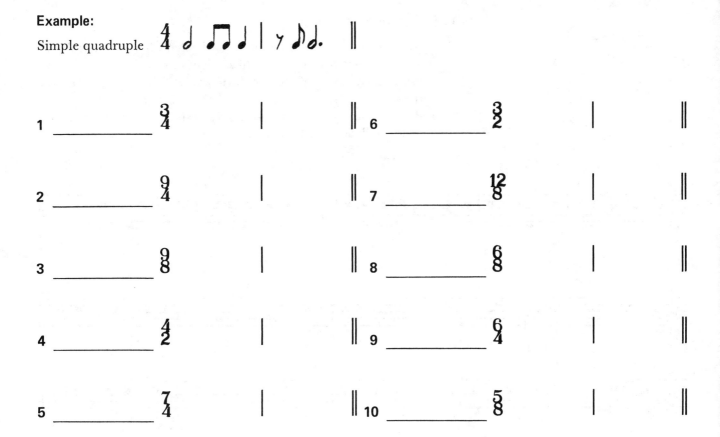

Simple quadruple

PRACTICE MATERIAL AND ASSIGNMENTS FOR PARTS B, C and D

A. Place the following pitches in the specified clefs, using half note values. Observe the correct placement of ledger lines and appropriate stem lengths and directions. Do not use the *ottava* sign to avoid ledger lines in this assignment.

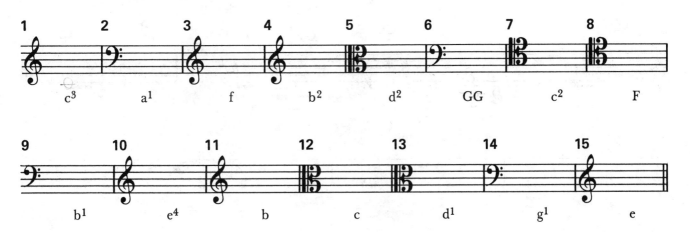

B. In each of the following:

1. Replace the tied values with a single value where acceptable. Be accurate with respect to the placement of dots.
2. Renotate as tied values any dotted values that tend to obscure the pulse.
3. Renotate in equivalent values any rests that are not in accordance with accepted practice.

C. Renotate the following passages to reflect the meter clearly and to
represent the correct use of beams.

5

SUGGESTIONS FOR AURAL DRILL

A. Your instructor will choose and play several melodic passages from the following:

> Text: Chapter Three
> pages 68-69: Exercise F
>
> Workbook: Chapter Two
> pages 7-8: Exercise B
> pages 13-14: Exercise E
>
> Workbook: Chapter Three
> pages 17-18: Exercise B

You are to identify the meter of each as simple or compound, triple or duple (quadruple).

B. Your instructor (or another student) will choose any four measures from the groups below to play in succession *in tempo* (moderately slow). You are to notate the rhythmic values.

For example, your instructor may choose measures 1, 7, 11, and 13 from Group 1, in which case, he or she will play:

NOTE: The same measure can be used more than once in these four-measure passages. For intermediate level difficulty, instructors can mix measures from the easy and more difficult groups.

1 Easy group:

Simple meter

Compound meter

2 More difficult group:

Simple meter

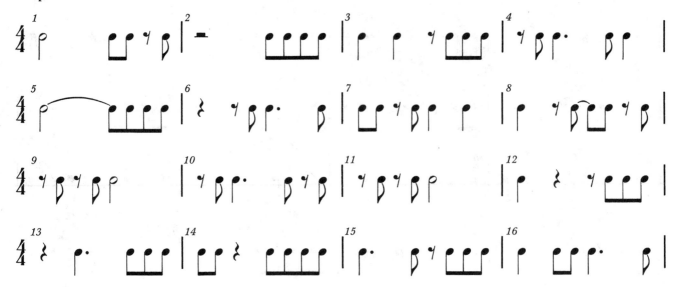

Compound meter

C. Several students will notate on the chalkboard four-measure passages constructed of the rhythmic measures from Exercise B above. Your class will then clap the rhythms of these passages at various tempos, as directed by your instructor.

TEST YOUR COMPREHENSION OF CHAPTER TWO

A. Classify the following meters as:

1. simple duple
2. simple triple
3. simple quadruple
4. compound duple
5. compound triple
6. asymmetric

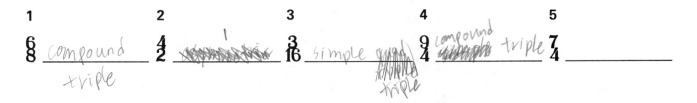

1 $\frac{6}{8}$ _compound triple_   **2** $\frac{4}{2}$ ~~scribbled~~   **3** $\frac{3}{16}$ _simple quad_   **4** $\frac{9}{4}$ _compound triple_   **5** $\frac{7}{4}$ _____

B. Select the term that most appropriately describes each of the following rhythmic patterns. Use each term once.

1. borrowed division
2. syncopation
3. cross rhythm
4. hemiola

1 _syncopation_   **2** _borrowed division_

3 _hemiola_   **4** _cross rhythm_

C. Several notational errors occur in the following excerpt. Identify and explain six.

	Location	Explanation
1	m.	beat
2	m.	beat
3	m.	beat
4	m.	beat
5	m.	beat
6	m.	beat

D. Write the meaning of each of the following signs.

1 *mp*   medium soft   4 ∧ accent

2 *ff* very louder   5 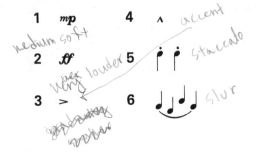 staccato

3 >   6 slur

Answers appear on page 362.

TERMS TO KNOW

chromatic	harmonic minor scale	reciting tone
chromatic scale	inversion	relative major/minor
cofinal	key signature	scale
compound intervals	major scale	simple intervals
diatonic	melodic minor scale	tetrachord
enharmonic interval	modes	tonic
enharmonic keys	natural minor scale	transposition
final	parallel major/minor	

A. Scales and Key Signatures

A *scale* (from the Italian *scala,* meaning "ladder") is the arrangement in ascending or descending order, of the pitch material that forms the basis of a musical composition. Although many different types of scales are possible, most of the music composed in Europe and the United States during the past three hundred years or so has had as its pitch basis a major or a minor scale.

A *major scale* is playable on the piano between any two Cs by striking, in ascending or descending order, only the white keys.

THE MAJOR SCALE

Illustration 3.1

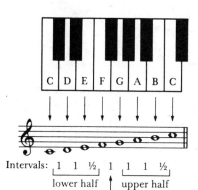

Intervals: 1 1 ½ 1 1 1 ½
lower half ↑ upper half
whole step separates the two "halves" of the scale

1 = whole step
½ = half step

Notice that this scale is composed of two intervallically identical four-note segments, called *tetrachords,* which are themselves separated by a whole step.

The resulting succession of intervals—$\overline{1\ 1}$ ½ $\overline{1\ 1}$ ½—constitutes a major scale.

Many melodies consist *solely* of the notes of the major scale.

Example 3.1   "O Tannenbaum" (German folk song)

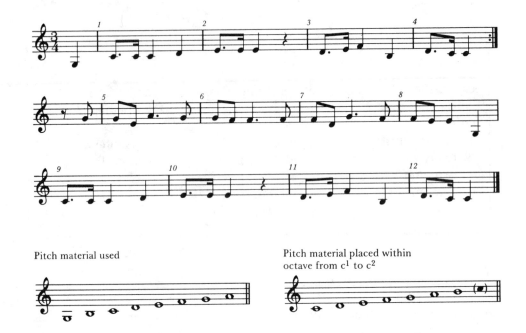

Pitch material used

Pitch material placed within octave from c¹ to c²

TRANSPOSITION   In order to duplicate the interval pattern of the major scale when beginning on a pitch other than C, certain chromatic alterations become necessary. Notice what happens if we attempt to construct a *new* major scale starting on the fifth degree of C major.

Illustration 3.2

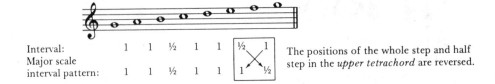

Interval:		1	1	½	1	1	½	1
Major scale interval pattern:		1	1	½	1	1	1	½

The positions of the whole step and half step in the *upper tetrachord* are reversed.

In order to maintain the interval pattern of the major scale, it is necessary to add a sharp before the F. This produces a *major scale* on G.

Illustration 3.3

G major scale

Interval: 1   1   ½   1   1   1   ½

The process of rewriting a scale, or a passage based on a scale, at a different pitch level is called *transposition*. If we continue to transpose the major scale by beginning on the *fifth* degree of each *new* scale, *an additional sharp* is required each time to preserve the half step between the seventh and eighth degrees.

Illustration 3.4

The major scale:

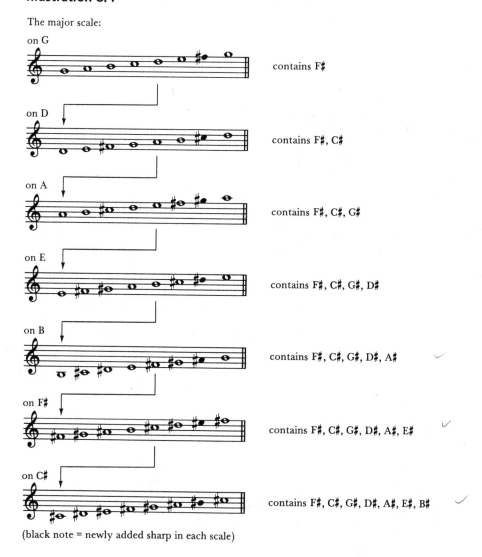

on G — contains F♯

on D — contains F♯, C♯

on A — contains F♯, C♯, G♯

on E — contains F♯, C♯, G♯, D♯

on B — contains F♯, C♯, G♯, D♯, A♯

on F♯ — contains F♯, C♯, G♯, D♯, A♯, E♯

on C♯ — contains F♯, C♯, G♯, D♯, A♯, E♯, B♯

(black note = newly added sharp in each scale)

In each case, the new sharp is the one added to the seventh scale degree.

If we now construct a new major scale beginning on the *fourth* degree of the C major scale—on F—a *different* alteration is required in order to preserve the proper interval structure.

Illustration 3.5

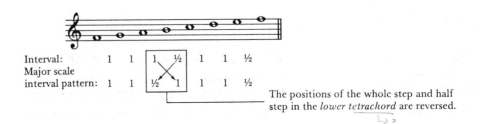

Interval:	1	1	1	½	1	1	½
Major scale interval pattern:	1	1	½	1	1	1	½

The positions of the whole step and half step in the *lower tetrachord* are reversed.

A *flat* must be added to the fourth scale degree in order to maintain the half step between the third and fourth degrees. This produces a *major scale* on F.

Illustration 3.6

F major scale

Interval:	1	1	½	1	1	1	½

If we continue to transpose the major scale by beginning on the *fourth* degree of each *new* scale, *an additional flat* is required each time to preserve the half step between the third and fourth degrees.

Illustration 3.7

The major scale

on F — contains Bb

on Bb — contains Bb, Eb

on Eb — contains Bb, Eb, Ab

on Ab — contains Bb, Eb, Ab, Db

on Db — contains Bb, Eb, Ab, Db, Gb

on Gb — contains Bb, Eb, Ab, Db, Gb, Cb

on Cb — contains Bb, Eb, Ab, Db, Gb, Cb, Fb

(black note = newly added flat in each scale)

In each case, the new flat is the one added to the fourth scale degree.

The first note of a major scale is called the *tonic*. It is the pitch of greatest stability and the focal pitch of most compositions that have that scale as their basis. In the melody of Example 3.1, the note C is heard as the tonic, or focal pitch, because it represents the final resting point of the melody and because of other reasons which we will consider in Chapter Five.

THE TONIC

The sharps or flats of the scale on which a piece is based usually are placed at the beginning of each staff. This is referred to as the *key signature*. Notice that there is a *precise manner of placement* for the sharps or flats of a key signature.

KEY SIGNATURES

Illustration 3.8

PLACEMENT OF SHARPS AND FLATS

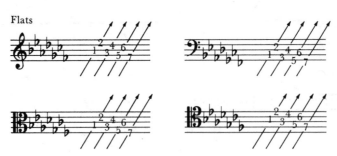

(Axis slants *downward to right* for all clefs except tenor.)

(Axis slants *upward to right* for *all* clefs.)

The names of the major scales and their key signatures are arranged in a circular pattern in the following illustration. By moving in both directions around this circle, we arrive at *the same scale, spelled enharmonically two different ways.*

Illustration 3.9

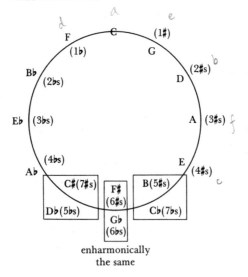

enharmonically
the same

This scale, spelled with either six sharps as F♯ major or with six flats as G♭ major, is the most distant from the C major scale in terms of common pitches. *Each shares only one tone in common* with the C major scale.

Illustration 3.10

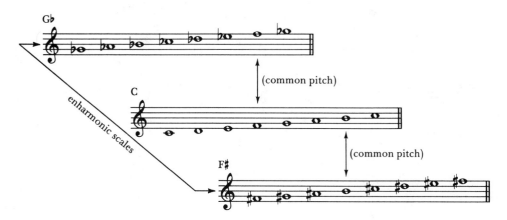

This same relationship holds true for any two scales located directly across the circle from each other, such as G and D♭, or E♭ and A.

Illustration 3.11

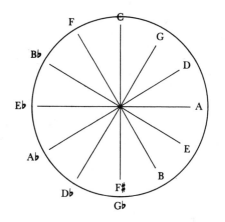

The most remote key relationships are directly across the circle from each other.

THE
MINOR
SCALE
FORMS

RELATIVE
MAJOR AND
MINOR
SCALES

By beginning on the sixth degree of any major scale and using all the same pitches, its *relative minor* scale is obtained. The term "relative" indicates that the two scales share the same key signature.

Illustration 3.12

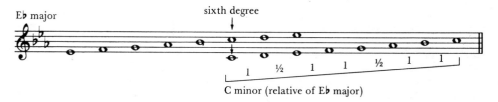

Notice that the interval order of this scale is different from that of the major scale.

The following chart lists the relative major and minor scales for key signatures up to seven sharps and seven flats.

Illustration 3.13

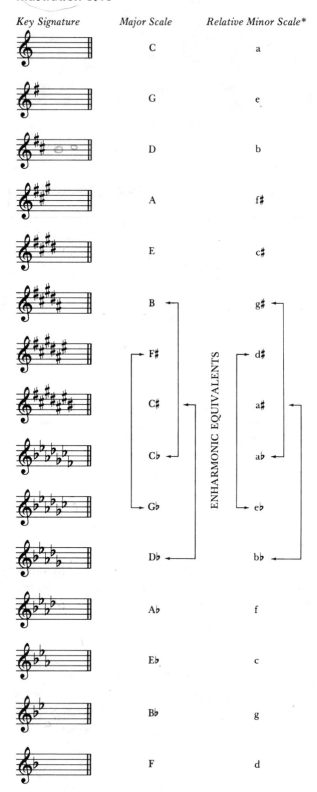

Key Signature	Major Scale	Relative Minor Scale*
	C	a
	G	e
	D	b
	A	f♯
	E	c♯
	B	g♯
	F♯	d♯
	C♯	a♯
	C♭	a♭
	G♭	e♭
	D♭	b♭
	A♭	f
	E♭	c
	B♭	g
	F	d

ENHARMONIC EQUIVALENTS

*When used alone, without the adjective "major" or "minor," capital letters designate major scales (or keys) and small letters designate minor scales (or keys).

NOTE: Arrows point to scales that are enharmonic equivalents.

The form of the minor scale that uses the *precise* pitch content of its relative major is called the *natural minor scale.* Following is a musical example using this form. **NATURAL MINOR SCALE**

Example 3.2 "O Come, Immanuel" (Gregorian chant)

In actual practice, this scale was rarely used without certain alterations.

The *harmonic minor scale* is a natural minor scale with the seventh degree raised one half step. **HARMONIC MINOR SCALE**

Illustration 3.14

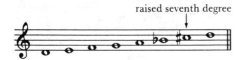

Raising the seventh degree creates an interval equal to three half steps between the sixth and seventh degrees. This interval gives the harmonic minor scale a unique sound. The raised seventh step also creates a strong push toward the tonic—scale degree eight. As we will learn in Chapter Four, this form of the scale was favored for *harmonic* structures. However, the extra large interval was considered somewhat awkward sounding in melodic passages and probably was difficult to sing as well. Therefore, a different form was favored for *melodic* structures.

The *melodic minor scale* is a natural minor scale with the sixth and seventh degrees raised by one half step *in ascent* and lowered to their natural minor positions in descent. **MELODIC MINOR SCALE**

Illustration 3.15

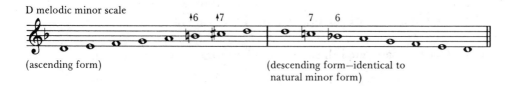

In the melodic minor scale, the upward push of the raised seventh is retained, but the extra large interval found in the harmonic minor form is avoided (by raising the sixth degree as well).

In all three minor scale forms, the lower tetrachord is identical. It is only the upper tetrachord that differs. Composers have treated the minor scale forms not as three separate structures but as different facets of a single scale. Consider the flexible use of the upper tetrachord in the following example.

Example 3.3   J. S. Bach: *Passacaglia in C Minor, BWV 582**

This movement is contained in its entirety in *Analytical Anthology of Music*, by this author (Alfred A. Knopf, Inc., 1984).

a. ascending form of the upper tetrachord used in *descent*
b. descending form of the upper tetrachord used in descent
c. descending form of the upper tetrachord used in descent
d. ascending form of the upper tetrachord used in *descent*
e. ascending form of the upper tetrachord used in ascent
f. ascending form of the upper tetrachord used in ascent
g. descending form of the upper tetrachord used in descent
h. ascending form of the upper tetrachord used in *descent*

NOTE: The bass line is based on the harmonic minor scale form.

A major and minor scale that share the same tonic are termed *parallel.* By beginning on the first degree of any major scale and adding three flats (or cancelling three sharps), the parallel minor scale (in its natural form) is obtained.

Illustration 3.16

F major   F (natural) minor

three flats added

A major   A (natural) minor

three sharps cancelled

G major   G (natural) minor

one sharp cancelled, two flats added

The parallel minor of a given major scale is always *three keys removed from it*—in the direction of more flats or less sharps.

FOR PRACTICE MATERIAL AND ASSIGNMENTS, TURN TO PAGE 63.

B. Modes

Our major and minor scales evolved from an earlier system of pitch organization called the *church modes*—different arrangements of whole steps and half steps within the octave that formed the basis of Gregorian chant and other medieval music. Modal melodies were notated largely without accidentals or key signatures. Following are the commonly used modes, built upon the pitches that permit their notation without flats or sharps. Notice that they constitute "white key scales" on D, E, F, G, and A respectively. Notice also that the half steps (E-F and B-C) are located in different places in each mode.

Illustration 3.17

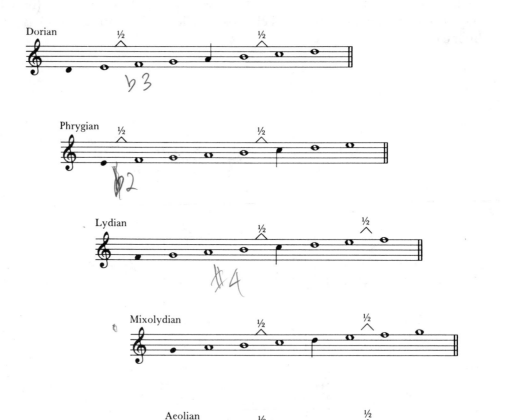

• = *Final:* the most important pitch of the mode—often the final pitch of the melody and otherwise a focal point

♩ = *Reciting tone* (or *cofinal*): the second most important pitch of the mode and a secondary focal point

NOTE: In all but the Phrygian mode, the reciting tone is the fifth degree.* Also, note that the Aeolian mode is identical in structure to the natural minor scale on A.

Following is a chant melody. Beneath it, the pitch material, the final and the mode are identified.

---

*The use of C instead of B as the reciting tone in the Phrygian mode reflects a cautious attitude toward the latter pitch in the Middle Ages. This was due to the interval formed by B and the F below it—the *tritone*—a dissonance generally thought to be capable of engendering immoral feelings and conduct.

Example 3.4 "Christe Redemptor omnium" (Gregorian chant)

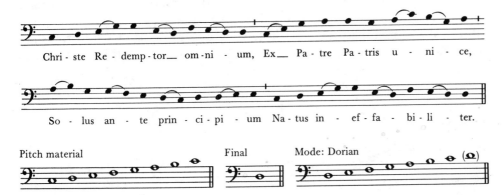

Chri - ste Re - demp - tor— om -ni - um, Ex— Pa - tre Pa - tris u - ni - ce,

So - lus an - te prin - ci - pi - um Na - tus in - ef - fa - bi - li - ter.

Pitch material   Final   Mode: Dorian

The following illustration shows the relationship between the modes and the present-day major and natural minor scales. For clarity, the modes have all been transposed to begin on C.

RELATIONSHIP TO SCALES
RELATIONSHIP TO SCALES

Illustration 3.18

Modes closely related to the major scale

Mode name	Mode built on C	Relationship to major scale
Lydian		Major scale with fourth degree raised one half step
Mixolydian		Major scale with seventh degree lowered one half step

Modes closely related to the natural minor scale

Mode name	Mode built on C	Relationship to natural minor scale
Dorian		Natural minor scale with sixth degree raised one half step
Phrygian		Natural minor scale with second degree lowered one half step
Aeolian		Identical to natural minor scale

Black note = the pitch that differs from the major or natural minor scale.

**EVOLUTION
OF MAJOR
AND MINOR
SCALES**

Our present-day major and minor scales evolved, over many years, from the church modes. This was due partly to the practice of altering certain pitches in performance to create half steps to the important modal degrees (the final and reciting tone). The following illustration shows how this may have happened, although the process was, no doubt, considerably more complex.

Illustration 3.19

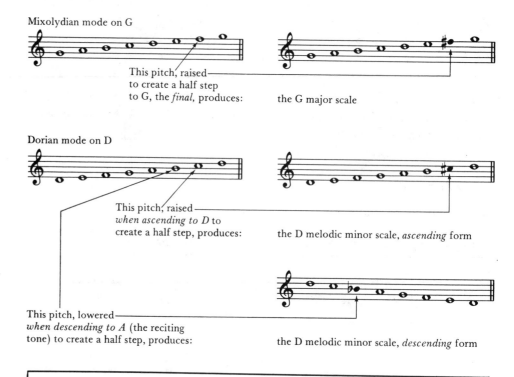

Mixolydian mode on G

This pitch, raised
to create a half step
to G, the *final,* produces:

the G major scale

Dorian mode on D

This pitch, raised
when ascending to D to
create a half step, produces:

the D melodic minor scale, *ascending* form

This pitch, lowered
when descending to A (the reciting
tone) to create a half step, produces:

the D melodic minor scale, *descending* form

FOR CLASS DISCUSSION:

In the Dorian mode chant melody on page 55, determine which of the pitches might have been altered in performance, and explain why.

FOR PRACTICE MATERIAL AND ASSIGNMENTS, TURN TO PAGE 70.

C. Intervals

As mentioned in Chapter One, the half step is the smallest interval commonly employed in our music. Because of this, it provides a convenient means by which to measure *other* intervals.

**NUMERICAL
VALUE**   All intervals are given a two-part designation—a numerical value and a qualifying term. The *numerical value* indicates the number of *letter names* spanned. For example, interval **a** in the following illustration is a third because it spans a total of three letter names (G, A, and B); interval **b** is a fifth because it encompasses five letter names (A, B, C, D, and E); and so on.

Illustration 3.20

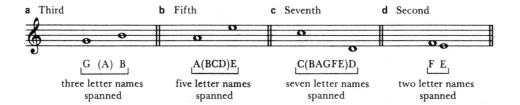

a Third	**b** Fifth	**c** Seventh	**d** Second
G (A) B	A(BCD)E	C(BAGFE)D	F E
three letter names spanned	five letter names spanned	seven letter names spanned	two letter names spanned

QUALITY

To this numerical designation, a qualifier is prefixed, which tells more precisely how large the interval is. This is necessary because two intervals that span the same number of letter names may span a different number of half steps. For example, interval **a** in the following illustration is *not* the same-size third as interval **b**.

Illustration 3.21

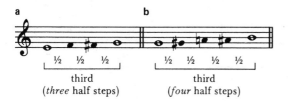

a	b
½ ½ ½	½ ½ ½ ½
third (*three* half steps)	third (*four* half steps)

The five qualifying terms used and their abbreviated symbols are:

major   M } apply to seconds, thirds, sixths and sevenths
minor   m }

perfect   P   applies to unisons, fourths, fifths and octaves

augmented + } can apply to all intervals*
diminished o }

The best way to understand how the numerical value and the qualifier are used together is to consider the intervals found in a single-octave major scale. From the following chart, you can see that in the major scale (within a *single octave*):

Seconds, thirds, sixths, and sevenths are either major or minor.

Unisons, octaves, fourths, and fifths are perfect.

There is one instance of an augmented fourth.

INTERVALS
OF THE
MAJOR SCALE

*Exception: A unison cannot be diminished. This is explained on page 61.

Interval	Abbreviation	Composed of:	Examples in C major scale (Scale degrees are indicated by numbers.)
Perfect unison	P1	a pitch and its duplication	
Minor second	m2	a half step	
Major second	M2	two half steps or one whole step	
Minor third	m3	three half steps (M2 plus m2 or P4 minus M2)	
Major third	M3	four half steps (M2 plus M2 or P4 minus m2)	
Perfect fourth	P4	five half steps (M3 plus m2)	
Augmented fourth	+4	six half steps (M2 plus M2 plus M2 or P5 minus m2)	
Perfect fifth	P5	seven half steps (P4 plus M2)	
Minor sixth	m6	eight half steps (P5 plus m2)	
Major sixth	M6	nine half steps (P5 plus M2)	
Minor seventh	m7	ten half steps (P8 minus M2)	
Major seventh	M7	eleven half steps (P8 minus m2)	
Perfect octave	P8	twelve half steps	

Remember that, in each and every case, the number of *letter names* spanned is reflected by the interval's numerical designation.

The intervals of the major scale, measured above and below the tonic, are shown below.

Illustration 3.22

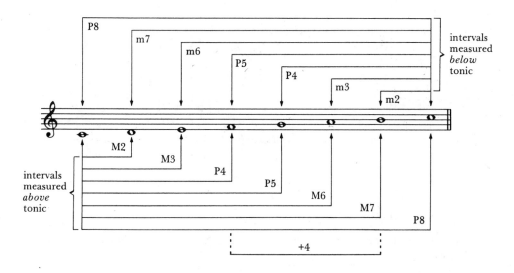

NOTE: All intervals of the major scale *measured from the tonic up* are either *major or perfect.*

All intervals of the major scale *measured from the tonic down* are either *minor or perfect.*

An interval's *quality* may be changed through the addition or subtraction of accidentals. However, the *number* of letter names spanned must remain the same or the interval's *quantity* (its numerical value) changes as well.

CHROMATIC
ALTERATION

- Major Intervals

ALTERATION
OF INTERVAL
QUALITY

   When made larger by a half step, a major interval becomes an augmented interval.

   The major third   becomes an augmented third (+3)   when the higher pitch is raised   or when the lower pitch is lowered.

   When made smaller by a half step, a major interval becomes a minor interval.

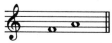

   The major third   becomes a minor third (m3)   when the higher pitch is lowered   or when the lower pitch is raised.

- Minor Intervals

When made larger by a half step, a minor interval becomes a major interval.

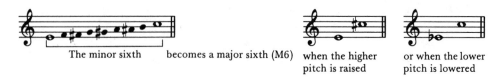

| The minor sixth | becomes a major sixth (M6) | when the higher pitch is raised | or when the lower pitch is lowered |

When made smaller by a half step, a minor interval becomes a diminished interval.

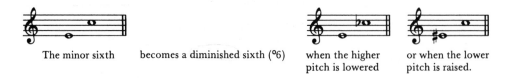

| The minor sixth | becomes a diminished sixth (°6) | when the higher pitch is lowered | or when the lower pitch is raised. |

- Perfect Intervals

When made larger by a half step, a perfect interval becomes an augmented interval.

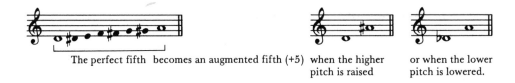

| The perfect fifth | becomes an augmented fifth (+5) | when the higher pitch is raised | or when the lower pitch is lowered. |

When made smaller by a half step, a perfect interval becomes a diminished interval.

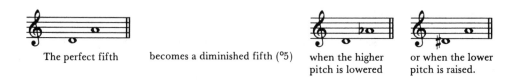

| The perfect fifth | becomes a diminished fifth (°5) | when the higher pitch is lowered | or when the lower pitch is raised. |

The following illustration shows the relationship between diminished, minor, major, augmented and perfect intervals.

Illustration 3.23

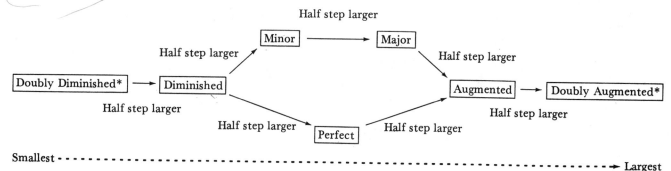

*Not commonly encountered.

Notice that:

1. Perfect intervals cannot be altered to form major or minor intervals.
2. Major and minor intervals cannot be altered to form perfect intervals.
3. A unison may be augmented but may not be diminished, since it can become no smaller than a unison.

Illustration 3.24

Just as two intervals may be of the same numerical value but of different quality, two intervals of different numerical values may sound identical. That is, they may comprise an identical number of half steps. Such intervals are *enharmonic*.

ENHARMONIC INTERVALS

Illustration 3.25

All are enharmonic, containing two half steps.

*Doubly augmented unison—a unison made larger by *two* half steps.

All are enharmonic, containing nine half steps.

†Doubly augmented fifth—a perfect fifth made larger by *two* half steps.

Enharmonic intervals can have the *same* numerical value and quality and yet be spelled differently.

Illustration 3.26

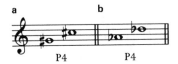

Here the *type* of interval is the same (a perfect fourth) but the pitches are spelled enharmonically.

INVERSION OF INTERVALS

Inversion of an interval involves octave transposition of one of the pitches so that the higher pitch becomes the lower pitch and vice versa.

Illustration 3.27

The designation of an interval's inversion can be easily determined.

1. Subtract its numerical value from 9.
2. Change the *quality* of the interval as follows.

- Major intervals invert to minor and vice versa.
- Augmented intervals invert to diminished and vice versa.
- Perfect intervals remain perfect.

Illustration 3.28

To find the inversion of:	Subtract numerical value from 9:	Change quality:	The inversion's designation is:
m2	9−2 = 7	m becomes M	M7
P4	9−4 = 5	P remains P	P5
°5	9−5 = 4	° becomes +	+4
+6	9−6 = 3	+ becomes °	°3

Besides numerical value and quality, intervals are often classified in other ways. One such classification indicates whether an interval is larger or smaller than an octave.

A *simple interval* is one contained within an octave.

A *compound interval* is larger than an octave.

SIMPLE VERSUS COMPOUND INTERVALS

For ease of reference, compound intervals are commonly reduced to simple intervals.

Intervals can be classified as diatonic or chromatic. *Diatonic intervals* are those formed by only the pitches of a given key. For example, in E♭ major, a diatonic interval can be formed by any two of the following pitches: E♭, F, G, A♭, B♭, C, D. *Chromatic intervals* involve some chromatic alteration (a flat, sharp, or natural) of one or both of the pitches.

DIATONIC VERSUS CHROMATIC INTERVALS

Intervals may also be classified as consonant or dissonant. *Consonance* refers to sounds that suggest a lack of tension—a feeling of repose or stability. *Dissonance* denotes sounds that suggest tension or unrest. While this is somewhat subjective and relative, the following classifications are in general use.*

CONSONANT VERSUS DISSONANT INTERVALS

Perfect consonances: the perfect unison, perfect fourth, perfect fifth, and perfect octave

Imperfect consonances: major and minor thirds and sixths

Dissonances: seconds, sevenths, and all augmented or diminished intervals

The ability to recognize and spell intervals fluently is a fundamental and useful musical skill. Your instructor will undoubtedly suggest a method that he or she feels to be most helpful. One possible method is outlined in Appendix Two (see page 344).

FOR PRACTICE MATERIAL AND ASSIGNMENTS, TURN TO PAGE 73.

PRACTICE MATERIAL AND ASSIGNMENTS FOR PART A

A. Write the following scales (in ascending form only, unless otherwise indicated), placing sharps or flats before the appropriate pitches. Be careful to observe the clefs. Then practice singing each, using a neutral syllable, numbers, or solmization syllables.

1 G major   **2** B harmonic minor

---

*These classifications were made by Franco of Cologne, writing around 1260. Certain later theorists regarded the perfect fourth as a dissonance rather than as a consonance, and musical usage in certain periods of music history bears this out. Further discussion appears in Appendix One.

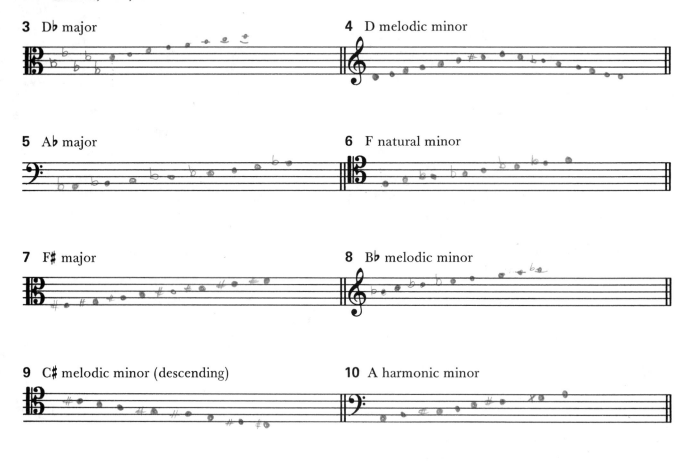

3 Db major

4 D melodic minor

5 Ab major

6 F natural minor

7 F# major

8 Bb melodic minor

9 C# melodic minor (descending)

10 A harmonic minor

B. Correct the errors in the following scales by changing, adding, or deleting accidentals. If no errors are present, indicate this with the notation *O.K.*

NOTE: More than one error may be present in a scale.

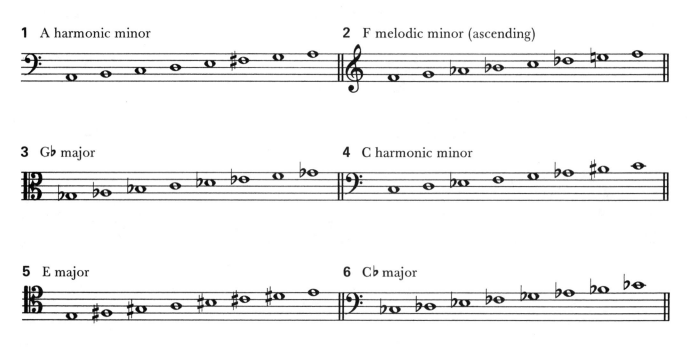

1 A harmonic minor

2 F melodic minor (ascending)

3 Gb major

4 C harmonic minor

5 E major

6 Cb major

7 F♯ natural minor   **8** A♭ harmonic minor

9 E♭ melodic minor (descending)   **10** D major

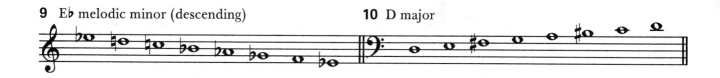

C. Write the signature of the key *most remote* from each of the given
   keys. Be sure to observe the correct placement of sharps and flats
   in the indicated clef.

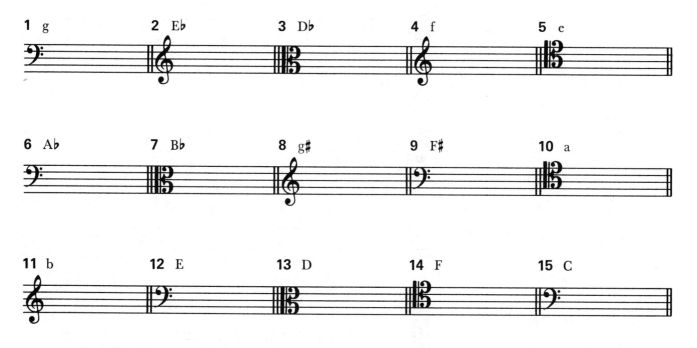

1 g   **2** E♭   **3** D♭   **4** f   **5** e

6 A♭   **7** B♭   **8** g♯   **9** F♯   **10** a

11 b   **12** E   **13** D   **14** F   **15** C

D. Construct the melodic minor scale (ascending form) in which:

1 A is the fifth degree

2 C♯ is the sixth degree

3 D is the third degree

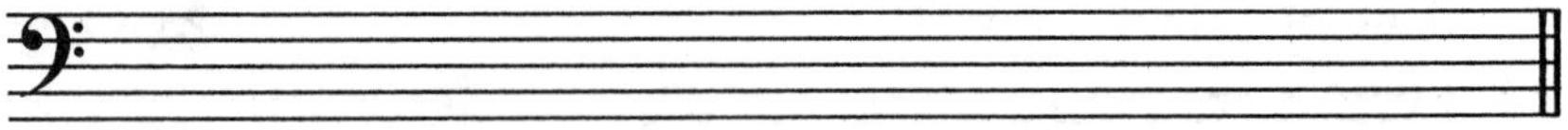

4 F♯ is the fourth degree

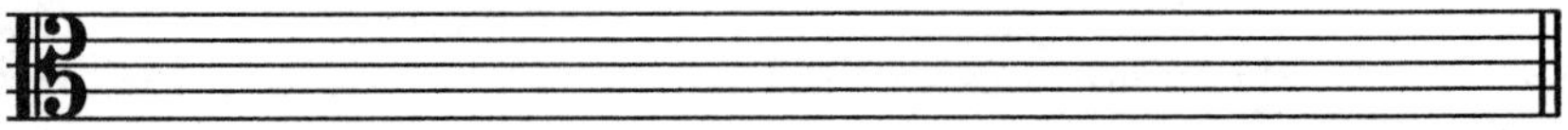

5 B♭ is the second degree

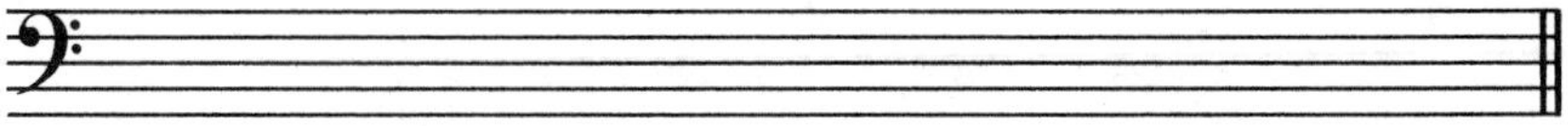

6 G♯ is the seventh degree

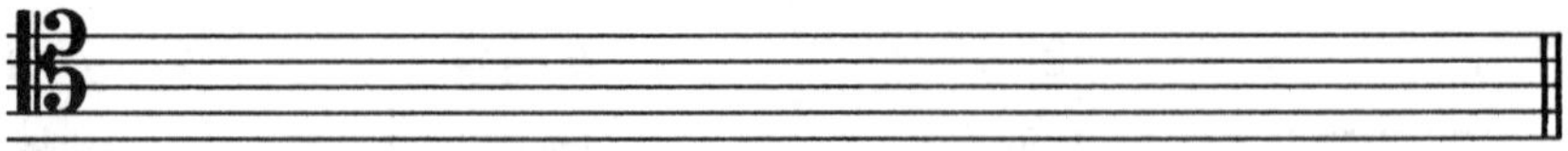

7 E is the sixth degree

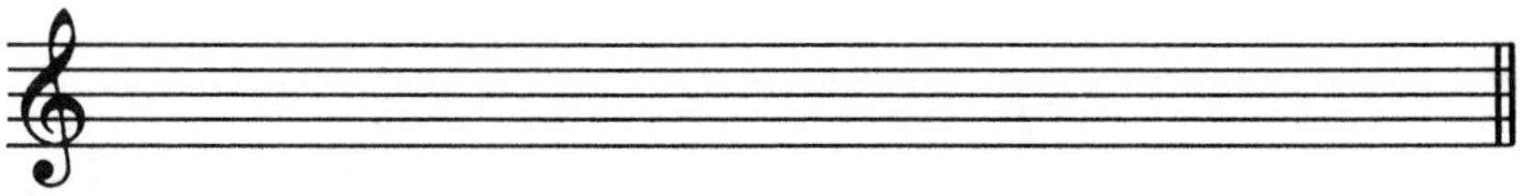

8 E♭ is the third degree

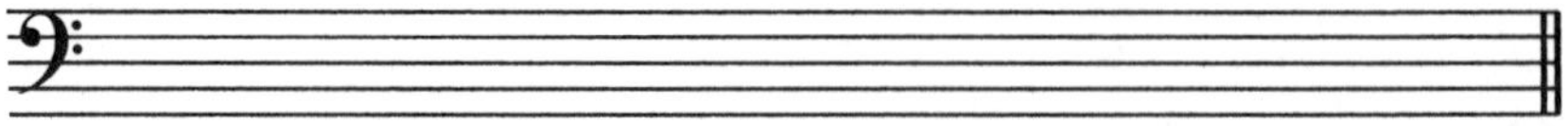

9 B is the third degree

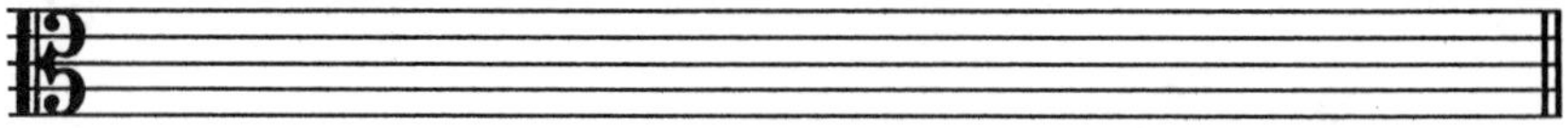

10 G is the sixth degree

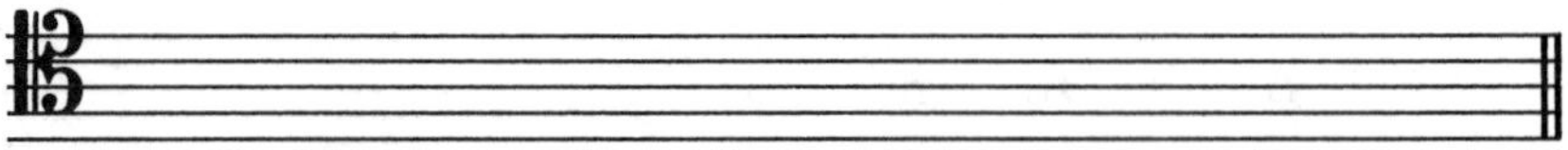

E. Name a scale (major or any minor scale form) in which each of the following appears:

1. as the upper tetrachord
2. as the lower tetrachord

If a particular pattern *does not* appear in any scale as an upper or lower tetrachord, place an *X* in the corresponding space.

Example:

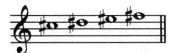

1. __F#__   (upper tetrachord)
2. __C#__   (lower tetrachord)

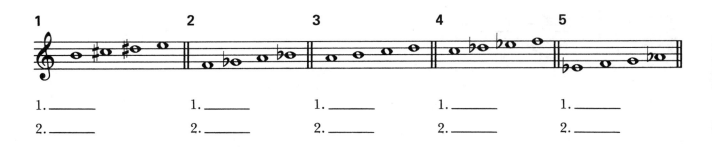

1. _____   1. _____   1. _____   1. _____   1. _____
2. _____   2. _____   2. _____   2. _____   2. _____

1. _____   1. _____   1. _____   1. _____   1. _____
2. _____   2. _____   2. _____   2. _____   2. _____

F. Above each pitch, place the number that corresponds to its position in the scale (degrees 1-7). Use the numbers 1 to 7 regardless of the octave in which the pitches appear. Then transpose each melody to the indicated key. The first melody is begun for you.

1 J. Strauss: *Tales from the Vienna Woods, Op. 325*

Transpose to the key of E♭.

2 Beethoven: *Piano Sonata, Op. 2, No. 3* (I)

Transpose to the key of D.

3 *Morris Dance* (English)

Transpose to the key of F.

4 Mozart: *Piano Sonata, K. 280* (II)

Adagio

Transpose to the key of d.

PRACTICE MATERIAL AND ASSIGNMENTS FOR PART B

A. Identify each of the modes and transpose each in the same clef so that it consists entirely of white keys.

Example:

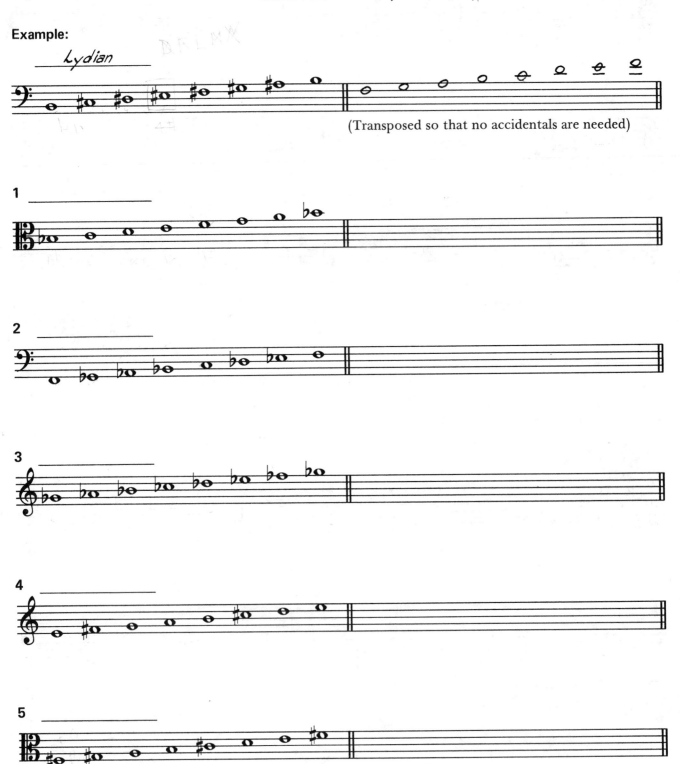

Lydian

(Transposed so that no accidentals are needed)

1

2

3

4

5

6

7

8

9

10

B. 1. Write the requested modes beginning on the final shown, adding accidentals where necessary.

2. Show the key signature that would be required to change the mode as specified.

Example:

Phrygian mode on:

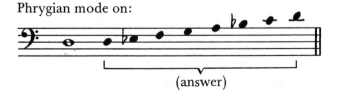

(answer)

Signature needed to change to Lydian:

(answer)

Additional suggestion: Sing each of the modes, using a neutral syllable or numbers (1-8).

1 Dorian mode on:

Signature needed to change to Phrygian:

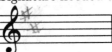

2 Mixolydian mode on:

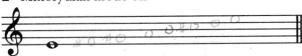

Signature needed to change to Dorian:

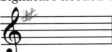

3 Lydian mode on:

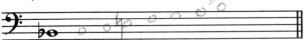

Signature needed to change to Mixolydian:

4 Phrygian mode on:

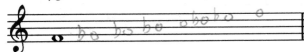

Signature needed to change to Lydian:

5 Aeolian mode on:

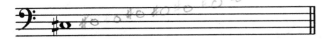

Signature needed to change to Phrygian:

6 Phrygian mode on:

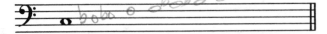

Signature needed to change to Mixolydian:

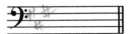

7 Mixolydian mode on:

Signature needed to change to Dorian:

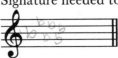

F6ABCDEf

8 Lydian mode on:

Signature needed to change to Aeolian:

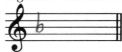

9 Dorian mode on:

Signature needed to change to Lydian:

10 Mixolydian mode on:

Signature needed to change to Phrygian:

C. From the designated pitches, practice singing, on *la,* the specified scales or modes. Sing each scale or mode upward and downward, proceeding immediately to the next, making the needed pitch adjustments. Practice each exercise until you can perform it without pause at ♩ = 120. Give yourself the beginning pitch on the piano or on your own instrument.

1. On C: major scale; Mixolydian mode; Lydian mode
2. On A: natural minor scale; harmonic minor scale; Dorian mode
3. On D: natural minor scale; Phrygian mode; melodic minor scale
4. On B♭: Lydian mode; Mixolydian mode; major scale
5. On C: major scale; natural minor scale; Dorian mode

PRACTICE MATERIAL AND ASSIGNMENTS FOR PART C

A. 1. Identify each interval and place the answer in the *first space* beneath it. Then designate the inversion of that interval in the *second space.*
2. Practice singing the original interval followed by its inversion.

M3 5⁺ 6⁺ M6 M2 m7 M6 1⁺ M2
M6 4° 3° M3 M7 M2 m3 8° m7

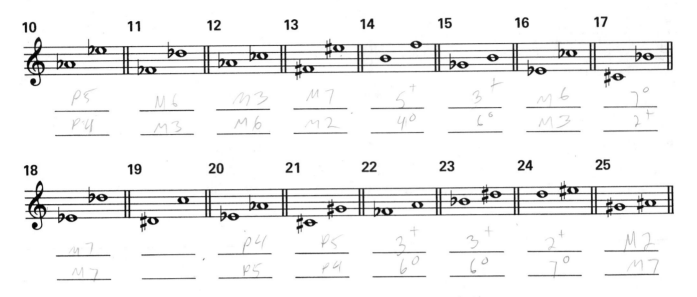

B. Spell the specified intervals above or below the given pitches. It will also be valuable to sing each interval after you write it. Do not alter the given pitch.

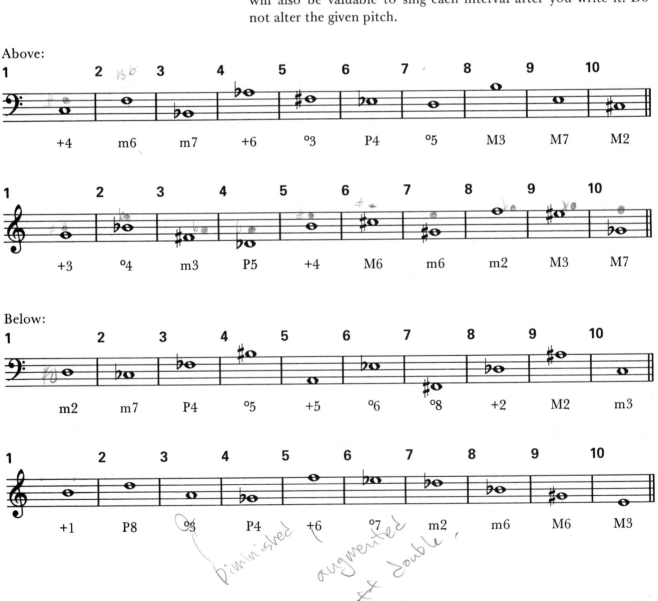

C. Respell the following intervals enharmonically in two different
ways. At least one of the respellings should result in a numerical
value different from the original. Give the numerical value and
quality of each enharmonic interval. The first one has been completed for you.

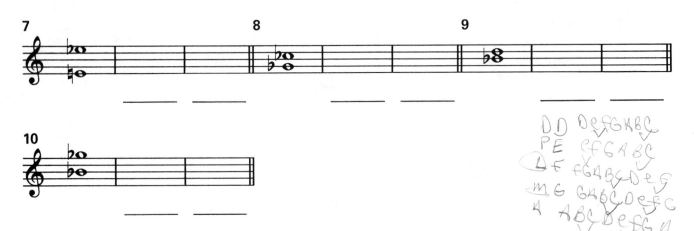

SUGGESTIONS FOR AURAL DRILL

A. Your instructor will play one pitch. You are to sing, beginning on that pitch, a major or minor scale (one of the three forms) as instructed.

B. Your instructor (or another student) will play various major or minor scales and church modes. You are to identify them.

C. Beginning on a given pitch, sing the following, in succession.

> natural minor scale
> Dorian mode
> Phrygian mode
> major scale
> Lydian mode
> Mixolydian mode

D. Your instructor will play two pitches simultaneously. You are to identify the interval as:

> simple or compound
> a perfect consonance, imperfect consonance, or dissonance

E. Your instructor will play several intervals. You are to identify each. These intervals might be grouped in different ways for study purposes, such as:

> 1. m2, M2, m3, M3
> 2. P4, +4, P5
> 3. m6, M6, m7, M7

or

> 1. P4, P5, P8
> 2. m3, M3, m6, M6
> 3. m2, M2, m7, M7

The two members of the interval can be played harmonically (simultaneously) or melodically (successively). Ideally, both manners of playing should be used.

TEST YOUR COMPREHENSION OF CHAPTER THREE

A. Identify the following scales or modes.

1 Phrygian

2 Aeolian

3 Lydian

4 Mixolydian

5 Dorian

B. Identify the major *and* minor keys indicated by each key signature.

1 Major key: B Minor key: g#

2 Major key: D Minor key: b

3 Major key: Ab Minor key: f.

4

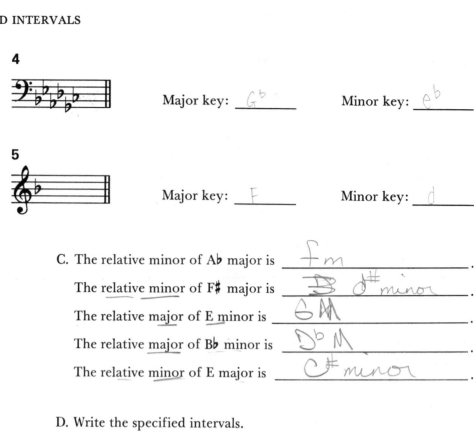

Major key: _G♭_   Minor key: _e♭_

5

Major key: _F_   Minor key: _d_

C. The relative minor of A♭ major is _f m_ .

The relative minor of F♯ major is _B d♯ minor_ .

The relative major of E minor is _G M_ .

The relative major of B♭ minor is _D♭ M_ .

The relative minor of E major is _C♯ minor_ .

D. Write the specified intervals.

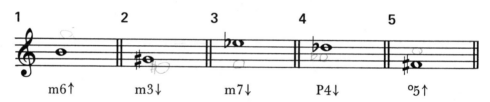

E. Match the intervals that contain the same number of half steps.

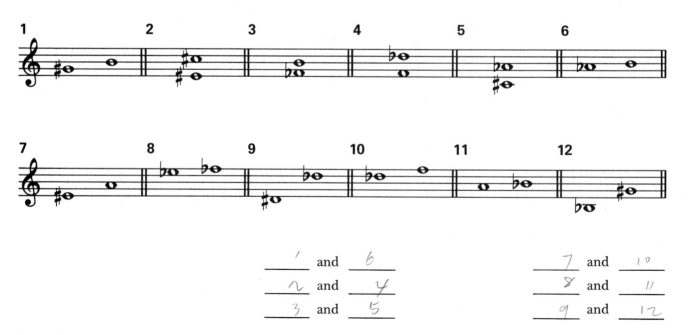

_____1__ and __6__   _____7__ and __10__

_____2__ and __4__   _____8__ and __11__

_____3__ and __5__   _____9__ and __12__

F. Notate two appearances of each interval in the indicated scales.

1 G major scale: M6

2 A♭ major scale: m3

3 D minor scale (harmonic): M6

4 E major scale: P4

5 E♭ minor scale (harmonic): P5

Answers appear on page 363.

CHAPTER FOUR
HARMONY

<table>
<tr><td colspan="2" align="center">TERMS TO KNOW</td></tr>
<tr><td>authentic cadence</td><td>imperfect authentic cadence</td></tr>
<tr><td>bass</td><td>perfect authentic cadence</td></tr>
<tr><td>chord</td><td>Phrygian cadence</td></tr>
<tr><td>continuo</td><td>plagal cadence</td></tr>
<tr><td>deceptive cadence</td><td>root</td></tr>
<tr><td>figured bass</td><td>root position</td></tr>
<tr><td>first inversion</td><td>second inversion</td></tr>
<tr><td>half cadence</td><td>soprano</td></tr>
<tr><td>harmony</td><td>triad</td></tr>
</table>

HARMONY AND CHORD

The word *harmony* can refer to the general effect of several musical lines in combination, or it can refer to any single combination of sounds. Harmony in the latter sense is more often referred to as a *chord*—a single sound comprising three or more pitches. (Two simultaneous pitches produce a *harmonic interval,* not a chord.) Following are some examples of chords.

Illustration 4.1

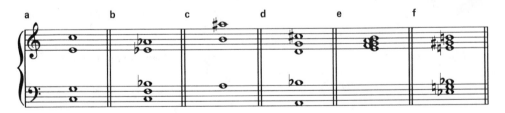

A. Triads

In the broadest sense, a triad is any three-note chord. In a more limited sense, a *triad* is any three-note chord in which the notes can be arranged to form two thirds, one immediately above the other. In this position, the lowest note is called the *root.*

Illustration 4.2

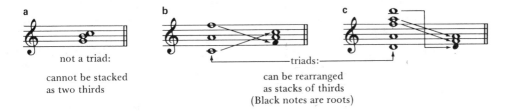

not a triad:

cannot be stacked
as two thirds

———————————triads:———————————

can be rearranged
as stacks of thirds
(Black notes are roots)

Notice that octave doublings are not considered to be additional chord tones in determining whether a chord is a triad.

The four most common triad types are shown below. Note the intervals present in each.

Illustration 4.3

Triad Quality	Example: Triad built on G	Symbol	Intervals Present
Major (M)	fifth / third / root	G	M3 P5 m3
Minor (m)	fifth / third / root	g	m3 P5 M3
Augmented (⁺)	fifth / third / root	G⁺	M3 ⁺5 M3
Diminished (°)	fifth / third / root	g°	m3 °5 m3

(Black notes are roots)

Observations:

1. An upper-case letter denotes a major triad.
2. A lower-case letter denotes a minor triad.
3. An upper-case letter followed by a ⁺ denotes an augmented triad.
4. A lower-case letter followed by a ° denotes a diminished triad.
5. The two upper chord members (the third and fifth) are so named because of their intervallic distance above the root.

STABILITY Of the four triad types, the major and minor triads have the greatest stability. Because of this, they have traditionally served as points of musical repose, or *resolution,* appearing at the ends of compositions or sections within compositions. Stability is directly related to intervallic makeup. In the major and minor triads, the interval formed by the root and fifth is a perfect consonance; this is not the case with diminished and augmented triads (see Illustration 4.3).

TRIADS IN MAJOR KEYS By constructing a triad on each of the seven tones of a major scale, the *diatonic triads* of that key are obtained. Each triad has a name that suggests its function within the key and its relationship to the other triads.

Illustration 4.4

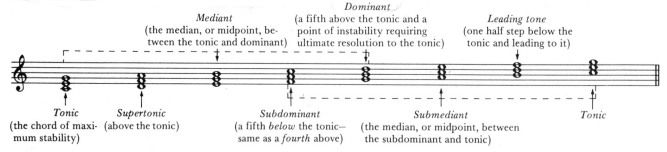

Mediant
(the median, or midpoint, between the tonic and dominant)

Dominant
(a fifth above the tonic and a point of instability requiring ultimate resolution to the tonic)

Leading tone
(one half step below the tonic and leading to it)

Tonic
(the chord of maximum stability)

Supertonic
(above the tonic)

Subdominant
(a fifth *below* the tonic— same as a *fourth* above)

Submediant
(the median, or midpoint, between the subdominant and tonic)

Tonic

NOTE: These names are also applied to the individual scale degrees upon which the triads are built.

FUNCTIONAL CHORD SYMBOLS In harmonic analysis, it is not enough to know the letter name of a triad, since a given triad's effect depends on the key of the music. For this reason, a system of chord symbology is used that reflects the chords' relationships within a key. In this system, Roman numerals are used to stand for the functional names.

Illustration 4.5

Key: C

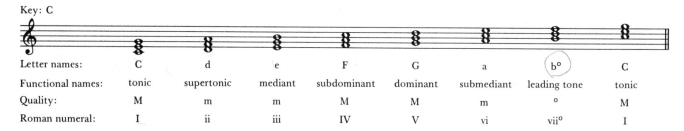

Letter names:	C	d	e	F	G	a	b°	C
Functional names:	tonic	supertonic	mediant	subdominant	dominant	submediant	leading tone	tonic
Quality:	M	m	m	M	M	m	°	M
Roman numeral:	I	ii	iii	IV	V	vi	vii°	I

Observations:

1. As with letter-name designations, upper-case numerals denote major triads while lower-case numerals denote minor triads.
2. The symbol $^+$ is used only with an upper-case Roman numeral and indicates an augmented triad (not present in the major scale). The symbol ° is used only with a lower-case Roman numeral and indicates a diminished triad.

3. Three of the triads in a major key are major—the I, IV and V.
4. Three of the triads in a major key are minor—the ii, iii and vi.

A greater variety of diatonic triads is possible in minor keys than in major keys, due to the variable sixth and seventh minor scale degrees. Following are the diatonic triads for each form of the minor scale.

TRIADS IN MINOR KEYS

Illustration 4.6

Natural minor

Letter names:	c	d°	E♭	f	g	A♭	B♭	c
Functional names:	same as for major						subtonic	tonic
Quality:	m	°	M	m	m	M	M	m
Roman numeral:	i	ii°	III	iv	v	VI	VII	i

Melodic minor
NOTE: Descending form is identical to natural minor form.

Letter names:	c	d	E♭+	F	G	a°	b°	c
Functional names:	same as for major							
Quality:	m	m	+	M	M	°	°	m
Roman numeral:	i	ii	III+	IV	V	vi°	vii°	i

Harmonic minor

Letter names:	c	d°	E♭+	f	G	A♭	b°	c
Functional names:	same as for major							
Quality:	m	°	+	m	M	M	°	m
Roman numeral:	i	ii°	III+	iv	V	VI	vii°	i

Observations:

1. There is only one version of the tonic. *This is the only chord that has no diatonic variant in a minor key.*
2. All the variations for the other chords result from the alteration of *either the sixth or seventh scale degrees* (the only scale degrees that change from one form of the minor scale to another): ii° or ii; III+ or III; iv or IV; v or V; VI or vi°; vii° or VII.

Certain minor-key triads appear more often than others. *Most* common are those of the harmonic minor scale, with one exception—the mediant. This chord appears less often as an augmented triad than as a major triad.

MOST COMMON MINOR-KEY TRIADS

This is because it is closely related to the tonic, as its relative major. Therefore, when we speak of minor-key harmonies, we are generally referring to a specific few chords, shown in the following example in C minor.

Illustration 4.7

i   ii°   III   iv   V   VI   vii°   i

TRIADIC INVERSION

With the chord root in the lowest position (called the *bass*), a triad is said to be in *root position.* Two other arrangements are possible—first inversion and second inversion. If the third of the chord is in the lowest position, the triad is in *first inversion.*

Illustration 4.8

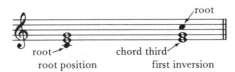

root position   first inversion

If the fifth of the chord is in the lowest position, the triad is said to be in *second inversion.*

Illustration 4.9

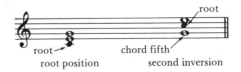

root position   second inversion

It makes no difference which pitch occupies the *highest* position in the chordal structure. The inversion is determined solely by the lowest pitch. The following triads are *all* in first inversion, regardless of the pitch appearing in the highest voice (called the *soprano*).

Illustration 4.10

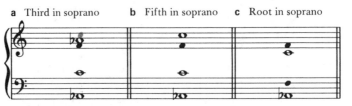

a Third in soprano   b Fifth in soprano   c Root in soprano

(Black note is the root)

The following triads are *all* in second inversion.

Illustration 4.11

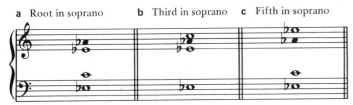

a Root in soprano   **b** Third in soprano   **c** Fifth in soprano

(Black note is the root)

For major and minor triads, root position is the most stable-sounding arrangement. One possible reason may be the stability of the perfect fifth, an interval present between the bass and an upper voice in root-position major and minor triads but *not* in their inversions.

STABILITY
OF ROOT
POSITION

FOR PRACTICE MATERIAL AND ASSIGNMENTS, TURN TO PAGE 90.

B. Chord Symbols and Figured Bass

A numerical superscript added to the symbol for a triad indicates whether it is in root position, first inversion or second inversion. The superscript indicates the intervals that appear above the lowest note of the chord. In root-position triads, these intervals are a third (indicated by a 3) and a fifth (indicated by a 5). However, because root-position triads are so common, the numerical superscripts for chords in this position are normally omitted.

Illustration 4.12

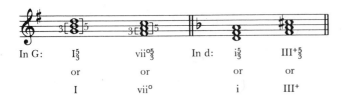

TRIADS
IN ROOT
POSITION

For triads in first inversion, the superscript $^6_3$ or simply ^{6} is used.

Illustration 4.13

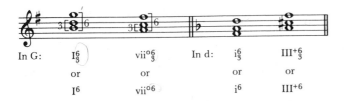

TRIADS
IN FIRST
INVERSION

For triads in second inversion, the superscript ⁶₄ is used.

Illustration 4.14

TRIADS
IN SECOND
INVERSION

Notice that three important pieces of information are conveyed through these chord symbols—the chord root, the chord quality, and the chord position (root position, first inversion, or second inversion). This method of symbolizing chords is derived from a seventeenth- and eighteenth-century practice called *figured bass notation*—a system of musical shorthand devised for keyboard parts, consisting of a bass line along with numbers below the notes to indicate the intervals to be added above. Known as the *continuo,* this part was interpreted (*realized*) by keyboard players who filled in the indicated harmonies according to their musical tastes and skill. The basic rules of figured bass notation follow.

**FIGURED
BASS**

1. The numbers appearing under a given bass note indicate the intervals to be added above that note. (The composers and performers of the time thought in terms of intervals only—*not chord inversion,* a concept unknown to all but the last generation of figured bass composers.)
2. The absence of a number under a bass note implies that a third and fifth are to be added above that note (i.e., a root-position triad).
3. The intervals to be added are diatonic—that is, *found within the key*—unless otherwise indicated through the presence of accidentals.

Illustration 4.15

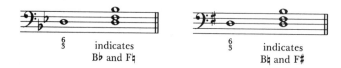

As with chord symbols, figured bass symbols give no indication as to *how* the notes are to be disposed above the bass, although occasionally, a symbol is expanded in order to show a desired doubling or omission of a chord member.

Illustration 4.16

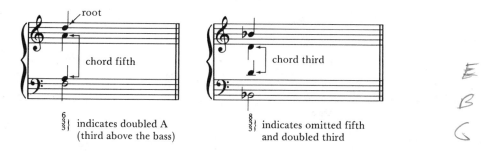

$\begin{smallmatrix}6\\3\\3\end{smallmatrix}$ indicates doubled A (third above the bass)

$\begin{smallmatrix}8\\3\\3\end{smallmatrix}$ indicates omitted fifth and doubled third

However, this matter largely was left to the performer, and abbreviated symbols are found much more often.

When a chord falls *outside* the key, accidentals are added to the figure, as shown below.

Illustration 4.17

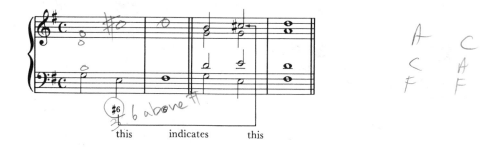

this   indicates   this

Two conventions are commonly applied in figured bass notation.

1. An accidental *by itself* applies to the *third above* the bass.

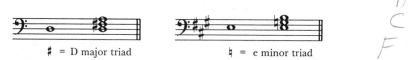

♯ = D major triad   ♮ = e minor triad

Observe the different meaning of these two symbols.

♭6 = A♭⁺ triad
3

$\begin{smallmatrix}6\\♭3\end{smallmatrix}$ = a° triad

2. A raised pitch (sharp or natural) is often indicated by a slash through the number to which it applies.

♯6   6♯   6   ♮6   6♮   6
These figures all mean   These figures all mean

Following is an example of a figured bass part and one possible realization.

Illustration 4.18

Realization:

FOR PRACTICE MATERIAL AND ASSIGNMENTS, TURN TO PAGE 94.

C. Harmonic Cadences

A *cadence* is a musical punctuation—a point of repose that separates musical thoughts. When a melody comes to a point of repose, the supporting harmonies at that point are called a *harmonic cadence*. The great majority of harmonic cadences can be reduced to four basic types—authentic, plagal, half, and deceptive.

AUTHENTIC CADENCE
The *authentic cadence* (V-I in major and V-i in minor) is the most common of all cadences. Two varieties traditionally have been distinguished. In the *perfect authentic cadence* (abbreviated PAC), the dominant and tonic chords are both in root position, and the tonic also appears in the highest voice. Owing to this strong melodic and harmonic motion to the tonic, the PAC is the most conclusive sounding of all cadences.

Illustration 4.19

Perfect authentic cadences

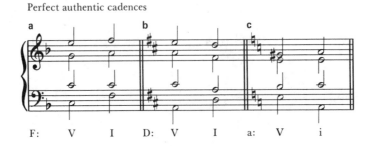

F: V I   D: V I   a: V i

The *imperfect authentic cadence* (abbreviated IAC), while still regarded as a conclusive cadence, is somewhat less so, because it lacks either the tonic resolution in the highest voice or the descending fifth (ascending fourth) to the tonic in the bass, or both. Unlike the PAC, it may involve the vii° in place of the V.

Illustration 4.20

Imperfect authentic cadences

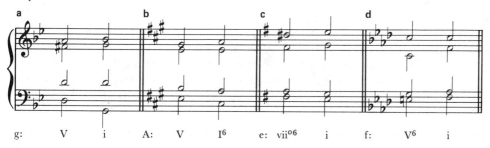

g: V   i   A: V   I⁶   e: vii°⁶   i   f: V⁶   i

   a Lacks tonic resolution in upper voice
   b Lacks descending perfect fifth in bass
   c Lacks descending perfect fifth in bass
   d Lacks descending perfect fifth in bass *and* tonic resolution in upper voice

Also conclusive, but less common than the authentic cadence, is the *plagal cadence* (IV-I in major and iv-i in minor), heard in the familiar "Amen" intoned at the end of hymns. Because the root movement is to the tonic from the *fourth* scale degree (rather than from the fifth) and because no leading tone is present, it is somewhat weaker than the authentic cadence.

PLAGAL CADENCE

Illustration 4.21

Plagal cadences

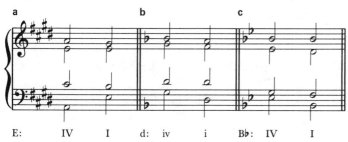

E: IV   I   d: iv   i   B♭:   IV   I

A *half cadence* is, in the broadest sense, one that ends *on any chord but the tonic.* In actual practice, the most common forms end on the dominant, as shown below. Of these, the first of the minor key cadences—iv⁶-V—has acquired a special name, the *Phrygian cadence.* This is due to the half-step descent in the bass, a common motion in Phrygian melodies.

HALF CADENCE

Illustration 4.22

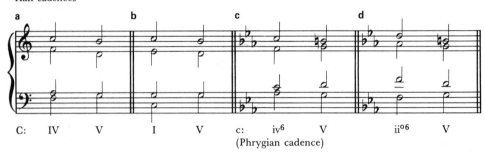

Half cadences

C: IV   V   I   V   c: iv⁶   V   ii°⁶   V
                                                   (Phrygian cadence)

The half cadence is an *inconclusive* cadence; that is, it implies continuation rather than finality. For this reason, half cadences normally are not used to end a musical work, although they *may* end a movement if another is to follow.

DECEPTIVE CADENCE   In the broadest sense, a *deceptive cadence* is one in which the dominant moves not to the expected tonic but elsewhere. Certain deceptive cadences have been favored more than others, the most common ending on the submediant.

Illustration 4.23

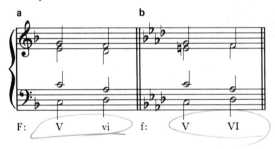

Deceptive cadences

F: V   vi   f: V   VI

FOR PRACTICE MATERIAL AND ASSIGNMENTS, TURN TO PAGE 96.

PRACTICE MATERIAL AND ASSIGNMENTS FOR PART A

A. Place an *X* in the space below each chord that is *not* a triad. For those chords that *are* triads:

1. Give the letter name of the root.
2. Rearrange the chord as a stack of thirds (root in the lowest position) with all pitches as close together as possible.
3. Eliminate all octave doublings.

Example:

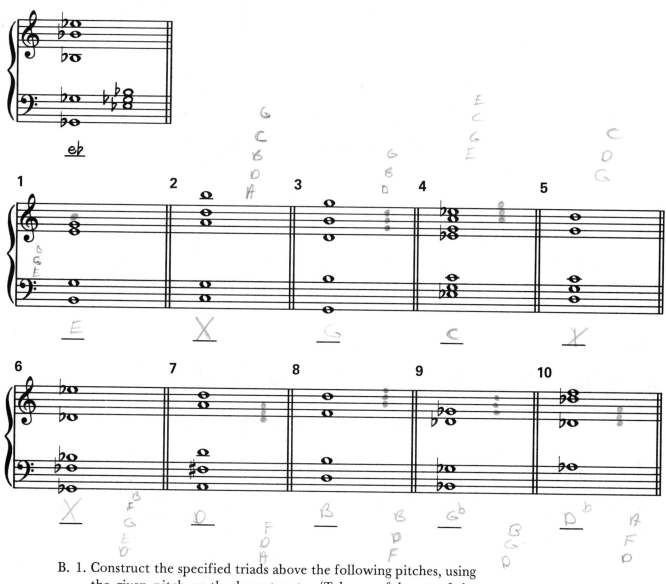

B. 1. Construct the specified triads above the following pitches, using
the given pitch as the lowest note. (Take careful note of the
clefs.)
   2. Play each triad on the piano.

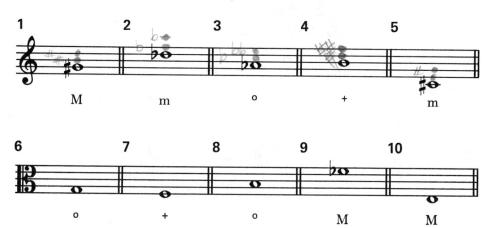

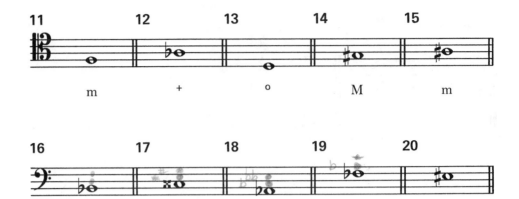

C. 1. Beneath each triad, place the chord symbol that indicates its letter name and quality.

2. Sing each triad, upward and downward from the root, as follows: 1-3-5-3-1.

D. Write the following triads in the inversion indicated. After you
have written each triad, play it on the piano and practice singing it
upward and downward from the lowest pitch, first using the numbers 1, 3, and 5 to designate the chord members and then using
their letter names.

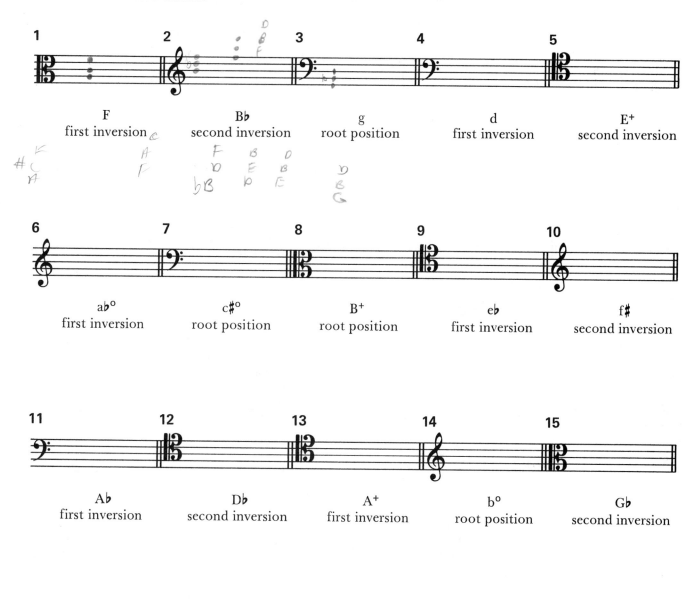

1	2	3	4	5
F	B♭	g	d	E⁺
first inversion	second inversion	root position	first inversion	second inversion

6	7	8	9	10
ab°	c#°	B⁺	eb	f#
first inversion	root position	root position	first inversion	second inversion

11	12	13	14	15
A♭	D♭	A⁺	b°	G♭
first inversion	second inversion	first inversion	root position	second inversion

16	17	18	19	20
e	g#°	c#	db	F#
first inversion	second inversion	root position	first inversion	second inversion

PRACTICE MATERIAL AND ASSIGNMENTS FOR PART B

A. Construct above the given bass note the triad that is indicated by the figures. Then identify by Roman numeral (with superscript if needed) its function in the given key.

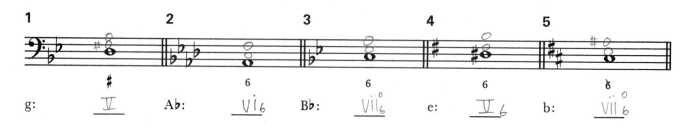

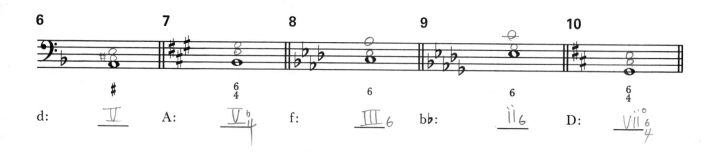

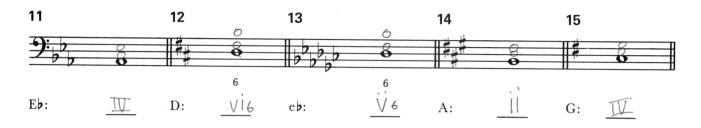

B. Show the figured bass symbol that would correctly represent each of the following chords. Observe the key signature for each and be sure to show accidentals in the figured bass symbol where necessary.

Example:

Suggestion: An excellent ear-training technique is to play the chord first, without studying its structure, and try to identify, by ear, the type (major, minor, augmented, or diminished).

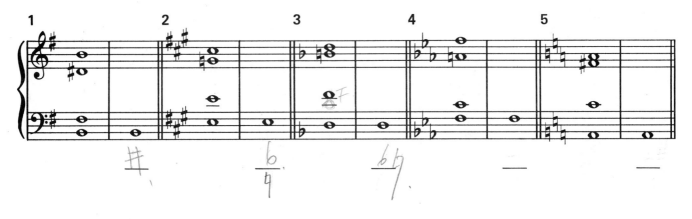

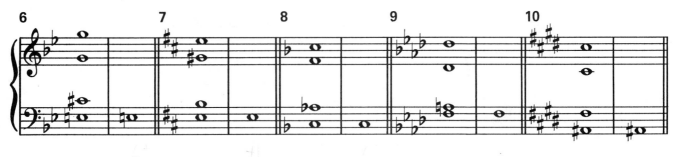

C. Notate:

1 The three major triads in the key of B♭

2 The two minor triads in the key of f♯ (harmonic form)

3 The two diminished triads in the key of g (harmonic form)

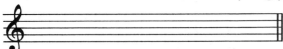

4 The two diminished triads in the key of e♭ (harmonic form)

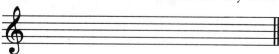

5 The three minor triads in the key of A♭

6 The submediant triad in the key of f

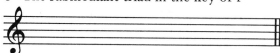

7 The three major triads in the key of d (the form most often used as a basis for harmonies)

8 The dominant in the key of g (descending form of melodic minor scale)

9 The three minor triads in the key of F♯

10 The augmented triad in the relative minor of E major

PRACTICE MATERIAL AND ASSIGNMENTS FOR PART C

In each of the following measures, indicate the chords by Roman numeral, with superscripts where necessary, and identify the cadences as perfect authentic (PAC), imperfect authentic (IAC), plagal, half, deceptive, or Phrygian.

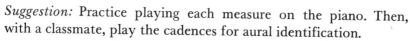

Suggestion: Practice playing each measure on the piano. Then, with a classmate, play the cadences for aural identification.

SUGGESTIONS FOR AURAL DRILL

A. List the numbers 1 to 10. Your instructor will play a succession of ten chords. Indicate whether each is a triad by placing a *Y* (yes) or an *N* (no) beside each number.

B. 1. Your instructor will play a succession of ten triads. After each is played, indicate which of the four basic triad types it is (M = major; m = minor; $^+$ = augmented; $^\circ$ = diminished).

2. Your instructor will play a pitch on the piano. Sing the triad type requested, using the given pitch as the root. Arpeggiate the triad upward and downward from the root as follows: 1-3-5-3-1.

C. 1. Your instructor will play pairs of root-position triads. Consider the first one to be a tonic and identify the second by Roman numeral designation.

2. Your instructor will play a major or minor triad, which you are to consider to be the tonic. He or she will then ask you to arpeggiate another triad in the key (ii, VI, and so on). Arpeggiate this triad upward and downward from the root as in B.2 above.

TEST YOUR COMPREHENSION OF CHAPTER FOUR

A. Identify the triads as major (M), minor (m), augmented ($^+$), or diminished ($^\circ$).

B. Write the requested triad, using the given pitch as the lowest note in the chord.

NOTE: The lowest note is *not necessarily* the root.

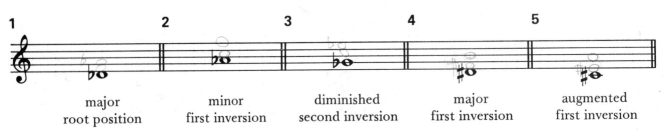

| major | minor | diminished | major | augmented |
| root position | first inversion | second inversion | first inversion | first inversion |

C. Place the correct Roman numeral and superscript beneath each triad. The key is specified for each.

D. Identify the cadences as PAC, IAC, plagal, half, deceptive, or Phrygian.

1 2 3 4 5

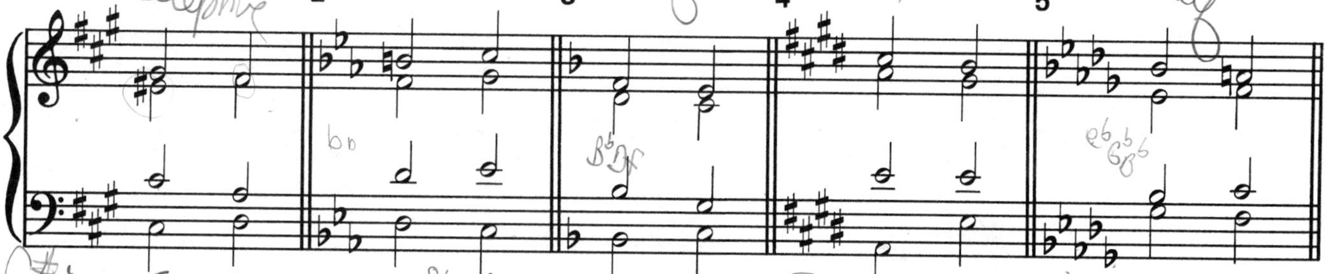

Cadence: ______ ______ ______ ______ ______

E. Add the key signature and supply the bass notes with figures that would indicate the following cadences. Then, in the blanks to the right, supply the Roman numerals.

1 Key: d authentic

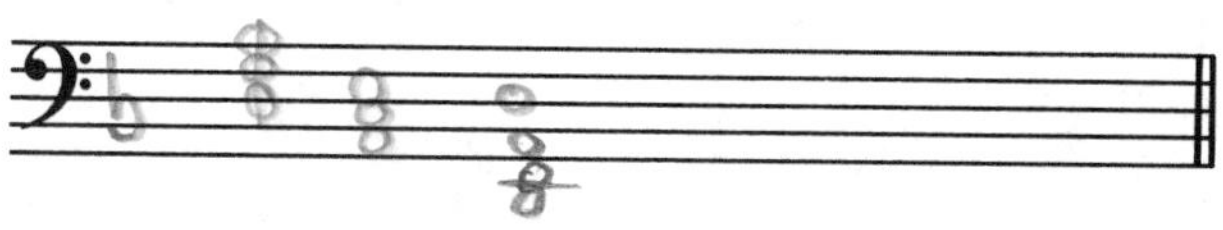

R.N. ______ ______

2 Key: F♯ half

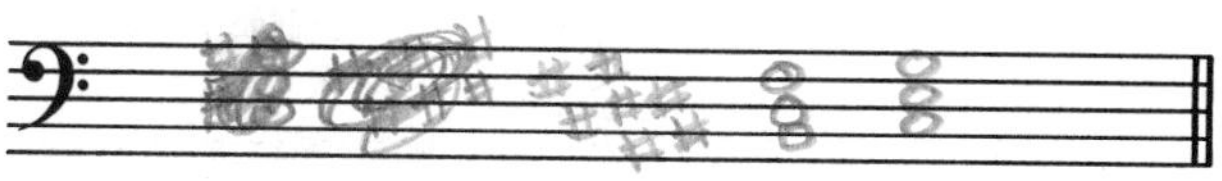

R.N. ______ ______

3 Key: g Phrygian

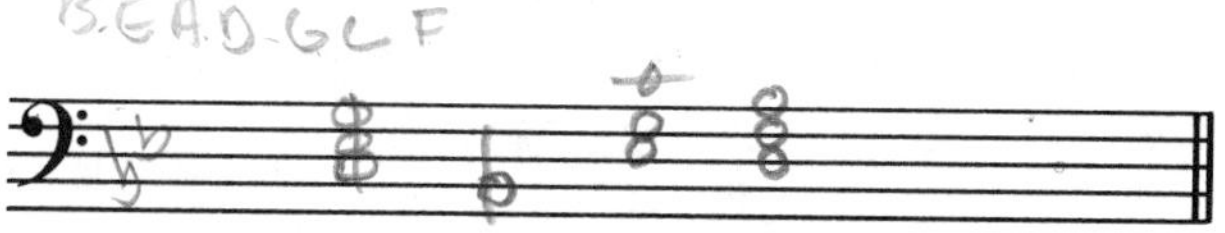

R.N. ______ ______

4 Key: A plagal

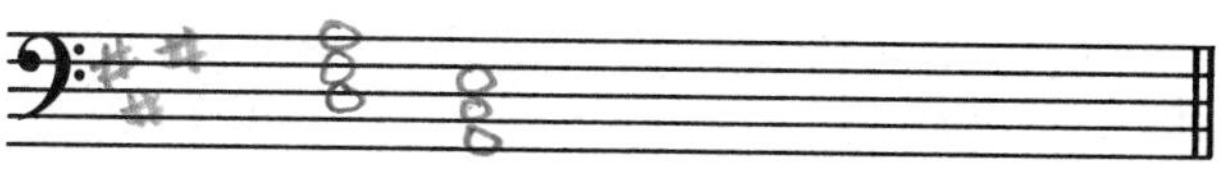

R.N. ______ ______

5 Key: e Phrygian

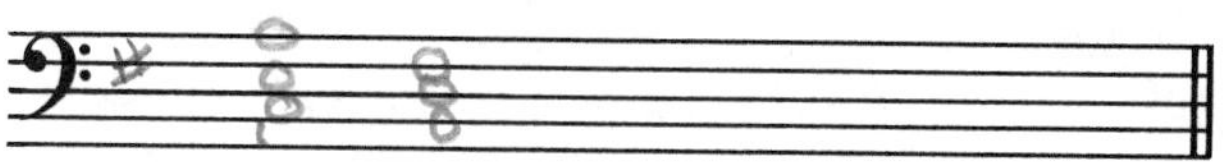

R.N. ______ ______

Answers appear on page 364.

CHAPTER FIVE
MELODY

In the majority of musical works, melody is the element that impresses us most immediately and remains longest in our minds. A melody is, in the most general sense, a succession of pitches in rhythm. These pitches are usually organized into one or more larger units. Thus, pitch, rhythm, and form are the essence of most melodies.

A. General Melodic Characteristics

CONTOUR　One of the more general aspects of a melodic line is its *contour*—its overall shape. Most melodies present a combination of certain basic contours, illustrated below.

Example 5.1

(a)　Mozart: *Piano Sonata, K. 332* (I)*

Ascending contour

*This movement is contained in its entirety in *Analytical Anthology of Music,* by this author (Alfred A. Knopf, Inc., 1984).

(b) Schumann: *Kinderscenen, Op. 15* (No. 6, "An Important Event")*

Descending contour

*This movement is contained in its entirety in *Analytical Anthology of Music,* by this author (Alfred A. Knopf, Inc., 1984).

(c) Handel: *Suite No. 9* from *Pièces pour le Clavecin, HWV 442* (Chaconne)

Archlike contour

(d) Chopin: *Mazurka, Op. 33, No. 3*

Inverted arch contour

(e) Schubert: *Piano Sonata, D. 960* (I)*

Stationary contour

*This movement is contained in its entirety in *Analytical Anthology of Music,* by this author (Alfred A. Knopf, Inc., 1984).

The inherent tension produced by a rising contour is probably both physiological and associative. For example, vocalists and certain instrumentalists, such as brass players, normally exert a little more effort to produce higher pitches. The relaxation accompanying the return to a lower register is experienced to some degree by the listener as well. As a result, melodic gestures are able to impart, through their contours, feelings of tension and repose.

Two compositional concerns related to contour are:

TENSION AND REPOSE

1. *Range:* the distance from the highest to the lowest pitch in a melody
2. *High and low points:* the highest and lowest pitches, which are often focal points of some importance

RANGE AND HIGH/LOW POINTS

INTERVAL
STRUCTURE

A more specific feature of a melody is its intervallic structure. Generally, *conjunct* (stepwise) motion is balanced by *disjunct* motion (movement by leap). Both types can be found in the excerpts of Example 5.1. In the following excerpt, two leaps separate areas of prevailingly conjunct activity.

Example 5.2 Wagner: *Die Meistersinger* (Prelude)*

*This excerpt is contained in piano reduction in *Examples for the Study of Musical Style*, by William R. Ward (Wm. C. Brown Company Publishers, 1970).

RHYTHM

Because every pitch must be given some durational value, rhythm is an inherent feature of a melody. Regardless of the general level of complexity, most melodies display a balance between similar and contrasting rhythms. Notice how, in the preceding example, the rhythmic repetition of mm. 1-2 at mm. 5-6 is balanced by the different rhythms of mm. 3, 4, and 7.

Illustration 5.1

In summary, composers are attentive, whether consciously or intuitively, to certain general melodic characteristics. These include contour, range, interval structure, and rhythm. In most (but not all) cases, composers seek a balance between the extremes.

B. Tonality and Harmonic Implication in the Melodic Line

TONAL
CENTERS

A tonal center is defined any time one pitch or chord is made to sound like a point of greater stability and importance than the other pitches or chords of a key. Most melodies composed prior to 1900 and a great many composed since are, in this sense, *tonal*. Tonal "centers of gravity" are usually created by:

1. emphasis on the first and fifth scale degrees (tonic and dominant)
2. melodic outlining of the tonic, dominant, and subdominant triads
3. resolution of *tendency tones*—pitches that have a strong inclination to move in a specific direction

In the melody that follows, the first and fifth scale degrees are established as focal pitches through:

1. the number of their appearances
2. their metric placement and duration
3. melodic leaps between the two pitches
4. their appearance as high or low points in the melodic line
5. their use as beginning and ending pitches

Example 5.3 Schubert: *"Trout" Quintet, D. 667 (IV)**

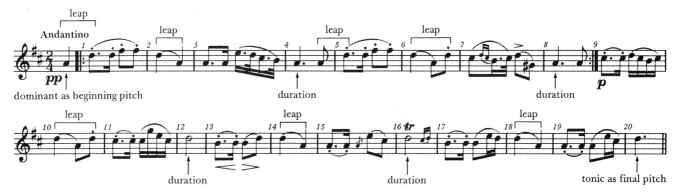

*This movement is contained in full score in *The Norton Scores, Vol. II,* third edition, by Roger Kamien (W. W. Norton & Company, Inc., 1977).

NOTE: The tonic appears as the downbeat in ten of the twenty measures.

In the following melody, notice how the tonic, dominant, and subdominant triads are outlined at various points. This lends a harmonic dimension to the melody. Generally, the more prominent the outlining of these triads, the more clearly defined is the tonality.

Example 5.4 Mozart: *String Quartet, K. 80* (Trio)

As with chords, there are tones of greater and lesser stability within a key system. The tones of *least* stability, and therefore with the greatest tendency to resolve, are most often those separated by a half step from a member of the tonic triad. These *tendency tones* are shown as black notes in the following illustration.

Illustration 5.2

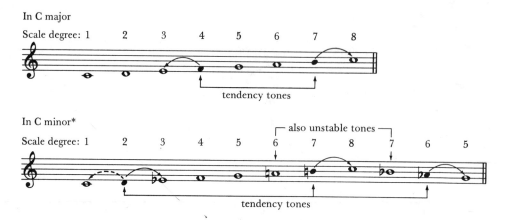

Following are some important points.

1. The normal tendency of each of these tones is toward a member of the tonic triad.
2. The need of each tendency tone to resolve is dependent on the harmonic structure. Their tendencies to resolve are usually greatest when the following chord is the tonic.
3. In minor, the attraction of the tonic is sufficient to pull the supertonic downward as often as upward.
4. The sixth and seventh degrees of the minor scale form a pair of unstable tones that are normally raised when their goal is the tonic and that remain in their natural minor state when their goal is the dominant.†

Illustration 5.3

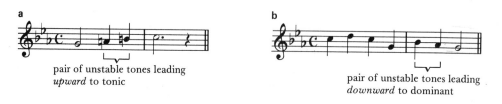

a

pair of unstable tones leading
upward to tonic

b

pair of unstable tones leading
downward to dominant

5. Pitches preceded by an accidental often function as *chromatic tendency tones,* the accidental serving to create a half step between that tone and the next. They normally resolve in the direction of their inflection.

---

*The melodic minor scale form is used here because it is the one most often encountered in melodic activity.

†The ascending sixth degree and the descending seventh degree (A♮ and B♭ in C minor) are not called tendency tones because they do not involve a half-step resolution. Nevertheless, they should be recognized as unstable tones. This is often true, as well, of the second degree in major and the fourth degree in minor.

Illustration 5.4

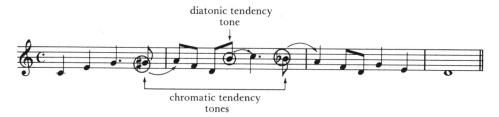

diatonic tendency
tone

chromatic tendency
tones

Tendency tones and their resolutions are shown in the following excerpts. Notice that the resolution of a tendency tone does not always occur immediately, but may be delayed by one or more beats. Also, tendency tones are not *always* resolved. These are ways in which a composer may create musical tension.

Example 5.5

(a)   Haydn: *String Quartet, Op. 17, No. 3, H. III:27* (III)

temporarily unresolved
tendency tone

(b)   Mozart: *Piano Concerto, K. 488* (II)

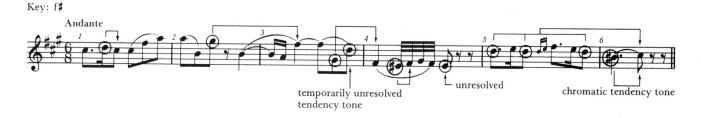

temporarily unresolved
tendency tone

unresolved

chromatic tendency tone

FOR PRACTICE MATERIAL AND ASSIGNMENTS, TURN TO PAGE 121.

C. Melodic Units

Melodic structure has many levels, the smallest being the individual pitches. A larger unit is the *figure,* which normally consists of from three to eight notes bound together in a distinctive rhythmic pattern. When a figure appears frequently in a melody, it is termed a *motive,* or *motif*—a short melodic-rhythmic gesture that, through its frequent use, serves a unifying function within a composition. The rhythmic features of a motive are generally retained more rigorously than the melodic features.

**FIGURE
AND
MOTIVE**

Example 5.6

(a) Chopin: *Prelude, Op. 28, No. 20**

*This prelude is contained in its entirety in Anthology for Musical Analysis, fourth edition, by Charles Burkhart (Holt, Rinehart and Winston, 1986).

(b) J. S. Bach: *English Suite No. 3, BWV 808* (Gavotte No. 1)*

*This movement is contained in its entirety in Anthology for Musical Analysis, fourth edition, by Charles Burkhart (Holt, Rinehart and Winston, 1986).

NOTE: The motive here might alternatively be considered ♪♪♩ , as the dashed brackets between the staves show. In musical analysis, alternative viewpoints are frequently acceptable, if reasonably explained.

PHRASE   A *phrase* is a larger unit—typically four to eight measures in length—in which musical ideas are developed into more complete thoughts.

Example 5.7

(a) Mozart: *Symphony, K. 183* (III)

A typical phrase length

(b) Brahms: *Symphony No. 3* (III)*

A comparatively long phrase (Phrase 2)

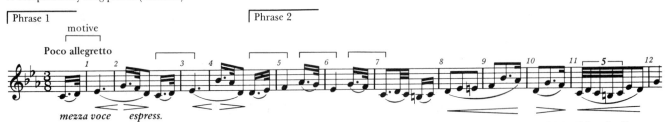

*This movement is contained in its entirety in The Norton Scores, Vol. II, third edition, by Roger Kamien (W. W. Norton & Company, Inc., 1977).

NOTE: This passage is unified by a recurring motive (bracketed).

Phrases are often composed of two or more units larger than a motive, termed *phrase members*—units often two measures in length which, in combination, create phrases.

Example 5.8 Mozart: *Eine Kleine Nachtmusik, K. 525* (I)*

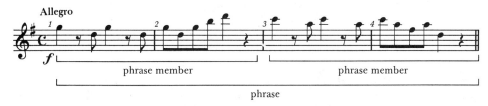

*This movement is contained in its entirety in *The Norton Scores, Vol. I,* third edition, by Roger Kamien (W. W. Norton & Company, Inc., 1977).

Most phrases end with a *cadence.* Like a grammatical punctuation, a cadence serves to separate ideas. It is often characterized by a momentary pause and a rise or fall in pitch. Melodic cadences are usually supported by harmonic cadences and may be conclusive, producing an effect similar to that of a period at the end of a sentence, or inconclusive, producing an effect similar to that of a comma. Between the most and least conclusive sounding cadences lie gradations. Following are some factors that affect the conclusiveness of a cadence.

1. *Pitch:* The tonic is the most conclusive of all cadence pitches.
2. *Harmony:* A pitch accompanied by the tonic triad usually sounds more conclusive than one accompanied by another chord.

Example 5.9 Haydn: *String Quartet, Op. 77, No. 2, H. III:82* (I)*

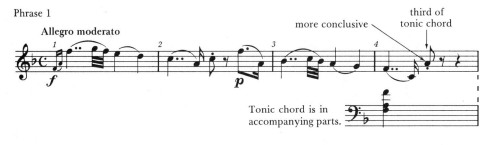

*This movement is contained in its entirety in *Analytical Anthology of Music,* by this author (Alfred A. Knopf, Inc., 1984).

Furthermore, a root-position tonic triad has a more stable and conclusive effect than an inversion. In fact, a tonic pitch in the melody accompanied by a tonic triad in inversion may sound less conclusive than a nontonic pitch in the melody accompanied by a root-position tonic triad.

Example 5.10   Haydn: *String Quartet, Op. 9, No. 1, H. III:19* (III)

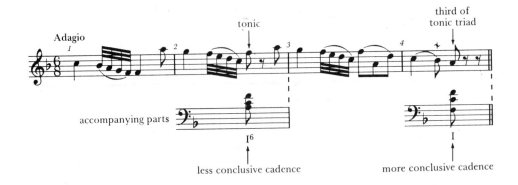

3. *Metric position:* Other factors being equal, a metrically strong cadence pitch sounds more conclusive than a metrically weak cadence pitch.

Example 5.11   Mozart: *Sonata for Violin and Piano, K. 403* (III)

4. *Rhythm:* An immediate continuation of rhythmic motion in the melody or continuing motion in the accompanying parts can weaken an otherwise conclusive-sounding cadence.

Example 5.12 Beethoven: *Piano Sonata, Op. 13* (III)*

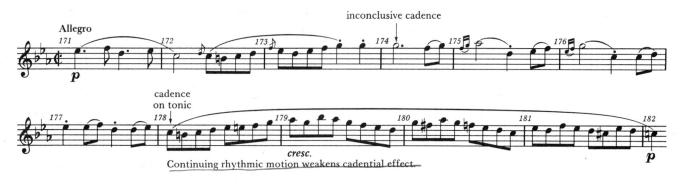

. *This movement is contained in its entirety in *Anthology for Musical Analysis,* fourth edition, by Charles Burkhart (Holt, Rinehart and Winston, 1986).

Although the most common method of ending a phrase is by a cadence, another way is to replace the cadence with the beginning of a new phrase. In this process, called *cadential elision,* the end of one phrase and the beginning of the next coincide. The technique is commonly used to create an uninterrupted flow in music where the melody moves from one part to another.

CADENTIAL ELISION

Example 5.13 Mozart: *Piano Sonata, K. 547a* (I)

cadence of first phrase

The phrases of a melody are related to each other in one of the following ways.

PHRASE RELATIONSHIPS

1. Repetition (exact or varied)

   In *exact repetition,* the second phrase is identical in melody and rhythm to the first. (Octave transposition is still regarded as exact repetition.)

   In *varied repetition,* the second phrase is composed of the same basic material as the first, but with some modifications, such as embellished melody tones or subtle rhythmic changes.

2. Similarity

In *similar phrases,* the second phrase is not a repetition of the first, but the two phrases are still alike in their general melodic characteristics (usually contour and/or rhythm).

3. Contrast

In *contrasting phrases,* the second phrase differs from the first quite obviously in such matters as rhythmic character, interval structure and/or contour.

Letters are used in the following way to symbolize the various phrase relationships:

SYMBOLIZING PHRASE RELATIONSHIPS

Same letter (a a): exact repetition

Same letter with "prime" mark (a a') or superscript (a a^1): varied repetition

Different letters (a b): phrases constructed of different material, *either similar or contrasting*

Examples of repeated, similar and contrasting phrases follow.

Example 5.14

(a)   Schubert: "Du bist die Ruh'," *D. 776**

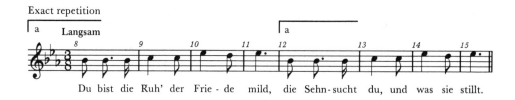

Du bist die Ruh' der Frie - de   mild,   die Sehn- sucht du, und   was   sie stillt.

*This song is contained in its entirety in *Schirmer Scores,* by Jocelyn Godwin (Schirmer Books, 1975).

(b)   Haydn: *String Quartet, Op. 9, No. 1, H. III:19* (I)

(c) Beethoven: *String Quartet, Op. 59, No. 1* (I)*

*This movement is contained in its entirety in *Analytical Anthology of Music*, by this author (Alfred A. Knopf, Inc., 1984).

(d) Beethoven: *Piano Sonata, Op. 26* (I)

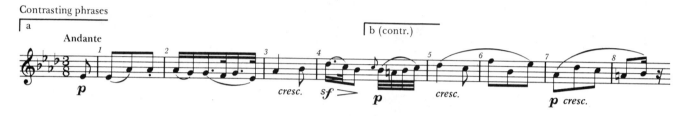

Phrases often combine to form still larger units. Perhaps the most common is the *period*—a unit comprising two (sometimes three) phrases, in which the final phrase provides a greater sense of completion than the first. The phrases within a period are dependent on each other and display an *antecedent-consequent* relationship—that is, the first phrase creates an effect similar to the first clause in a compound sentence (the antecedent) and the final phrase provides the concluding clause (the consequent). It is the greater conclusiveness of the final cadence that binds two or more phrases together to form a period.

THE PERIOD (2 phrases)

Periods are described as:

Parallel: The phrases begin in a similar or identical manner and are usually alike in contour and rhythm, but the final phrase ends more conclusively than the first.

Contrasting: The phrases differ, usually in contour and rhythm and, possibly, in length as well.

Following are examples of parallel and contrasting periods.

Example 5.15

(a) Mozart: *Sonata for Violin and Piano, K. 376* (III)

Parallel period (Second phrase begins *exactly* like the first phrase.)

inconclusive cadence

conclusive cadence

(b) Haydn: *Symphony No. 101, H. I:101* (IV)*

Parallel period (Second phrase begins with material *similar to*, but not identical with, first phrase.)

inconclusive cadence

conclusive cadence

*This movement is contained in its entirety in *Anthology for Musical Analysis,* fourth edition, by Charles Burkhart (Holt, Rinehart and Winston, 1986).

(c) Beethoven: *Piano Sonata, Op. 13* (II)*

Contrasting period (Second phrase differs from first phrase in rhythm and contour.)

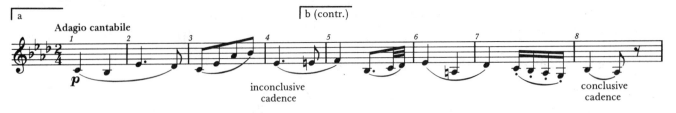

inconclusive cadence

conclusive cadence

*This movement is contained in its entirety in *The Norton Scores, Vol. I,* third edition, by Roger Kamien (W. W. Norton & Company, Inc., 1977).

THREE-PHRASE PERIODS   Less common than the two-phrase period is the three-phrase period. In it, the final phrase ends more conclusively than the preceding phrases. Most often, at least one of the phrases is contrasting.

Example 5.16 Rossini: *Il Barbiere di Siviglia* (Overture)

Three-phrase period

*This overture is contained in its entirety in *The Norton Scores, Vol. I,* third edition, by Roger Kamien (W. W. Norton & Company, Inc., 1977).

The most common four-phrase unit is the double period. In it, the final phrase ends more conclusively than *any* of the preceding phrases.

DOUBLE PERIODS 2 periods.

Example 5.17 Beethoven: *Piano Sonata, Op. 26* (I)

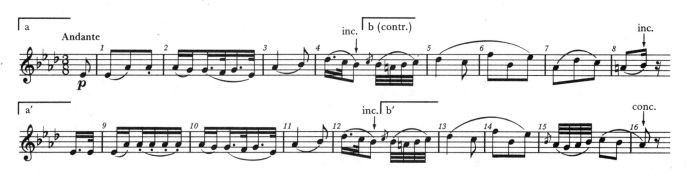

FOR PRACTICE MATERIAL AND ASSIGNMENTS, TURN TO PAGE 126.

D. Techniques of Melodic Development

The ways in which a melodic line is developed can be considered from the standpoint of two opposing principles—unity and variety—which composers seek to balance through repetition and contrast. One technique involves the varying of phrase lengths. This is sometimes accomplished by adding onto a phrase—*phrase extension*—or deleting from it—*phrase compression.*

The most common form of phrase extension is the *cadential extension*, expansion of a phrase at its cadence by emphasizing and prolonging the final pitch or chord (usually the tonic or dominant) for an extra measure or so.

PHRASE EXTENSION

Cadential extensions themselves can be repeated; they can constitute as little as the last couple of notes of the phrase or as much as the last couple of measures.

Example 5.18*
(a) Mozart: *Piano Sonata, K. 332* (I)

(b) Haydn: *Piano Sonata, H. XVI:34* (I)

*Both of the movements in this example are contained in their entirety in *Analytical Anthology of Music,* by this author (Alfred A. Knopf, Inc., 1984).

Phrase compression is a technique employed on repetition of a phrase in which some portion of the phrase is omitted or otherwise shortened. **PHRASE COMPRESSION**

Example 5.19   Haydn: *Piano Sonata, H. XVI:21* (I)

Phrase: a (6 measures)
Allegro

a′ (4 measures)   *compression*

Portion of phrase *a* from * on is omitted at this point.

Another technique of melodic development is *sequence*—the immediate or nearly immediate repetition of a melodic figure, motive, or phrase by the same instrument or voice part at a different pitch level. Sequences are classified in two ways.   **SEQUENCE**

Real: an intervallically exact transposition of a musical idea. Because real *different key* sequences often occur when moving from one key area to another,* they *may* require accidentals, although this is not always the case.

Illustration 5.5

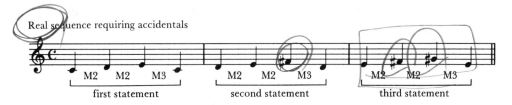

Real sequence requiring no accidentals

M2   M2   M3   M2   M2   M3
first statement   second statement

Real sequence requiring accidentals

M2   M2   M3   M2   M2   M3   M2   M2   M3
first statement   second statement   third statement

*Movement from one key area to another, termed *modulation,* is discussed in Chapter Twelve.

Tonal: a sequence in which the *quality* of certain intervals (but *not* their numerical designation) is changed. Tonal sequences are more common than real sequences. They also remain diatonic in a single key more often than do real sequences.

Illustration 5.6

Tonal sequence

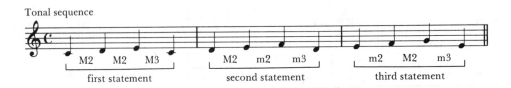

NOTE: The numerical designation for each interval is maintained, but the qualities change, with each repetition of the melodic figure remaining diatonic in C major.

The following musical excerpts contain real or tonal sequences.

Example 5.20

(a) Mozart: *Die Entführung aus dem Serail, K. 384* (Act III: Romance)*

Real sequence

Key: D

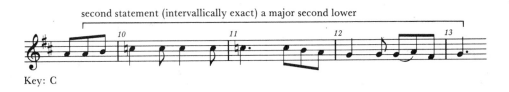

Key: C

*This movement is contained in its entirety in *Analytical Anthology of Music,* by this author (Alfred A. Knopf, Inc., 1984).

NOTE: The real sequence a step lower results in a tonality change one step lower as well.

(b) Handel: *Suite No. 7* from *Pièces pour le Clavecin, HWV 432* (Passacaglia)

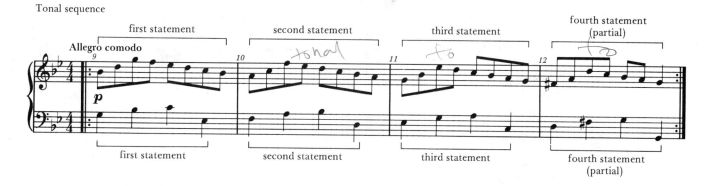

NOTE: All statements of the melodic idea are diatonic in a single key—
G minor.

(c) F. Couperin: *Les quatre nations* ("L'Italienne")

NOTE: This sequence does *not* remain diatonic in the original key (C minor), but moves to A♭ in the third and fourth measures of the excerpt and then to F minor. Because each statement is not intervallically identical, this is classified as a tonal sequence.

Either type of sequence—real or tonal—may be modified rhythmically or by changes in pitch *other than* those constituting a tonal sequence.

MODIFIED SEQUENCE

Illustration 5.7

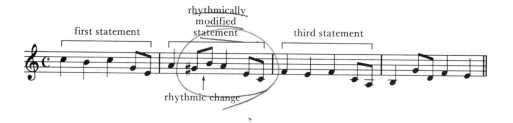

In addition, we can identify *partial sequences,* in which some part of a melodic idea is repeated sequentially while another part is not.

PARTIAL SEQUENCE

Illustration 5.8

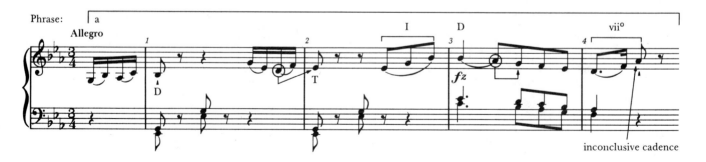

E. Melodic Analysis

In this chapter, many aspects of the melodic line have been considered. In outline form, they provide a basis for the analysis of any melody.

OUTLINE FOR MELODIC ANALYSIS

A. General Melodic Characteristics
 1. contour (including total range, overall shape and high/low points)
 2. interval structure (conjunct versus disjunct motion)
 3. rhythm

B. Tonality and Harmonic Implications
 1. tonic/dominant emphasis
 2. triadic outlining
 3. tendency tones and their resolutions

C. Melodic Units
 1. motives (if present)
 2. phrase structure

D. Techniques of Melodic Development
 1. phrase extension and compression
 2. sequence

The following excerpt has been analyzed using this outline as a guide. The left-hand part has been included so that the melody may be heard in its harmonic context.

Example 5.21   Haydn: *Piano Sonata, H. XVI:49* (I)

Analytical markings:

T = tonic pitch

D = dominant pitch

= tendency tone and resolution

= triads outlined by adjacent pitches
    (Specific chord indicated by Roman numeral above the bracket.)

Analysis
Haydn: *Piano Sonata, H. XVI:49* (I)

GENERAL MELODIC CHARACTERISTICS

This melody consists of two ascents, approximately an octave each, at mm. 1-4 and mm. 4-8, followed by a rapid rise to the high point and a gradual descent. This is shown by the *solid black line* in the illustration below. The *overall* shape (a more general contour) is shown by the *broken line* to be an asymmetric arch (with a longer ascent than descent).   **CONTOUR**

Illustration 5.9

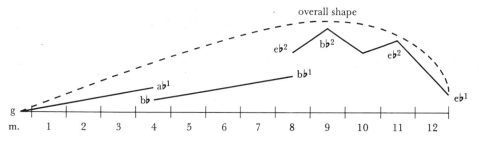

Conjunct and disjunct motion are rather evenly balanced in this melody.   **INTERVAL STRUCTURE**

RHYTHM   Prevailing rhythmic values are the eighth note and sixteenth note. The rhythmic pattern of mm. 1-4 is repeated in mm. 4-8. The final four measures are entirely different. Rhythmically, therefore, this melody is characterized by *both* similarity and contrast.

TONALITY AND HARMONIC IMPLICATIONS

TONIC/DOMINANT EMPHASIS   This melody very clearly implies a tonic E♭ through the means listed on page 102. Tonic and dominant pitches (indicated by a T and D in the music) are clearly emphasized at several points. Notice that one of these is the high point of the line and the other is the end point (the cadence pitch).

TRIADIC OUTLINING   Brackets above the music indicate the triads outlined by adjacent pitches. In addition, notice how tonic and dominant triads are outlined over a slightly larger time span by certain emphasized pitches.

Illustration 5.10

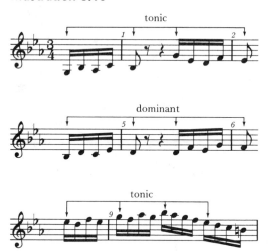

This *large-scale arpeggiation* is discussed further in Chapter Six.

TENDENCY TONES   Tendency tones have been indicated by an arrow leading from the circled tone to the tone of resolution. Most of the tendency tones are resolved.

MELODIC UNITS

MOTIVES   The only prominent motive is: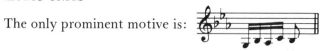

Its rhythm and general melodic shape appear on the anacrusis to m. 1, in m. 1, in m. 4, and in m. 5.

PHRASE STRUCTURE   The melody constitutes a three-phrase period, as indicated by the long brackets on the music.

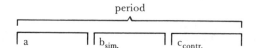

Notice that the only conclusive-sounding cadence is the final one, which ends on the tonic pitch. Because the consequent phrase is distinctly different from the two antecedent phrases, the unit is a *contrasting* period.

MELODIC DEVELOPMENT

The motive of mm. 4-5 is repeated sequentially in mm. 5-6.

SEQUENCE

Illustration 5.11

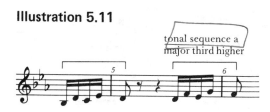

Although the repetition is not immediate, one can regard mm. 6-8 as a modified tonal sequence of mm. 2-4. The word *modified* is included because the embellishment appearing in m. 8 is not present in the original statement.

Illustration 5.12

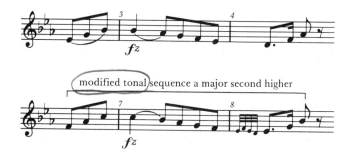

No examples of phrase compression or extension exist in this melody.

PHRASE EXTENSION OR COMPRESSION

FOR PRACTICE MATERIAL AND ASSIGNMENTS, TURN TO PAGE 129.

PRACTICE MATERIAL AND ASSIGNMENTS FOR PARTS A AND B

A. In the following melodies:

1. Identify the contour for each bracketed segment, using the terms ascending, descending, arch, inverted arch, or stationary.
2. Describe the overall intervallic organization, using the terms prevailingly conjunct, prevailingly disjunct, or evenly balanced.
3. Indicate the scalar basis and tonic.
4. Identify any recurrent rhythmic patterns.

NOTE: Circled tones are chromatic pitches and should be disregarded in determining the scalar basis and tonic. The melodies do not *necessarily* begin and end on the tonic.

Example: J. S. Bach: *French Suite No. 6, BWV 817* (Menuet)*

*This movement is contained in its complete form on page 309 of this volume.

Intervallic organization: *Prevailingly conjunct*

Scalar basis: *E major*

Tonic: *E*

Recurrent rhythmic patterns: *(used throughout)*

1   Mozart: *Le Nozze di Figaro, K. 492* (Act I: No. 9)

Intervallic organization: D15

Scalar basis: C maj

Tonic: C

Recurrent rhythmic patterns:

2 Haydn: *String Quartet, Op. 76, No. 2, H. III:76* (I)

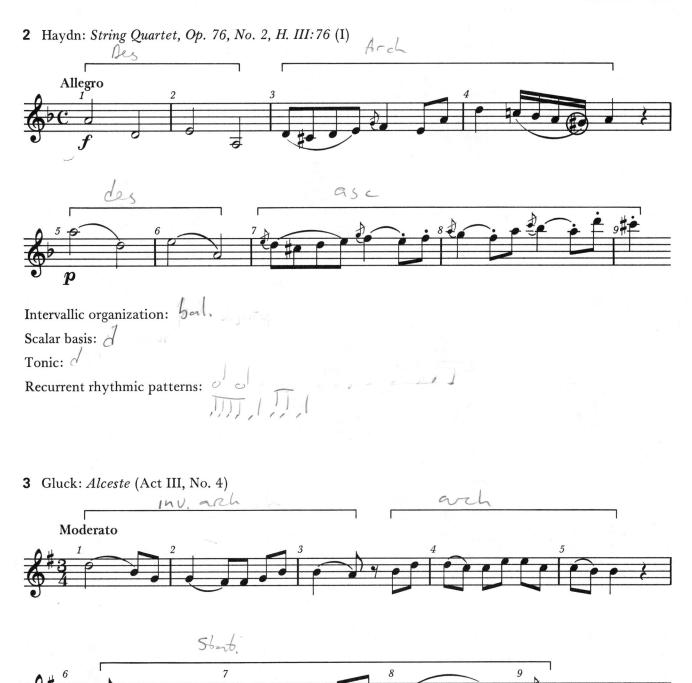

Intervallic organization: *bal.*

Scalar basis: *d*

Tonic: *d*

Recurrent rhythmic patterns:

3 Gluck: *Alceste* (Act III, No. 4)

Intervallic organization: *bal*

Scalar basis: *G*

Tonic: *G*

Recurrent rhythmic patterns:

4 Verdi: *Nabucco* (Act IV)

Intervallic organization: Con

Scalar basis: g

Tonic: g

Recurrent rhythmic patterns: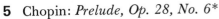

5 Chopin: *Prelude, Op. 28, No. 6**

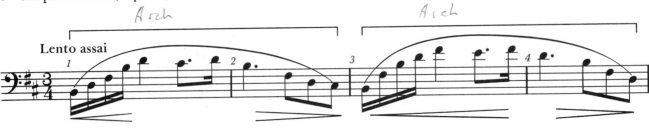

*This prelude is contained in its entirety in *Anthology for Musical Analysis,* fourth edition, by Charles Burkhart (Holt, Rinehart and Winston, 1986).

Intervallic organization: bal

Scalar basis: b

Tonic: b

Recurrent rhythmic patterns:

B. Show the tonal and harmonic implications in the following excerpts.

1. Indicate by T or D the points at which the tonic and dominant pitches are strongly emphasized, and indicate the means of emphasis.

2. Bracket any triadic outlining.

3. Circle the tendency tones and draw an arrow pointing to their notes of resolution, if present.

Example Mozart: *Concerto for Horn and Orchestra, K. 447* (I)

1 Tchaikovsky: *Symphony No. 6* (I)

2 Beethoven: *Piano Sonata, Op. 13* (III)*

*This movement is contained in its entirety in *Anthology for Musical Analysis,* fourth edition, by Charles Burkhart (Holt, Rinehart and Winston, 1986).

3 Mozart: *Symphony, K. 114* (I)

PRACTICE MATERIAL AND ASSIGNMENTS FOR PART C

A. In each of the following two-phrase excerpts:

1. Identify the unifying motive, if one is present.
2. Label all cadences with a C (conclusive) or an I (inconclusive).
3. Show the relationships between the phrases:

   a a   exact repetition

   a a′   varied repetition

   a b$_{sim.}$ similar material

   a b$_{contr.}$ contrasting material

4. Indicate whether or not the phrases in combination form a period.

1 Mozart: *Symphony, K. 543* (III)

Trio

2 Haydn: *Piano Sonata, H. XVI:35* (I)

3 *Prayer of Thanksgiving* (Dutch hymn)

4 Chopin: *Mazurka, Op. posth. 67, No. 4**

*This work is contained in its entirety in *Anthology for Musical Analysis,* fourth edition, by Charles Burkhart (Holt, Rinehart and Winston, 1986).

5 Bellini: "Ah! perche non posso odiarti" from *La Sonnambula*

B. Using the motives given, compose melodies for your own instrument according to the following specifications. Be sure to use correct notational practices. (You may wish to refer back to page 25 for notational guidelines.)

1. Using this motive:

Compose:

    a. a contrasting period consisting of two four-measure phrases of predominantly conjunct motion

    b. two similar phrases that do not form a period, in which disjunct motion predominates

    c. two phrases with a balance of conjunct and disjunct intervals, in which the cadence of the first phrase is overlapped by the beginning of the second phrase. The first phrase should have an ascending contour and the second phrase should have a descending contour.

2. Using this motive:

Compose:

    a. a parallel period consisting of two eight-measure phrases

    b. a three-phrase period consisting of four-measure phrases which would be symbolized:

period

| a | a' | b_{sim.} |

PRACTICE MATERIAL AND ASSIGNMENTS FOR PARTS D AND E

A. Bracket the cadential extension in each of the following phrases and indicate whether it represents an extension of tonic or dominant harmony.

1 Haydn: *Piano Sonata, H. XVI:47* (III)

Key: E

2 Mozart: "Durch Zärtlichkeit und Schmeicheln" from *Die Entführung aus dem Serail, K. 384**

Key: A

*This movement is contained in its entirety in *Analytical Anthology of Music,* by this author (Alfred A. Knopf, Inc., 1984).

3 Mozart: *Piano Sonata, K. 282* (Menuetto I)

Key: B♭

B. Compose two sequential repetitions to the melodic patterns given according to the directions for each.

1 Tonal sequence a major second downward

2 Real sequence a perfect fifth upward

3 Tonal sequence a diatonic third downward

4 Modified tonal sequence a diatonic third upward

5 Modified real sequence a major third downward

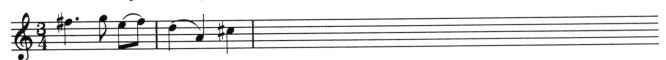

SUGGESTIONS FOR AURAL DRILL

A. Your instructor will choose four measures at random from the following group and will play the pitch series in quarter-note values, in a key of his or her choice. Given the beginning pitch, you are to notate the rest of the pitches.

Example: Instructor chooses measures 1, 7, 11, and 13 and the key of G. You should notate:

1				2				3				4			
1	5	4	5	4	6	2	3	5	1	8	3	1	5	3	2

5				6				7				8			
2	3	1	5	4	4	3	2	5	4	2	7	8	7	8	3

9				10				11				12			
6	4	7	5	3	4	5	6	8	3	4	5	1	1	5	5

13				14				15				16			
3	5	8	5	3	1	2	5	4	3	2	3	2	2	5	5

17				18				19				20			
5	3	4	2	6	7	8	1	1	8	7	8	8	5	4	3

B. Your instructor will choose four measures from the following group. He or she will give you the tonic pitch. You are to sing the entire pitch series in quarter-note values.

Example: Instructor chooses measures 3, 5, 9, and 10 and a tonic pitch of C. You should sing:

1				2				3				4			
1	2	3	1	3	2	1	8	1	3	2	1	5	4	3	3

5				6				7				8			
2	2	3	4	4	3	2	7	5	5	3	8	4	3	2	2

9				10				11				12			
5	6	4	2	1	1	2	3	3	8	6	4	2	3	4	5

13				14				15				16			
7	8	5	8	8	6	4	8	1	4	6	4	2	7	5	3

17				18				19				20			
1	6	4	2	5	4	3	2	1	3	5	3	8	3	5	3

C. Your instructor will choose one of the following series of arpeggiations, using a rhythmic pattern and key of his or her choice. You will be given the key and meter signature. Notate the pitches and rhythms.

Example: The instructor may play Series 1 in the key of B♭, using this rhythm:

You should then notate this:

1

| 1 | 3 | 5 | 1 | 8 | 6 | 4 | 6 | 7 | 7 | 5 | 2 | 8 | 5 | 3 | 1 |

2

| 1 | 8 | 5 | 3 | 2 | 4 | 7 | 4 | 3 | 8 | 5 | 5 | 4 | 2 | 3 | 1 |

3

| 5 | 2 | 7 | 5 | 8 | 1 | 5 | 3 | 4 | 1 | 4 | 6 | 5 | 3 | 1 | 8 |

4

| 5 | 8 | 5 | 3 | 4 | 8 | 6 | 4 | 5 | 1 | 3 | 8 | 5 | 5 | 3 | 1 |

5

| 4 | 4 | 8 | 6 | 5 | 1 | 3 | 8 | 7 | 5 | 5 | 7 | 8 | 3 | 5 | 1 |

TEST YOUR COMPREHENSION OF CHAPTER FIVE

A. Write the tendency tones found in each of the following scales.

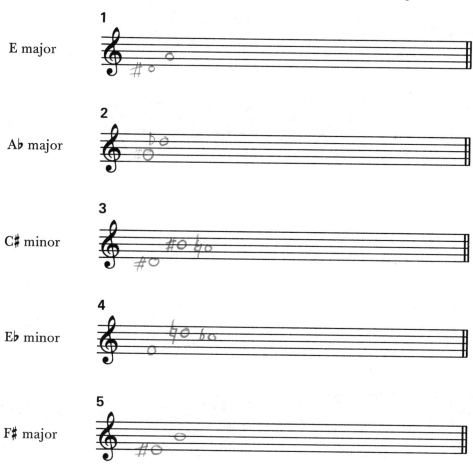

E major   1

Ab major   2

C# minor   3

Eb minor   4

F# major   5

B. For each two-phrase excerpt, select the most appropriate descriptive term from *both* categories 1 and 2.

1. a. a a
   b. a a′
   c. a b$_{sim.}$
   d. a b$_{contr.}$

2. a. phrases form a period
   b. phrases do not form a period

1 Mozart: *Piano Concerto, K. 488* (I)

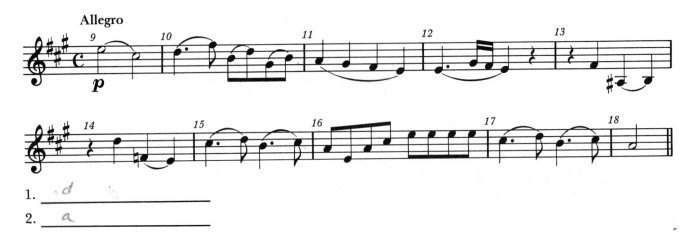

1. _____ d _____

2. _____ a _____

2 *March* (Polish)

1. _____ b _____

2. _____ a _____

3 Chopin: *Waltz, Op. 69, No. 2*

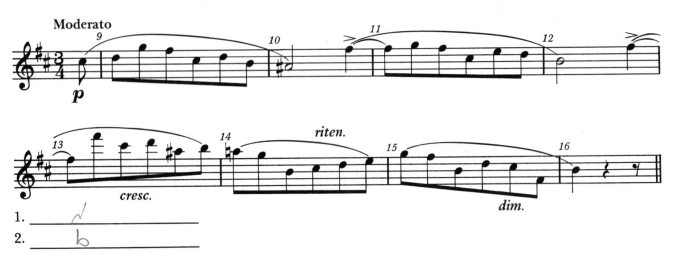

1. _____ d _____

2. _____ b _____

C. Bracket each repetition of the melody pattern and identify the
   sequence as:

1. real
2. tonal
3. modified real or tonal
4. partial

Indicate the level of transposition.

1 Beethoven: *Piano Sonata, Op. 10, No. 1* (I)

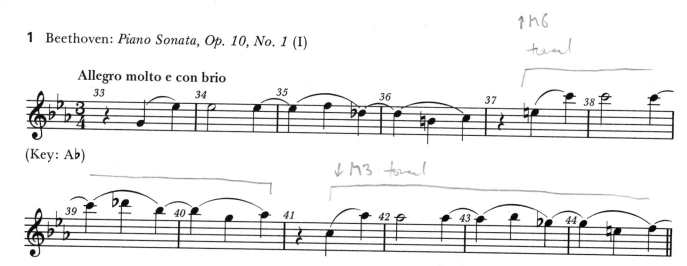

(Key: A♭)

2 Schumann: *Carnaval, Op. 9* (No. 4, "Valse noble")

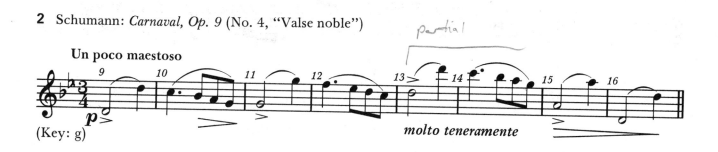

(Key: g)

3 Schubert: "Gute Nacht," No. 1 from *Die Winterriese, D. 911*

(Key: F)

D. Name two ways in which a phrase can be developed.

extension, compression

E. Circle or supply the most appropriate answers to describe the following melody.

1 A tonal center is created by (circle each technique that applies):

  a. tonic-dominant emphasis
  b. melodic outlining of tonic, dominant, and subdominant triads
  c. resolution of tendency tones

2 The most distinctive rhythmic motive can be found in __1, 5__.
   (measure numbers)

3 The interval structure is:

  a. prevailingly conjunct
  b. prevailingly disjunct
  c. evenly balanced

4 The passage contains:

  a. sequence
  b. repetition
  c. cadential extension

Handel: *Sonata No. 3 for Two Violins and Continuo, Op. 5, HWV 398*

Answers appear on page 364.

CHAPTER SIX
FURTHER ASPECTS OF MELODIC CONSTRUCTION

TERMS TO KNOW

anticipation	large-scale arpeggiation	retardation
appoggiatura	neighbor tone	step progression
changing tone	nonchord tone	structural tone
embellishing tone	passing tone	supporting tone
escape tone	pedal point	suspension
	prolongation	

A. The Underlying Structure of Melody

In Chapter Five, we examined the general characteristics of melodic lines and certain aspects of their organization, such as the motive, phrase, and period. In this chapter, we will discuss in greater detail the relationships among the melodic tones.

It may be helpful to begin with an analogy. In a sentence, not all the words are equally important to our understanding. Rather, the noun and verb convey the primary information, while adjectives, adverbs, modifying phrases, and the like elaborate on this information, providing nuances, qualifications, and so on. Similarly, in a melody, some tones provide the basic structure—the "primary information"—while others serve to embellish and amplify. Consider the following musical example.

Example 6.1 Schubert: *Waltz, Op. 18a, No. 5, D. 145*

*This excerpt can be found with its harmonic accompaniment in *Music for Study,* second edition, by Murphy, Melcher and Warch (Prentice-Hall, Inc., 1973).

Notice how the melody revolves around the F♯ (the dominant) in this two-phrase period. In five of the eight measures, this tone is given dynamic, agogic, and tonal accents. In the last two measures, there is a motion away from the F♯ toward the tonic, B. Notice that this motion is stepwise—through D and C♯ in m. 7. We might, then, characterize the underlying structure of this melody as a *prolonged* F♯ with an eventual descent to the tonic, as shown below.

Illustration 6.1

By viewing the melody in this way, we purposely omit all those embellishments—the "adjectives," "adverbs" and so on—that make this melody unique, that, in fact, make it interesting. On balance, however, we gain a larger perspective—an understanding of its basic thrust and direction. The tones that provide this direction can be called *structural tones,* because they form the underlying structure of the melody.

Two different melodies may display an identical or similar underlying structure. Consider the next example.

Example 6.2 Haydn: *String Quartet, Op. 3, No. 5* (III)

Again, the melody revolves around the dominant—this time, F—which is stressed in one way or another in four of the excerpt's first six measures. Following this prolongation of F is a stepwise descent to the tonic B♭ through D and C in mm. 7-8.

Illustration 6.2

Even with what appear to be identical underlying structures, the melodies of Examples 6.1 and 6.2 sound quite different. Aside from the fact that one is major and one is minor, it is the melodic detail—the embellishing tones—that provide the individuality. We will now consider these important components of the melodic line.

FOR PRACTICE MATERIAL AND ASSIGNMENTS, TURN TO PAGE 153.

B. Embellishing Tones

Embellishing tones are tones of secondary importance in a melodic line. They are usually not part of the harmonic structure and are therefore called *nonchord tones* when they appear in a harmonic context. They are usually of short duration and receive little emphasis through pitch and metric placement. They usually create a dissonance* against a more important pitch in another voice, and they usually resolve by step to a more important pitch in the same voice.

The most common type of embellishing tone is the *passing tone* (PT), which links two more important tones of different pitch through stepwise motion. A passing tone may be accented, which means that it is stronger metrically than the tone that immediately follows, or unaccented. It may appear ascending or descending in any voice of the texture. It may also be chromatic or diatonic.

PASSING TONE

Illustration 6.3

Two voices

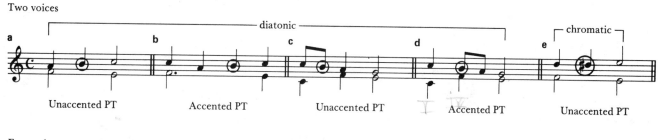

Four voices

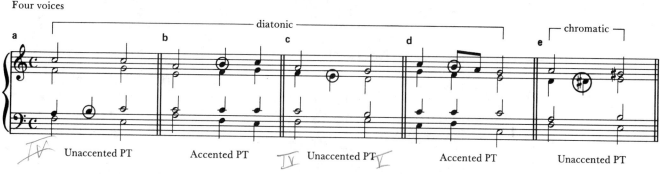

*Consonant and dissonant intervals were identified on page 63. Although the perfect fourth was classified *theoretically* as a consonance, in actual practice, it was treated as a dissonance in two-voice writing, as were seconds and sevenths.

CONSECUTIVE PASSING TONES   Occasionally, two or more passing tones may appear in direct succession. These are called *consecutive passing tones.*

Illustration 6.4

NEIGHBOR TONE   A *neighbor tone* (*auxiliary tone*) is an embellishing tone that occurs stepwise between a more important tone and its repetition. It may be accented or unaccented and may appear above (abbreviated UN) or below (abbreviated LN) a more important tone in any voice of the texture. Like the passing tone, it may be diatonic or chromatic.

Illustration 6.5

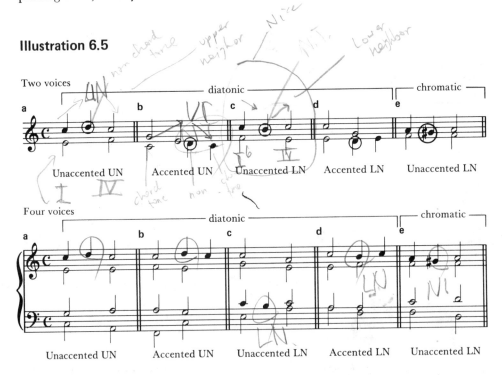

INCOMPLETE NEIGHBOR TONE AND APPOGGIATURA   An *incomplete neighbor tone* (abbreviated IN) resembles only the final part of a neighbor tone pattern (the stepwise resolution). The approach to the incomplete neighbor tone is by leap. When an incomplete neighbor tone appears in a stronger metric position than its resolution, it is known as an *appoggiatura* (APP).* In most cases, the approach (by leap) and the resolution (by step) are in opposite directions.

*Some theorists make no distinction between the IN and APP, referring to *all* leap-step configurations as appoggiaturas.

Illustration 6.6

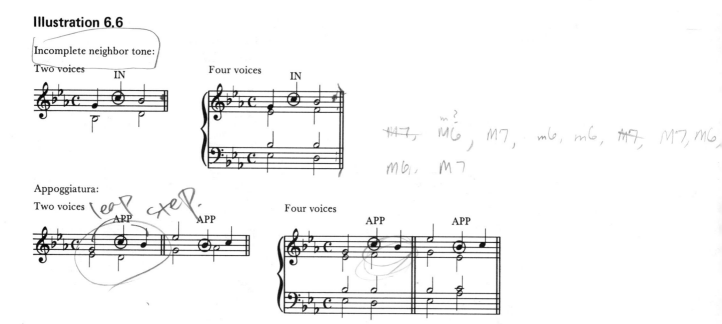

The following example contains passing tones, neighbor tones and an appoggiatura.

Example 6.3   Beethoven: *Piano Sonata, Op. 10, No. 3* (I)

An *escape tone* (abbreviated ET) is a rhythmically weak embellishing tone that is approached by step and left by leap, in a manner opposite that of the incomplete neighbor.

ESCAPE TONE

Illustration 6.7

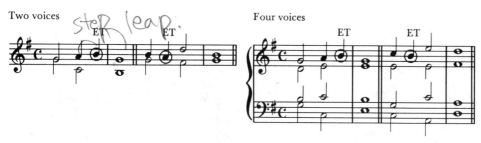

*Although the major third formed here by the two voices is not a *dissonance,* the A♯ lower neighbor is not part of the B minor harmony implied by the left-hand part. It is, therefore, a nonchord tone.

CHANGING TONE

A *changing tone* is a two-note embellishing figure (abbreviated CT) involving the pitches a step above *and* below a more important tone and its repetition. It is, in essence, a combination of upper and lower neighbor tones.

Illustration 6.8

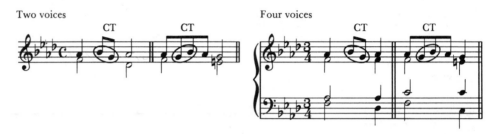

Two voices   Four voices

> **FOR CLASS DISCUSSION**
>
> *The following example contains changing tones at two points. The first is identified. Identify the second changing tone figure as well as the passing tones present.*

Example 6.4   Scheidt: *Bergamasca*

ANTICIPATION

An *anticipation* (abbreviated ANT) is a melodic embellishment most often found at cadences, in which one voice moves to a tone of the next chord ahead of the other voices. The anticipation is dissonant with the harmony against which it first appears. When the other voices move to form the new chord, the note that constituted the anticipation is repeated, *but it is no longer dissonant.* Anticipations usually occur in the uppermost voice. In four-part vocal settings, they sometimes appear in the tenor voice as well.

Illustration 6.9

Two voices   Four voices

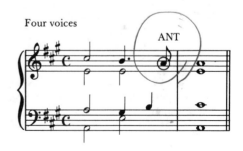

FOR CLASS DISCUSSION

The following example contains an anticipation and escape tones. Locate and identify these and all other embellishing tones in the passage.

Example 6.5 Handel: *Menuet, HWV 516a*

A *suspension* (SUS) is a dissonance that results when one voice is delayed   **SUSPENSION**
in its stepwise movement downward.

Illustration 6.10

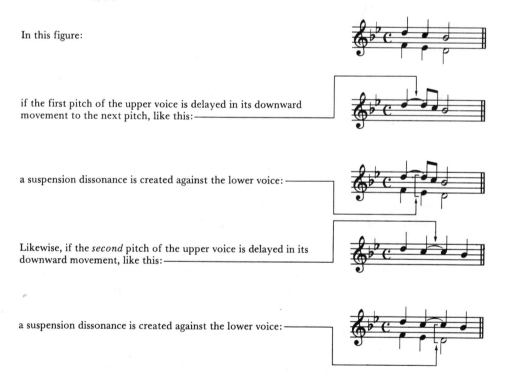

In this figure:

if the first pitch of the upper voice is delayed in its downward movement to the next pitch, like this:———————

a suspension dissonance is created against the lower voice:———

Likewise, if the *second* pitch of the upper voice is delayed in its downward movement, like this:———————

a suspension dissonance is created against the lower voice:———

Suspensions may be regarded as having three parts: ✳

1. *Preparation:* The note that is delayed (suspended) first appears as a consonance or as a member of the harmony.
2. *Dissonance:* The dissonance is created as the suspended tone fails to move to the next pitch at the same time as the other voices.

3. *Resolution:* The stepwise downward motion of the suspended tone is to a pitch consonant with the other voices.

Typically, the suspension dissonance is stronger metrically than its resolution.

Illustration 6.11

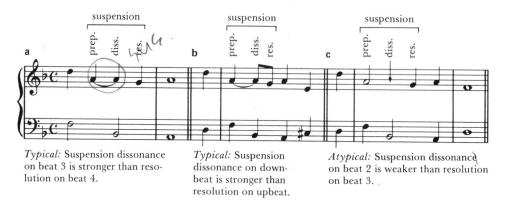

Typical: Suspension dissonance on beat 3 is stronger than resolution on beat 4.

Typical: Suspension dissonance on downbeat is stronger than resolution on upbeat.

Atypical: Suspension dissonance on beat 2 is weaker than resolution on beat 3.

The four most common suspension figures are: 9-8, 7-6, 4-3 and 2-1. In a two-voice texture, these numbers indicate the intervals formed between the voices *at the points of dissonance and resolution.* In textures of more than two voices, the figures show the intervals formed by the dissonant voice and its resolution, measured against the lowest voice. Note that the 9-8 suspension is a 2-1 suspension in which one or more octaves separate the dissonant voice and the bass.

Illustration 6.12

Observations:

1. Although very common, the tie is not necessary. Absence of a tie results in a *rearticulated suspension.*
2. The 2-1 suspension can be changed to a 9-8 suspension in **d** above by exchanging the soprano and tenor parts.

In another suspension figure—the 2-3—the suspension is *in* the lowest voice rather than *above* it. The figure indicates the intervals formed by the lowest voice and the voice with which it is initially dissonant. In four voices, these intervals are usually a ninth and a tenth, but the figure 2-3 is nevertheless employed (in preference to 9-10).

Illustration 6.13

BASS — 2-3.

9-8. 76 43 21

NOTE: The 2-3 suspension is the only one in which the interval at the point of resolution (a third) is *larger* than at the point of suspension (a second).

One final suspension figure is the 6-5. Although neither the 6 nor the 5 represent a dissonance, the first note of the figure is normally not regarded as part of the harmony.

Illustration 6.14

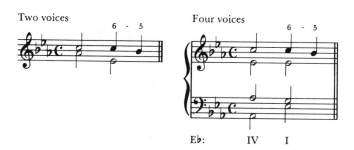

A *retardation* (RET) is an upward-resolving suspension. This relatively infrequent embellishment occurs most often as a 2-3 or 9-10 figure (measured above the lowest voice), but other types are possible as well (7-8, for example). The 2-3 retardation should not be confused with a 2-3 *suspension*.

RETARDATION

Illustration 6.15

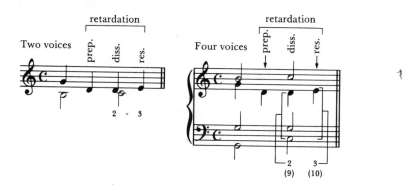

Occasionally, in a suspension, the bass (and possibly the harmony as well) changes at the point of resolution. Such suspensions over a change of bass or change of chord create unusual suspension figures, such as 9-3 or 7-8.

Illustration 6.16

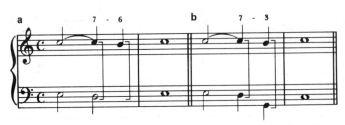

(The change of bass in **b** causes the 7-6 suspension to be re-figured as a 7-3 suspension.)

SIMULTANEOUS EMBELLISHING TONES

Embellishing tones can occur individually or simultaneously with one another. If of the same type, simultaneous embellishing tones are called *double passing tones*, *double neighbor tones*, and so on. Following is an example of a double anticipation followed by a double suspension.

Example 6.6   Josquin: *Ave Maria, gratia plena**

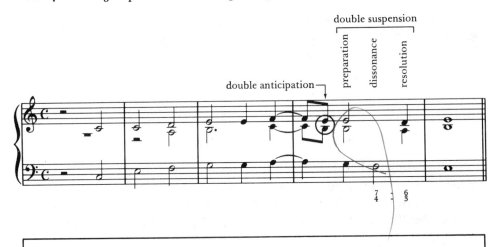

FOR CLASS DISCUSSION

The following musical excerpt contains a double passing tone (marked) along with a variety of other embellishing tones. Locate and describe:

   1. the bass suspension in m. 1
   2. the two neighbor tones and two incomplete neighbor tones on the upper staff in m. 2
   3. a neighbor tone and an incomplete neighbor tone in m. 3
   4. an additional passing tone in m. 4

*Text omitted from example.

Example 6.7   Handel: "How beautiful are the feet," No. 37a from *Messiah*

A *pedal point* is a note that is sustained or repeated while the other voices of the texture change pitch, usually creating dissonances against it. Actually, the pedal point is most often a structural pitch, against which the other voices are more properly regarded as the embellishments. Although it may appear in *any* part of the texture, it most often appears in the lowest voice. The name *pedal point* derives from a technique frequently used in early organ music, wherein a sustained note on the pedal keyboard provided a background for improvisatory passages on the manuals.

PEDAL POINT

Example 6.8   Schumann: *Album for the Young, Op. 68* (No. 17, "Little Morning Wanderer")

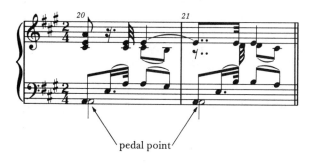

*This composition is contained in its entirety in *Anthology for Musical Analysis,* fourth edition, by Charles Burkhart (Holt, Rinehart and Winston, 1986).

FOR PRACTICE MATERIAL AND ASSIGNMENTS, TURN TO PAGE 154.

C. Large-Scale Melodic Relationships

In this section, we will examine more closely the relationships among the most important tones of a melody (the structural tones) and the role of the less important tones. To do so, we must first amplify some familiar terms and introduce a few new concepts.

STRUCTURAL TONES

Structural tones are the most important pitches of a melody. They serve as focal points toward, from, or around which the other pitches move. Structural tones tend to be:

1. longer and/or metrically stronger than other pitches
2. more important by virtue of their positions at the beginning or end of a phrase or as the highest or lowest pitch of the phrase
3. supported by the underlying harmonic structure

The importance of the tonic triad is evident in the fact that members of the tonic chord are frequently heard as structural tones.

EMBELLISHING TONES

Embellishing tones have been covered in Part B of this chapter. Their essential characteristics are listed on page 139. A final characteristic is that embellishing tones rarely end a phrase.

SUPPORTING TONES

Supporting tones are pitches that lie somewhere between structural and embellishing tones in importance. Supporting tones:

1. are usually (not always) members of the underlying harmonic structure
2. are generally longer and stronger than embellishing tones
3. are sometimes elaborated by an embellishing tone

In the examples that follow, special notations are used to show structural, supporting, and embellishing tones.

MELODIC REDUCTION

> ♩ = structural tone
>
> ♪ = supporting tone
>
> • = embellishing tone
>
> ♩ ♩ = connection to show that a single tone dominates a particular time span even though other pitches intervene
>
> *NOTE:* Immediate pitch repetitions are not shown.

The underlying harmonic structure is indicated on a separate staff. The resulting representation of the melody is termed a *melodic reduction.* The reduction procedure used in Example 6.10(a) is explained, measure by measure, following the excerpt.

Example 6.9

(a) Schubert: *Symphony No. 9* (II)

Observations:

m. 17: The E is structural. Not only is it the first pitch of the melody, it is the longest and metrically strongest of the measure. The Cs are members of the underlying harmony and are longer and stronger than the embellishing tones. They are therefore designated supporting tones.

m. 18: Even though the A has a certain prominence as the highest pitch, it stands as a support to the E, which dominates the three-measure time span. The final D is a supporting tone—not an embellishing tone—because it is supported by its own harmony.

m. 19: The E is structural. Immediate pitch repetitions are not shown in a reduction.

m. 20: F, the metrically strongest pitch, is structural. Note that it is a member of the G⁷ harmony.* Even though the final F is very short and unaccented, it is designated as a structural tone. This may seem inappropriate; however, the pitch F dominates the entire measure. The final F is but a continuation of the effect of the first F—similar to an immediate repetition—and it is still part of the underlying harmony. While the pitch A is not part of the harmony, it is stressed through a tonal accent and it is repeated. It is therefore more important than a mere embellishment and is shown as a supporting tone.

m. 21: The same considerations apply as in m. 20.

m. 22: The first two Cs are represented as a structural tone. However, the third is not because it is not supported by the harmony (notice the chord change at that point). The B, D, and F are all part of this harmony. However, none of these pitches is long or strong enough to be regarded as a structural tone.

m. 23: The Es are structural because of their duration (through repetition).

m. 24: The A is structural as the final note of the passage.

*This type of seventh chord is explained in Chapter Eight. For now, you need only be aware that the F is part of the chord.

(b) Brahms: *Academic Festival Overture, Op. 80*

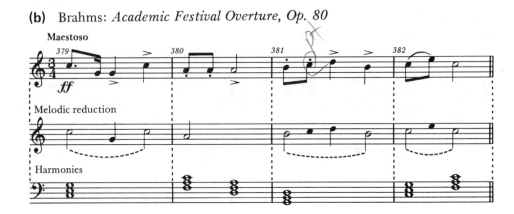

(c) Rameau: *Nouvelles Suites de Pièces de Clavecin, Book II* (Minuet II)

Many melodies—perhaps most—invite several analyses. Opinions may at times differ regarding the precise importance of all but the strongest of structural tones and the weakest of embellishing tones. In m. 5 of Example 6.9(c), the supporting tones are so designated because they are part of the harmonic structure and they appear on downbeats. Even so, they are of no greater duration than the embellishing tones that separate them.

MELODIC PROLONGATION In Example 6.9(a-c), the structural tones connected by the broken ties are said to be *prolonged,* that is, they remain melodic focal points for, perhaps, several measures, even though other pitches intervene. *Melodic prolongation* is the elaboration and extension of a structural tone through supporting and embellishing tones. Following is an example of a more extensive prolongation.

Example 6.10 Brahms: *Intermezzo, Op. 117, No. 1*

A sense of overall direction is imparted to a melody when there is a clear relationship between its more important pitches. This relationship often proves to be a stepwise one. The term *step progression* is used to describe these large-scale stepwise motions. Although step progressions do not always involve *only* structural tones, these are usually the most clearly heard.

Example 6.11   J. S. Bach: *English Suite No. 3, BWV 808* (Gavotte I)

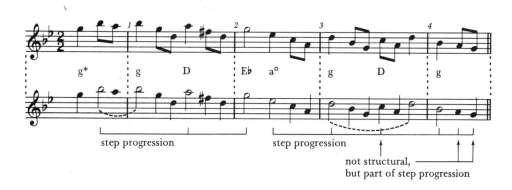

*Harmonies are indicated by letter name designations.

More than one step progression may exist simultaneously within a single melodic line.

Example 6.12   "We Wish You a Merry Christmas" (English)

*Harmonies are indicated by letter name designations.

Because the bass line is so frequently melodic in character, step progressions in this voice are common. The following example shows simultaneous step progressions in the soprano line as well as a step progression in the bass line.

Example 6.13   Handel: *Suites de Pièces pour le Clavecin, HWV 516a*
(Minuet)

**LARGE-SCALE
ARPEGGIATION**

Somewhat less common, perhaps, than step progressions are *large-scale arpeggiations*—chordal outlining involving nonadjacent pitches (often structural tones) over the course of several measures. In the following examples, arrows indicate the notes that form large-scale arpeggiations. (Dotted lines show pitch prolongations.) The harmonies are indicated by letter name designations.

Example 6.14

(a)   Mozart: *String Quartet, K. 80* (Trio)

NOTE: Measure-for-measure triadic outlining in this passage is illustrated on page 103.

(b)   Chopin: *Mazurka, Op. 68, No. 3*

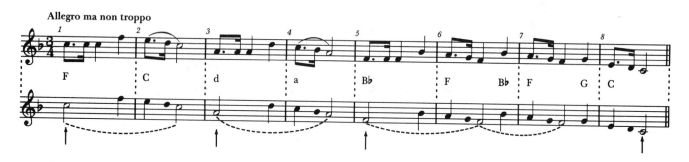

In summary, several points should be stressed regarding step progressions and large-scale arpeggiations.

1. Step progressions and large-scale arpeggiations create the large-scale motion that imparts a sense of logic and direction to a melodic line.
2. The more important the pitches constituting a step progression or large-scale arpeggiation, the stronger will be the sense of overall melodic direction and purpose.
3. Because step progressions and large-scale arpeggiations tend to involve the more important melodic pitches, it is often helpful first to identify the structural and supporting tones before looking for these other relationships.

FOR PRACTICE MATERIAL AND ASSIGNMENTS, TURN TO PAGE 157.

PRACTICE MATERIAL AND ASSIGNMENTS FOR PART A

In a manner similar to the illustrations in Part A, identify the underlying structure in the following melodies. Notate as half notes only the most important tones—those which provide the basic focal points and direction of the melody. Also indicate the means by which these important pitches are stressed.

NOTE: Your solutions may differ in certain details from those of your classmates, depending on how many notes of lesser importance you show (as stemless noteheads).

Example: Mozart: *Symphony No. 40, K. 550* (I)

Underlying structure

1 Dvořák: *Symphony No. 9, Op. 95* (IV)

2 Chopin: *Nocturne, Op. 55, No. 1*

3 Beethoven: *Dance*

PRACTICE MATERIAL AND ASSIGNMENTS FOR PART B

A. Circle and identify the embellishing tones in each of the following musical passages. Also indicate chord function, position, and quality with Roman numerals for each chord. Chords not yet discussed in the text are marked with *X*s. You may disregard these chords.

1 J. S. Bach: "Schmucke dich, O liebe Seele"

2 Weber: *Castor et Pollux, Op. 5*

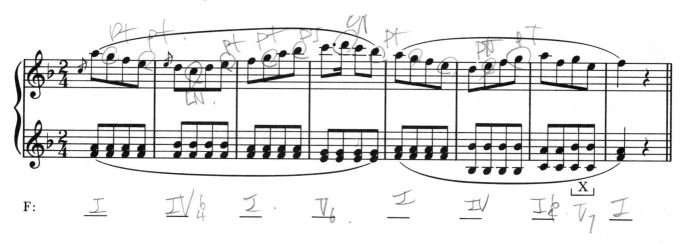

3 J. S. Bach: "In dulci jubilo"

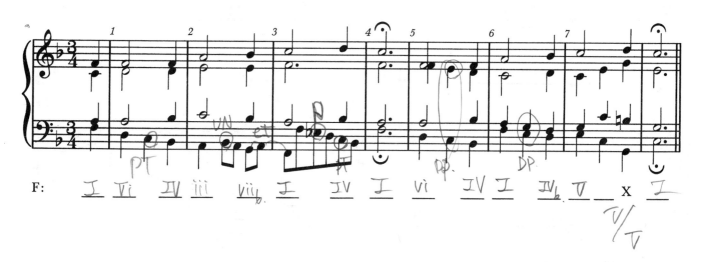

B. Add the specified embellishing tones in the indicated voice. To do so, you may have to change the rhythmic value of the note immediately preceding or following the indicated point or to displace a note by half a beat or a beat.

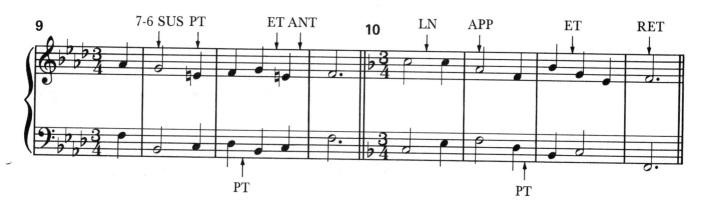

PRACTICE MATERIAL AND ASSIGNMENTS FOR PART C

A. For each of the following melodies, make a reduction that shows structural, supporting and embellishing tones and prolongations, if present. The harmonic structure is indicated beneath each melody. Remember that embellishing tones are usually distinguishable because they are *not* part of the harmonic structure, and that structural and supporting tones are distinguished from each other primarily on the basis of length and strength.

1 "Cockles and Mussels" (Irish)

2 J. C. F. Bach: *Menuet*

3 Beethoven: *Symphony No. 5* (II)

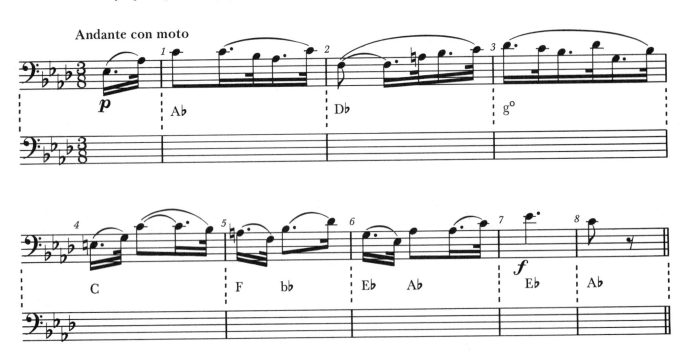

B. In the following melodies, use brackets to show step progressions and arrows to show large-scale arpeggiations. The Schubert example below illustrates the procedure.

Example: Schubert: *Sonata in B Major, D. 575* (IV)

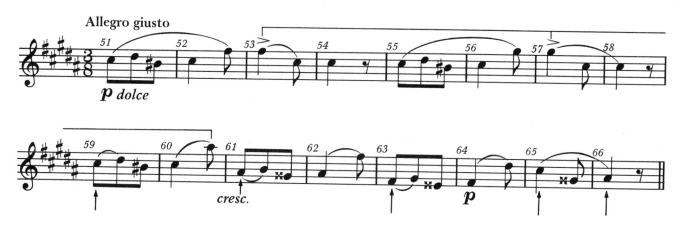

1 Handel: "How beautiful are the feet," No. 37a from *Messiah*

2 Handel: *Suite No. 8* from *Suites de Pièces pour le Clavecin, HWV 441* (Courante)

3 Mozart: *String Quartet, K. 464* (III)

4 Verdi: "La donna e mobile" from *Rigoletto* (Act IV)

5 Mozart: *Piano Sonata, K. 331* (II)

TEST YOUR COMPREHENSION OF CHAPTER SIX

A. Add the requested embellishing tones in the *upper* voice.

B. Complete the following suspensions (two voices only).

C. Provide a reduction of the following melody, showing structural, supporting, and embellishing tones in the manner prescribed in this chapter.

Schumann: *Fantasiestucke, Op. 12, No. 4*

D. In the following melody, bracket the step progressions and indicate by arrows the large-scale arpeggiations.

March (German)

Answers appear on page 365.

CHAPTER SEVEN
VOICE LEADING

HARMONY AND VOICE LEADING

Harmony consists not only of the particular chords that a composer uses but also the way in which these chords are connected. As we perform or listen to a succession of harmonies, we hear not only individual chords but also the melodic motion between the top notes of adjacent chords, between the second highest notes, and so on down to the bass. Composers often seek to connect the harmonies of a phrase in such a way that each individual vocal or instrumental part forms an effective melody. This is *most* important for the highest and lowest parts since they are generally the ones most easily heard.

The techniques of chord connection are referred to as *voice leading* (since each melodic "voice," or musical line, is successively "led" from a tone of one chord to a tone of the next) or *part writing* (since a series of harmonies is generated by simultaneous melodic parts). In Western music from approximately 1650 to 1900, certain basic voice-leading principles have generally been followed. These norms, the subject of this chapter, are most easily observed and mastered through choral music of hymnlike nature because it is melodically concise and rhythmically uncomplicated.

THE CHORALE

The *chorale,* a hymn tune in which several stanzas of verse are sung to the same music, originated in the Lutheran Church during the sixteenth century. Many composers made harmonizations of chorale melodies for four-part chorus. Such settings also were incorporated within several larger types of compositions, such as the cantata and the Passion, by J. S. Bach and his contemporaries. Bach's harmonizations exhibit many features of eighteenth-century harmonic practice that have remained influential to the present day. For this reason, a study of the chorale long has been considered an important aspect of a musician's training.

Throughout this text, four-part examples are notated on the grand staff, with the soprano and alto parts in the treble clef and the tenor and bass parts in the bass clef. Observe the stem directions.

Illustration 7.1

Soprano
Alto

Tenor
Bass

A. Melodic Principles in the Chorale Style

1. Chorale lines, except for the bass, generally cover a narrow range of about an octave and move predominantly in stepwise motion.
2. The *total* range of each of the four basic voice types is:

CHARACTERISTICS OF THE INDIVIDUAL LINES

Illustration 7.2

Soprano   Alto   Tenor   Bass

NOTE: The range of each voice is about an octave and a fifth, the tenor and bass approximately duplicating the soprano and alto an octave lower.

3. Except for the bass, the lines rarely include leaps larger than a fifth and rarely leap twice consecutively in the same direction, except when outlining a triad.
4. The bass line has a wider range than the other voices and is often more disjunct because it functions not only as a melodic line but also as a harmonic support.
5. Nondiatonic intervals (those not to be found among the pitches of a given major or minor scale), as well as the augmented second and augmented fourth, are rare.

Most of these principles are evident in the following two phrases from a chorale harmonization by J. S. Bach.

Example 7.1 J. S. Bach: "Aus meines Herzens Grunde"

FOR PRACTICE MATERIAL AND ASSIGNMENTS, TURN TO PAGE 179.

B. Voicing a Single Chord

The *voicing* of a chord is the manner in which the tones of a harmony are distributed among the four parts. Perhaps most basic to the distribution of a three-note chord among four parts is the decision of which note to double. Tendency tones and chromatically altered tones (those tones outside the key) usually are not doubled because of their instability, and their need for a specific resolution.* For the same reason, chord tones that form an augmented or diminished interval with some other note of the triad are normally not doubled. Beyond these general considerations, the best choice is usually determined by the triad's position and type.†

DOUBLING

1. Major and Minor Triads

   a. In root position:

     For root-position triads, the most frequently doubled tone is the root. Alternatively, the fifth may be doubled, and less often, the third.

Illustration 7.3

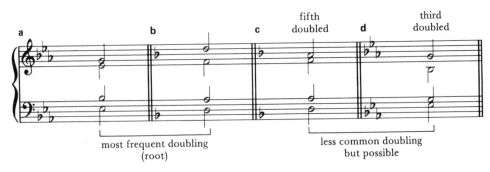

*For purposes of doubling, regard the fourth scale degree as a tendency tone only when it is a member of a viiº.

†In Part C of this chapter, you will learn that the melodic considerations of each of the voices can also determine which note is doubled.

b. In first inversion:

There is more latitude in the doubling of triads in first inversion than in root position or second inversion. Often, the choice of doubled tone depends on melodic factors, such as the desired shape or direction of a line. Still, we frequently find the soprano doubled, with the doubled bass an alternate possibility (provided, of course, that these tones are not tendency tones).

Illustration 7.4

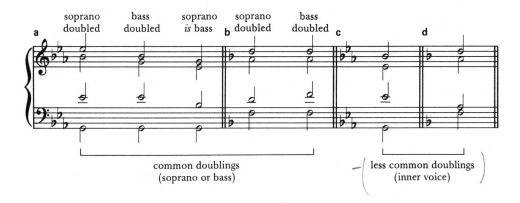

c. In second inversion:

In second-inversion triads, the overwhelming preference is to double the bass, which is the fifth of the chord.

Illustration 7.5

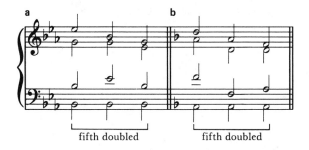

2. Diminished and Augmented Triads

Diminished and augmented triads are generally found *only in first inversion,* probably because the third of the chord (i.e., the bass) is the only chord member *not* a part of the unstable interval in these chords. For this reason also, the third is most often the doubled tone.

Illustration 7.6

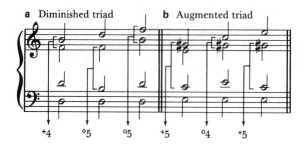

The following diagram showing preferred chord tone doublings may prove useful.

Major and Minor triads			Augmented and Diminished triads
Root position	First inversion	Second inversion	
R	S	B	3
	B		

Notice that, because the root in a root-position triad is in the bass, and because the third in an augmented or diminished triad is normally in the bass, a safe generalization regarding doubling is:

When in doubt, double the bass (unless it is a leading tone or other tendency tone).

3. Optional Doubling

If circumstances do not permit any of the more common doublings just described, an optional practice is to *omit* a chord tone. The preferred note to omit is the fifth, with either the root tripled or the root and third doubled (so long as they are not tendency tones). In second inversion, optional doublings are generally avoided.

Illustration 7.7

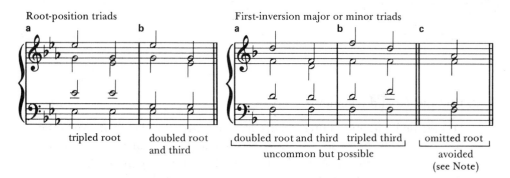

NOTE: In **c**, without the root, the chord will probably sound like an F major triad with an omitted fifth.

Spacing refers to the distance between adjacent voices of a triad or other chord. The sound ideal for most harmonic music is a homogeneous blending of the voices. This is best achieved by keeping the voices fairly equidistant from each other. The following types of homogeneous spacing may be used.

1. Close Structure

In close structure, the soprano, alto, and tenor are spaced as close together as possible.

Illustration 7.8

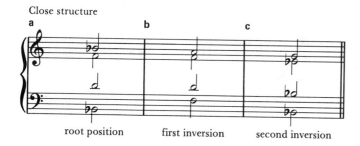

Close structure

root position   first inversion   second inversion

2. Open Structure

In open structure, the soprano, alto, and tenor are *not* as close together as possible. Because of this, an octave or more usually separates the soprano and tenor.

Illustration 7.9

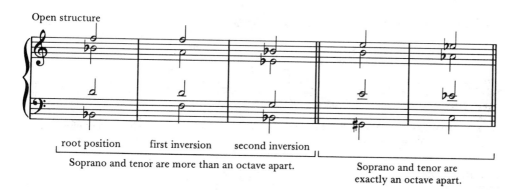

Open structure

root position   first inversion   second inversion

Soprano and tenor are more than an octave apart.   Soprano and tenor are exactly an octave apart.

Even within a short composition such as a chorale, chord structure can be changed for many reasons, such as the melodic contour of the individual lines. One of the most common points for a change is a repeated chord. Perhaps the most important guideline regarding spacing is this:

To maintain a homogeneous blending of voices, do not allow the space of more than an octave between either the soprano and alto or the alto and tenor.

This blend factor is not so apparent when chords are played on the piano as when they are sung by men's and women's voices. This is because sympathetic vibration of the strings constituting the upper harmonics of the chord tones helps to fill in the gaps and thicken the sound on the piano. Then too, the piano lacks the timbral distinction that exists between human voice types.

Sing and compare the following examples.

Illustration 7.10

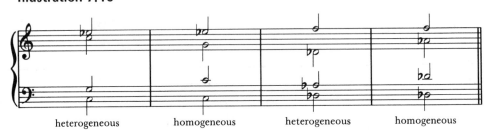

| | heterogeneous | homogeneous | heterogeneous | homogeneous |

FOR PRACTICE MATERIAL AND ASSIGNMENTS, TURN TO PAGE 181.

C. Chord Connection

Between any two voices, four types of connecting motion are possible.

Illustration 7.11

TYPES OF
MOTION

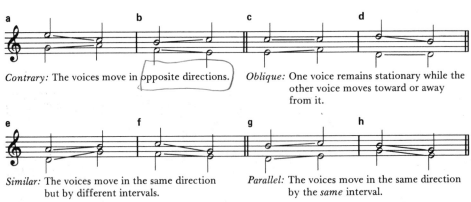

Contrary: The voices move in opposite directions.

Oblique: One voice remains stationary while the other voice moves toward or away from it.

Similar: The voices move in the same direction but by different intervals.

Parallel: The voices move in the same direction by the *same* interval.

Notice that:

1. In parallel motion, the numerical value of the interval between the two voices is maintained although its *quality* may change. That is, a major sixth may change to a minor sixth, as in **g** above.
2. When both voices repeat their respective pitches

this is *not* considered parallel motion because there is actually no motion.

3. Where one voice sustains a pitch while the other voice changes, the sustained tone may be regarded as a repeated pitch.

 = oblique motion

INDEPENDENCE OF CONTOUR AND COUNTERPOINT

In the chorale harmonizations of J. S. Bach, the soprano and bass move predominantly by contrary and oblique motion. This gives the outer lines an *independence of contour* and facilitates the part writing of the inner voices.

Following, in general order of importance, are some observations concerning chord-to-chord connections.

GUIDELINES FOR CHORD CONNECTION

1. Tendency tones in the soprano or bass are usually resolved (in the same voice). In the inner voices, however, the resolution is sometimes avoided in order to form a complete harmony.

Illustration 7.12

a

Common   Less common

C: V   I   V   I

leading tone resolved   leading tone unresolved

b

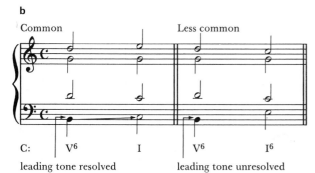

Common   Less common

C: V^6 I   V^6 I^6

leading tone resolved   leading tone unresolved

c

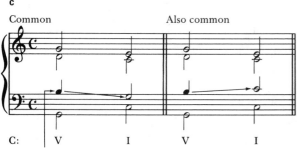

Common   Also common

C: V   I   V   I

Leading tone *in inner voice* unresolved in order to move to fifth of tonic (completing the chord).   Leading tone *in inner voice* resolved, resulting in optional doubling of tonic chord.

NOTE: Many times, the leading tone in an inner voice will be resolved despite the unusual doubling that may result. At such points, the linear (melodic) aspect of the music takes precedence over the vertical (harmonic) dimension.

2. When two voices forming the interval of a perfect fifth, perfect octave, or perfect unison move to pitches that form an identical interval, the result is termed *consecutive fifths, octaves, or unisons.** This practice is avoided.

Illustration 7.13

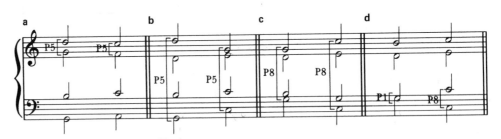

NOTE: All of these are avoided. In **d**, the perfect unison moving to a perfect octave between the same voices is also to be avoided due to the *nearly* identical sound of the two intervals.

When two voices forming a perfect fifth, octave, or unison remain stationary on their respective pitches, this is *not* considered objectionable since, in effect, there is no motion within the voices.

Illustration 7.14

NOTE: Although the perfect fifths appear consecutively in the same two voices, this is *not* objectionable because the two voices do not move.

The consecutive fifth restriction does *not* apply when one of the fifths is not perfect.

*These are also known as *parallel* fifths, octaves, or unisons.

Example 7.2   J. S. Bach: "In dulci jubilo"

A related matter concerns *direct fifths or octaves*—the approach to these intervals through similar motion. Direct fifths and octaves *approached by leap in both voices* generally are avoided. This problem is most pronounced when it involves the outer voices.

Illustration 7.15

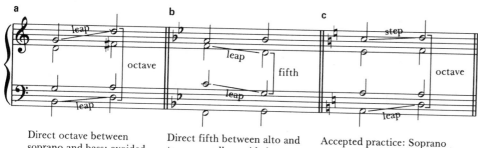

Direct octave between soprano and bass: avoided

Direct fifth between alto and tenor: usually avoided

Accepted practice: Soprano moves *by step* rather than by leap.

The only perfect interval that may appear consecutively between two voices is the perfect fourth. However, consecutive fourths between *the two lowest voices* are generally avoided (as are consecutive fourths in a two-voice texture).

Example 7.3   J. S. Bach: "Mach's mit mir, Gott, nach deiner Güt' "

3. *Voice crossing* is avoided by maintaining the normal vertical disposition of the voices—soprano above alto, alto above tenor, and tenor above bass.

Illustration 7.16

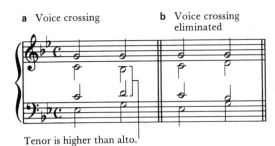

a Voice crossing

b Voice crossing eliminated

Tenor is higher than alto.

4. *Voice overlap*—allowing a voice to move above the preceding pitch of a higher voice or below the preceding pitch of a lower voice—generally is avoided.

Illustration 7.17

Voice overlap: This bass pitch is higher than the preceding tenor pitch.

Because voice crossing and overlap tend to obscure the linear motion of the individual parts, they are commonly avoided. When they do occur, they are usually of short duration and result from melodic considerations. In the following passage, for example, voice crossing in m. 4 permits the resolution of the chromatic tendency tone C♯ in the same voice. In m. 1, the voice overlap between the tenor and bass could have been avoided had Bach written the bass an octave lower. However, to do so, he would have had to break up the ensuing stepwise descent, since the last note or two would extend beyond the normal range of the bass voice.

Example 7.4 J. S. Bach: "In dulci jubilo"

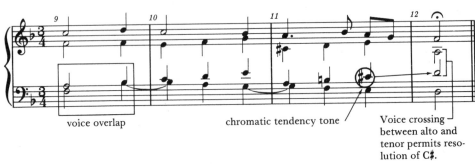

voice overlap

chromatic tendency tone

Voice crossing between alto and tenor permits resolution of C♯.

In the following pages, we will consider how these voice-leading principles are applied to each type of diatonic chord relationship.

Chords whose roots lie a fifth apart (or its inversion, the fourth) contain a common tone. Typically, the common tone is retained in the same voice in both chords, and the other tones move to the nearest member of the following chord that permits a common doubling.

Illustration 7.18

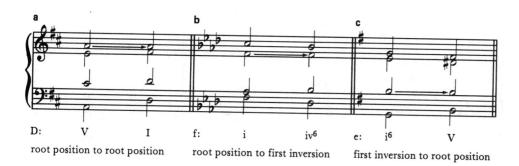

D: V   I   f: i   iv⁶   e: i⁶   V

root position to root position   root position to first inversion   first inversion to root position

Sometimes it is not desirable to move all the chord tones to the nearest possible member of the following harmony. A typical situation is a change of structure. Often, the third of one chord moves to the third of the next chord *in the same voice.*

Illustration 7.19

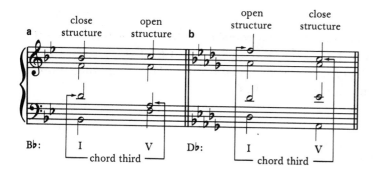

NOTE: The common tone is still retained in the same voice.

CHORDS IN THIRD RELATIONSHIP

Chords whose roots are related by the interval of a third (or its inversion, the sixth) have *two common tones.* Because of this, the resulting sense of harmonic motion is not very pronounced, and composers therefore sometimes employ leaps in several of the voices in order to provide a greater feeling of harmonic change. Often, a change of structure is involved.

Illustration 7.20

Common tones retained (sense of harmonic motion not pronounced)

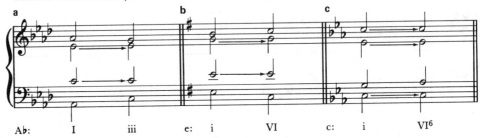

Common tones not retained (greater feeling of harmonic motion)

CHORDS IN SECOND RELATIONSHIP

In *second relationship,* no common tones exist between the two chords. Because all voices must move, the potential for consecutive fifths, octaves, or unisons is greater than in other chord relationships. Often, the three upper voices move in contrary motion to the bass.

Illustration 7.21

NOTE: Soprano, alto, and tenor move in contrary motion to the bass.

When two or more first-inversion triads appear in succession, consistent doubling of either the soprano or the bass can result in consecutive octaves and fifths. A solution is to double the soprano and bass in alternation.

Illustration 7.22

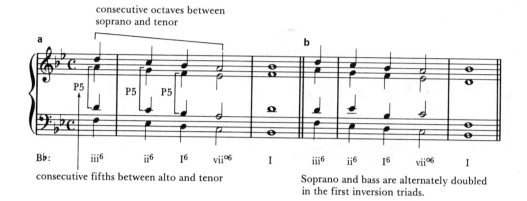

consecutive octaves between soprano and tenor

a   b

Bb: iii⁶   ii⁶   I⁶   vii°⁶   I   iii⁶   ii⁶   I⁶   vii°⁶   I

consecutive fifths between alto and tenor

Soprano and bass are alternately doubled in the first inversion triads.

Nonchord tones enhance the smoothness of chord connections and add a dissonant element to the musical texture. Because they are merely melodic embellishments, they usually do not substantially affect the basic chord connections. Consider the following examples.

Illustration 7.23

a Without nonchord tone   **b** With nonchord tone

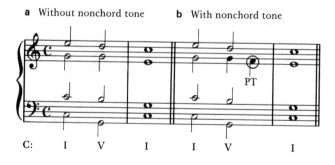

C: I   V   I   I   V   I

a Without nonchord tone   **b** With nonchord tone

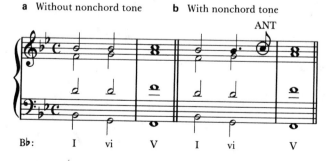

Bb: I   vi   V   I   vi   V

Notice that the presence of the nonchord tone does not change the basic voice leading of the passage. For this reason, nonchord tones cannot be used as a means of avoiding a basic voice-leading problem. In the following example, the addition of an anticipation in the soprano does not alleviate the consecutive fifths effect produced on the strong beats of the measure.

Illustration 7.24

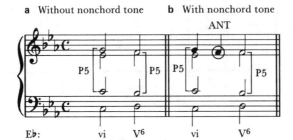

On the other hand, the addition of nonchord tones should not *create* voice-leading problems that otherwise would not exist. In the following illustration, the added passing tone creates consecutive perfect fifths between the soprano and alto.

Illustration 7.25

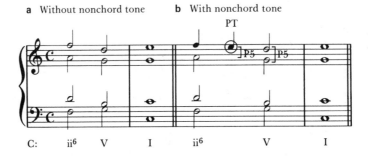

Suspensions require some further explanation. Since a suspension is but a delayed motion in one voice as it moves to the next chord tone, the doubling *at the point of resolution* is normally that which would occur if there were no suspension.

Illustration 7.26

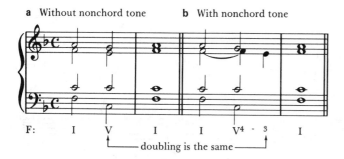

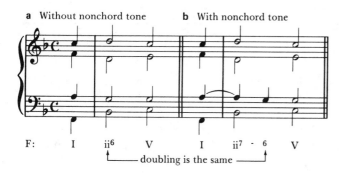

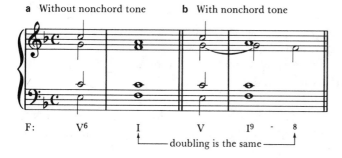

Notice that the suspension figure itself (which also would appear in the figured bass line of a continuo part) usually suggests the type of chord that occurs at the point of resolution. That is, a 4-3 indicates a root-position triad *at the point of resolution;* a 7-6 indicates a first-inversion triad *at the point of resolution;* a 9-8 indicates a root-position triad *at the point of resolution.*

Composers continually make choices that enhance either the melodic (linear) or the harmonic (vertical) aspect of their music. This is but one example of the balance between melodic and harmonic forces that characterizes much part music.

Many of the foregoing observations concerning doubling, spacing and chord connection are illustrated in the following musical example.

Example 7.5 Praetorius: "Herr Gott, dich loben alle wir" from *Musae Sionae*
(melody by Louis Bourgeois, 1551)*

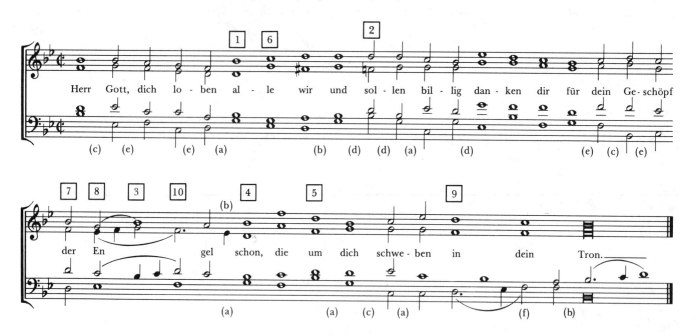

Observations on doubling in Example 7.5:

1. The vast majority of chords are in root position; in most of those cases, the root (bass) is the doubled tone. In only five instances is another chord member doubled. These exceptions are numbered 1 through 5.

2. Four triads appear in first inversion (numbered 6 through 9). For chords 7, 8, and 9, the bass is the doubled note. For chord 6, the inner voice is doubled.

3. There is only one second-inversion triad (numbered 10). In it, the bass (the chord fifth) is doubled.

This example also illustrates typical chord connection procedures. The letters (a) through (f) are used in the example to identify points that illustrate the following.

a. change of structure (page 167)
b. chord connection: tendency tones (page 169)
c. chords in fifth relationship (page 173)
d. chords in third relationship (page 174)
e. chords in second relationship (page 174)
f. a 4-3 suspension with normal doubling at the point of resolution (page 177)

*You may recognize this melody as the familiar "Old One Hundred," sung as the Doxology in certain Church services.

D. Part Writing Checklist

Following is a set of guidelines for part writing based on the procedures described in this chapter.

1. Keep all voices within their respective ranges.

THE INDIVIDUAL LINES

2. Avoid large melodic leaps, nondiatonic intervals, augmented seconds and fourths, and consecutive leaps in the same direction (except for arpeggiations).
3. Use common doubling procedures when possible.

VOICING A SINGLE CHORD

4. Avoid doubling tendency tones.
5. Use homogeneous spacing, changing from open to close structure (or vice versa) for variety, to produce more fluent voice leading, or to keep the voices within their respective ranges.
6. Strive for independent contour (predominantly contrary and oblique motion) between the outer voices.

CHORD CONNECTION

7. Resolve all tendency tones that appear in the outer voices.
8. Avoid consecutive perfect fifths, octaves, or unisons between the same two voices.
9. Avoid voice crossing and overlap.
10. Finally, when a part-writing problem seems insurmountable, one of the following options may still be available:
    a. Change the structure or inversion of the chord.
    b. Use optional doubling.
    c. Change the harmony.

FOR PRACTICE MATERIAL AND ASSIGNMENTS, TURN TO PAGE 182.

PRACTICE MATERIAL AND ASSIGNMENTS FOR PART A

A. Given the harmonic structure, complete the following melodies in chorale style (melody only), observing the principles discussed in Part A (pp. 162-164). (A dash indicates a repeated harmony.) Play and sing each melody when you have completed it, listening carefully to determine if the part you have written sounds consistent with the given part.

1

F: I V I IV V — I   IV I V vi IV V I   V vi IV ii I V I

2

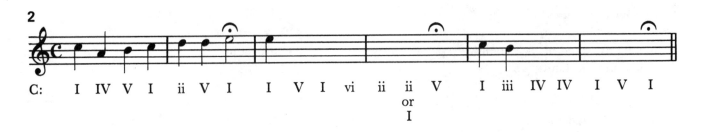

C: I IV V I ii V I   I V I vi ii ii V   I iii IV IV I V I

                                        or
                                        I

3

A: I — IV V   I IV V — I V   I V I V vii° I vi

  ii V — I   V — I IV V I IV vi V   I

4

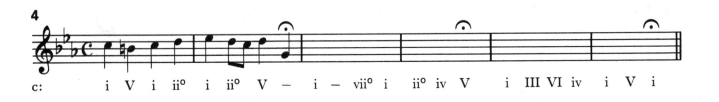

c: i V i ii° i ii° V — i — vii° i ii° iv V   i III VI iv i V i

B. Play and sing the following melodies. Then identify those features *not* in keeping with the melodic principles of the chorale style.

1

2

PRACTICE MATERIAL AND ASSIGNMENTS FOR PART B

A. Write the following chords for four voices, in both close and open structure, using common doublings. Be sure to keep each voice within its proper range. The soprano is given for each chord. Play each chord on the keyboard and note carefully the difference in sound between close and open structure.

NOTE: One of these ten chords cannot be notated in close structure without violating a fundamental principle of doubling. Identify the chord and explain the problem.

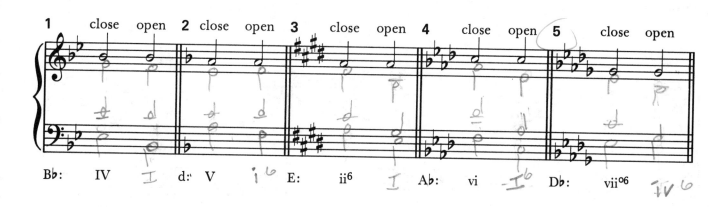

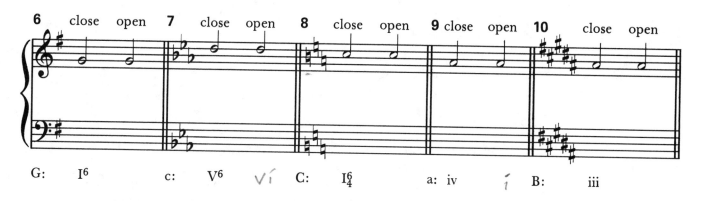

B. Identify the following chords by function (Roman numeral), inversion (superscript), and structure (C for close and O for open). Then, retaining the same soprano and bass pitch, re-voice the chord in a different structure.

Key:	c♯	B♭	G	b	F
Chord:	—	—	—	—	—
Structure:	—	—	—	—	—

Key:	e	D♭	f♯	E♭	b♭
Chord:	—	—	—	—	—
Structure:	—	—	—	—	—

PRACTICE MATERIAL AND ASSIGNMENTS FOR PART C

A. Identify the type of motion (*C*ontrary, *O*blique, *S*imilar, *P*arallel, *R*epetition) between each note of the soprano and bass in the following chorale fragments.* At certain points, one voice sustains a pitch while the other changes pitch. In such cases, regard the sustained note as a repeated pitch.

Suggestion: An excellent ear-training procedure is to play one part at the piano while singing the other.

*From Bach-Riemenschneider, *371 Harmonized Chorales and 69 Chorale Melodies.*

1 J. S. Bach: "Nur mein Jesus ist mein Leben"

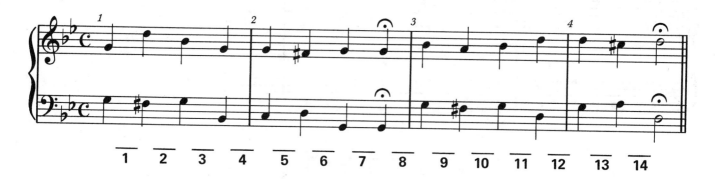

2 J. S. Bach: "Ermuntre dich, mein schwacher Geist"

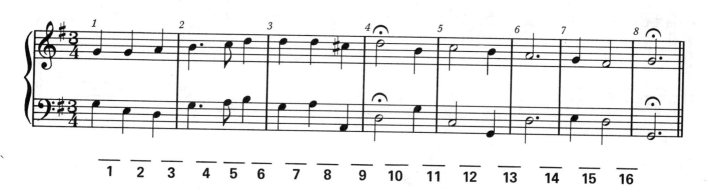

B. Add the alto and tenor voices to the following soprano-bass frame-
works, observing all part-writing guidelines. Then provide harmonic analysis.

1

Key ___ : ___ ___ ___ ___ ___ ___ ___ ___

2

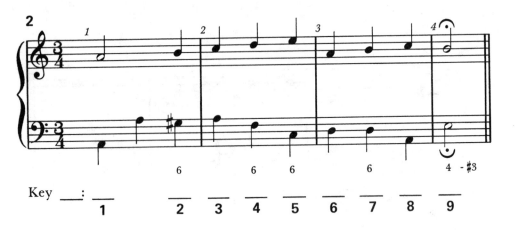

Key ___:
1 2 3 4 5 6 7 8 9

3

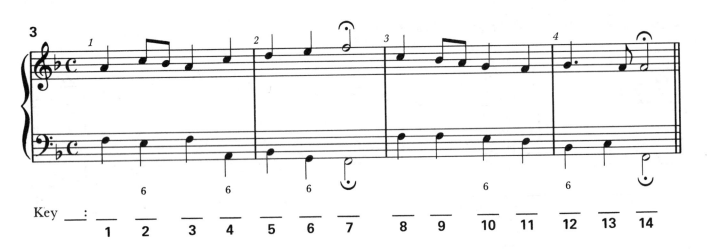

Key ___:
1 2 3 4 5 6 7 8 9 10 11 12 13 14

C. Provide harmonic analysis of the following chorale fragments, labeling all nonchord tones and indicating chord structure (C for close, O for open) as well. Disregard any material enclosed in boxes, since it contains harmonies not yet discussed.

1 J. S. Bach: "Wer weiss, wie nahe mir"

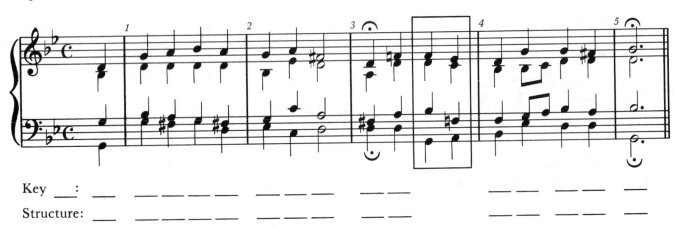

Key ___: ___ ___ ___ ___ ___ ___ ___ ___ ___ ___
Structure: ___ ___ ___ ___ ___ ___ ___ ___

2 J. S. Bach: "Werde munter, mein Gemüte"

Key ___: _ _ _ _   _ _ _ _   _ _ _ _   _ _ _ _

Structure: _ _ _ _   _ _ _ _   _ _ _ _   _ _ _ _

SUGGESTIONS FOR AURAL DRILL

A. Your instructor will play chords selected at random from the exercises at the end of the chapter, such as Exercise A on page 181, Exercise B on page 182, or Exercise C on page 184. Identify the quality (M, m, +, °), inversion (R, 1, 2) and structure (O, C) for each chord.

B. Your instructor will notate several four-voice chords on the chalkboard, which you are to copy on manuscript paper and number. Your instructor will play a second chord to follow each of these chords. You are to notate the second chord. Notate the outer voices first, followed by the inner voices.

C. Your instructor will play short, two-voice passages chosen from your text or workbook. Given the beginning pitch for both the soprano and bass voices, you are to notate the two-voice passage. Sources for two-voice passages are:

Text, pages 183-184 (Exercises A and B); pages 184-185 (outer voices only)

Workbook, pages 58-60 (outer voices); page 64

TEST YOUR COMPREHENSION OF CHAPTER SEVEN

A. Identify the structure for each chord as close or open. Then, re-taining the same soprano and bass notes, re-voice the chord in the opposite structure.

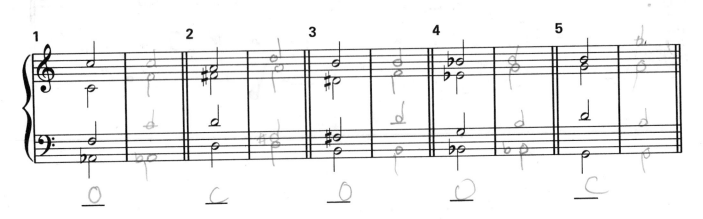

B. Place an *X* above those chords *not* doubled according to the common doubling procedures summarized on pages 164-166.

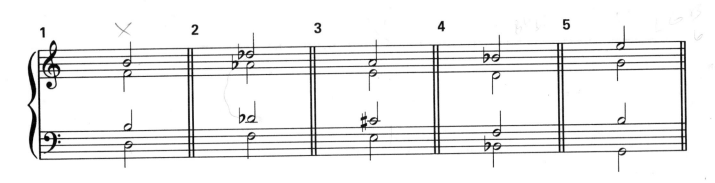

C. Write for four voices the triad indicated, using the specified structure and appropriate doubling.

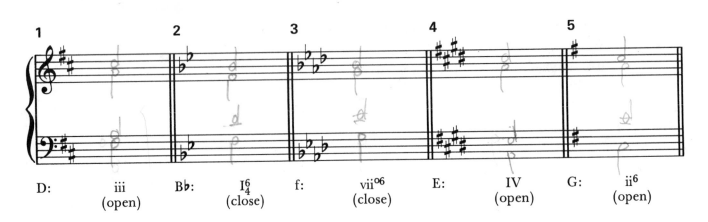

D: iii   Bb: I⁶₄   f: vii°⁶   E: IV   G: ii⁶
       (open)   (close)   (close)   (open)   (open)

D. Using *only consonances,* provide an upper voice that exhibits the specified motion against the given bass note.

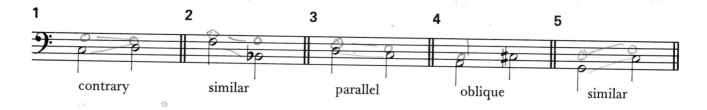

E. Part write the following two-chord successions in four voices, using appropriate voice-leading procedures.

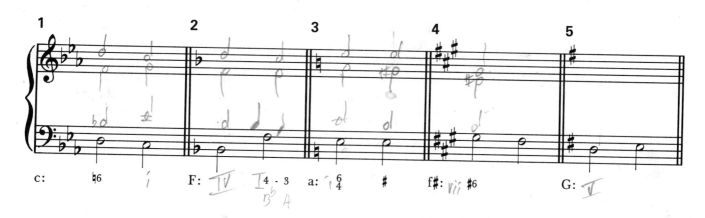

Answers appear on page 366.

CHAPTER EIGHT
FUNCTIONAL TONALITY;
PRINCIPLES OF HARMONIZATION

TERMS TO KNOW

arpeggiated six-four chord
cadential six-four chord
functional tonality
harmonic rhythm
passing six-four chord
pedal six-four chord

pre-dominant
progression
repetition
retrogression
seventh chord
six-four chord

A. Functional Tonality

In Chapter Six, we examined several means by which melodies acquire a tonal focus. One of the more important ways is through harmonic implication. Harmonies are generally related to each other in a system called *functional tonality*. The principles of this system governed harmonic practice from roughly 1650 to 1900 and beyond (depending on the musical style). They may be summarized in this way.

1. The music revolves around focal points called *tonal centers*.
2. These tonal centers are established through the function, or behavior, of the various chords.
3. Each of the triads within a given key bears a unique relationship to the tonic triad (which is the tonal center) and has a stronger tendency to lead to certain chords than to others.

The behavior of the individual chords is rather like a "chain of command," which is governed by the overwhelming strength of the descending-fifth root movement, as in the dominant-to-tonic motion. If, for example, all the chords of a major or minor key are arranged so that each moves to the chord whose root is a fifth below it, the following patterns result.

Illustration 8.1

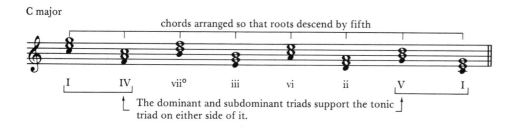

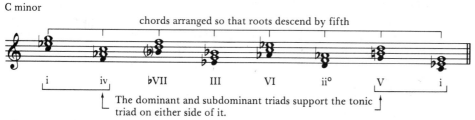

Black notes = chord roots

In this chordal hierarchy, a chord's relationship to the tonic is determined by its distance from it, measured in descending fifths, and its most natural behavior is to move *toward the tonic through a series of descending-fifth root movements.* The mediant, for example, would normally arrive at the tonic not directly, but by way of the submediant, supertonic, and dominant in turn.

THE CHORDAL HIERARCHY

Illustration 8.2

(circle of 5th's movement)

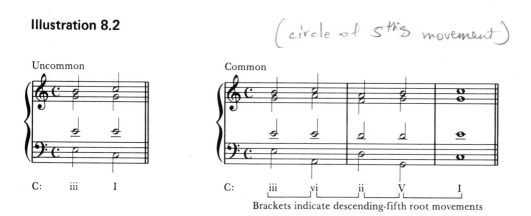

Brackets indicate descending-fifth root movements

In practice, there are a few exceptions.

1. The vii° is not *nearly* so distant from the tonic as Illustration 8.1 might suggest. This is because its root, the leading tone, has a very strong pull

THE vii° AND V

toward the tonic. Moreover, the fifth of the triad is a tone with a very strong tendency to move downward to the third of the tonic.

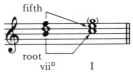

Arrows show tendencies of the root and fifth.

(The vii° thus acts (functions) as a dominant: It is a chord that leads directly to the tonic. For this reason, it is *functionally* related to the dominant.) As a matter of fact, the V and the vii° are very often heard together, in the form of a *dominant seventh chord.*

Illustration 8.3

THE DOMINANT SEVENTH CHORD

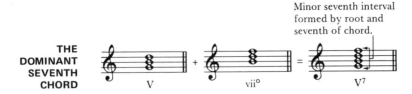

Minor seventh interval formed by root and seventh of chord.

Notice that the fifth of the vii° forms the interval of a seventh above the root of the V—hence, the name seventh chord. It is often used in place of the pure dominant triad.

THE IV AND ii

2. Although it sometimes precedes the tonic, as in the plagal cadence, the (IV more often functions as a *pre-dominant*—a chord that leads directly to the dominant—and is therefore grouped with the supertonic. As with the V and vii°, the ii and IV (ii° and iv in minor) are often heard together, in the form of a *supertonic seventh chord.*

Illustration 8.4

THE SUPERTONIC SEVENTH CHORD

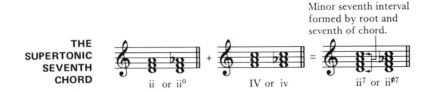

Minor seventh interval formed by root and seventh of chord.

Note the symbol $^{\emptyset 7}$, which denotes the *diminished* supertonic triad with the added seventh. These and other seventh chords are discussed in detail in Chapters Ten and Eleven.

It may be helpful to view the chords of a key as a sort of tonal planetary system with the tonic as its center.

Illustration 8.5

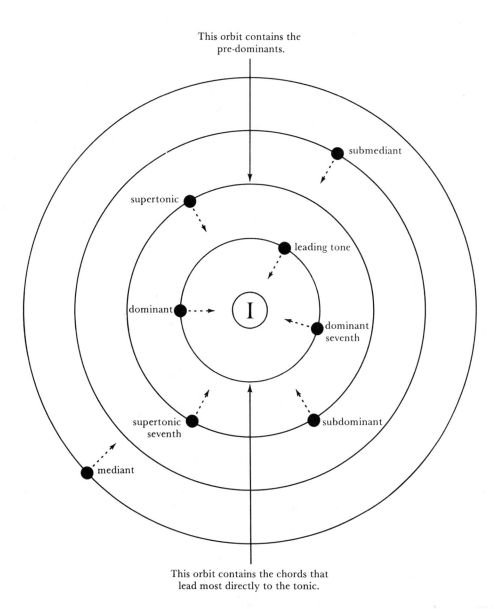

This orbit contains the pre-dominants.

This orbit contains the chords that lead most directly to the tonic.

A chord in any orbit tends most strongly toward a chord in the next orbit inward. The farther the chord is from the tonic (the musical center of gravity), the weaker the pull of the tonic on it.

HARMONIC MOTION   Harmonic motion is of the following types.

1. A *progression* constitutes forward harmonic motion, in which a chord advances to a chord functionally closer to the tonic.

Illustration 8.6

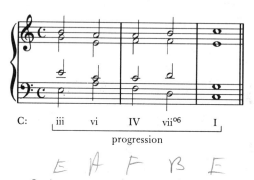

C: iii   vi   IV   vii°⁶   I

progression

E   A   F   B   E

2. A *retrogression* constitutes harmonic motion away from the tonic, in which each chord moves to a chord more remote from the tonic.

Illustration 8.7

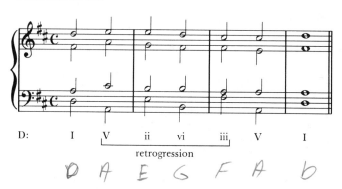

D: I   V   ii   vi   iii   V   I

retrogression

D   A   E   G   F   A   b

3. *Repetition* involves a chord followed either by itself or by another chord of the same function, such as V-vii° or IV-ii.

Illustration 8.8

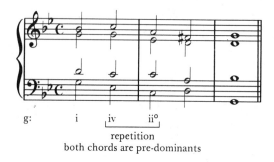

g: i   iv   ii°

repetition
both chords are pre-dominants

4. Movement *from* the tonic triad itself constitutes the final type of harmonic motion. This has no special name. The tonic triad may lead to any other chord.

While any musical work will likely contain all types of harmonic motion, progression is the most common. Chords connected by the strong descending-fifth root movement have a particularly satisfying sense of propulsion. On the other hand, chords connected by *ascending*-fifth root movement (retrogressions) somehow sound less natural, since they deny the attraction of the tonic. One fairly common retrogression, however, is found in the form of the deceptive cadence (discussed on page 90).

Example 8.1 Mozart: *Piano Sonata, K. 332* (I)

NOTE: While technically a retrogression, this movement from V⁷ to vi has a satisfying sense of resolution. This is probably because the vi has two tones in common with the tonic, and in fact can serve as a substitute for the tonic. The two common tones provide a resolution for the two tendency tones (scale degrees 4 and 7) in the V⁷ (right-hand part, last measure).

In most musical works, the harmonies change with some regularity, creating a series of rhythmic patterns that constitute the *harmonic rhythm* of a piece. Although some music (certain folk songs, for example) employs a single harmonic rhythm throughout, it is more common to find a variety of patterns. Tempo, meter, and style are all important factors that determine harmonic rhythm, which can range from a chord change on every beat to a chord change every measure or so. Generally, harmonies change at the *beginning* of a measure. They also can change at metrically strong points *within* a measure as well. Some common harmonic rhythms in 4/4 are:

HARMONIC RHYTHM

Illustration 8.9

The harmonic rhythm is shown below the music in the following example.

Example 8.2   Brahms: *Symphony No. 3, Op. 90* (II)

COMMON HARMONIC PATTERNS

Certain harmonic patterns have been used extensively. Several are shown below.

1. In major: ii⁶-V-I
   In minor: ii°⁶-V-i

   This pattern became common at cadences in the seventeenth and eighteenth centuries and remains one of the most convincing ways to end a phrase of tonal music.

Example 8.3   Handel: *Suite No. 1* from *Suites de Pièces pour le Clavecin, HWV 434* (Aria con variazioni)

2. In major: I (or iii)-vi-ii-V-I
   In minor: i (or III)-VI-ii°-V-i

   This is simply an expansion of the previous formula, involving downward-fifth root movement. It may end on the tonic, repeat, or move elsewhere.

Example 8.4   J. S. Bach: *Cantata, Wachet Auf, BWV 140* (I)

3. In major: I (or vi)-iii-IV-I (or V)

This pattern is similar to pattern 2. However, the IV is substituted for the ii^6, and the use of the iii permits a more conjunct bass line.

Example 8.5 Mozart: *Le Nozze di Figaro* (Act II, No. 10)

4. In major: I-V^6-vi-iii^6 (or I$^6_4$)
   In minor: i-v^6-VI (or iv^6)-V (or i$^6_4$)

The most important feature of this pattern is the descending bass line, which moves stepwise from the tonic to the dominant. This bass line, or one of several variants, formed the foundation of many seventeenth- and eighteenth-century compositions and was called a *ground bass*. (Ground bass compositions are discussed in Chapter Fifteen.)

Example 8.6 J. S. Bach: *French Suite No. 5, BWV 816* (Gavotte)

It was pointed out in Chapter Four that two chord types exist for every scale degree except the tonic in minor tonalities. Generally speaking, the most frequently used chords are those of the harmonic minor scale. The alternative chords result when one of the individual voices moves upward or

HARMONIC VARIANTS IN MINOR

downward through the upper four notes of the melodic minor scale. Alternative triads using the *raised sixth* scale degree therefore tend to precede a chord containing the *raised seventh* degree (the dominant or leading tone triad).

Illustration 8.10

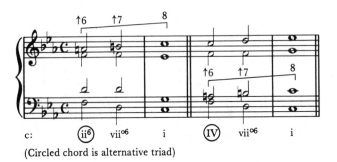

(Circled chord is alternative triad)

Alternative triads using the *lowered seventh* degree tend to precede a chord containing the *natural minor sixth* degree.

Illustration 8.11

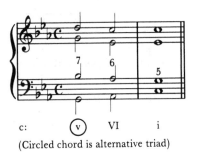

(Circled chord is alternative triad)

FOR PRACTICE MATERIAL AND ASSIGNMENTS, TURN TO PAGE 202.

B. The Six-Four Chord

The fourth harmonic pattern given in the previous section lists the tonic six-four chord as an option. In actual practice, triads appear in second inversion much less frequently than they do in root position or first inversion. This is perhaps due to the unstable sound that results from the placement of the interval of the fourth between the bass and the root. Composers have used second-inversion triads in the following ways.

1. The Cadential Six-Four Chord

This chord often appears between the supertonic and the dominant in cadential formulas, as follows: ii6-I$^6_4$-V. Typically, the tonic six-four chord is metrically stronger than the dominant, to which it resolves. In four-voice textures, the bass is usually doubled. The sixth above the bass resolves by step downward to the fifth above the bass, and the fourth above the bass resolves by step downward to the third above the bass.

Illustration 8.12

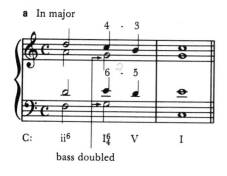
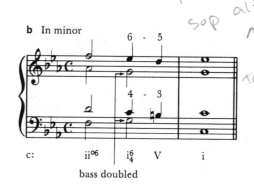

a In major

b In minor

C: ii6   I$^6_4$ V   I

c: ii°6   i$^6_4$ V   i

bass doubled

bass doubled

NOTE: The six-four chord on beat 3 is metrically stronger than its resolution on beat 4.

Note that once the resolution takes place, the tonic six-four chord changes identity and becomes a root-position dominant (with normal doubling). This suggests that the cadential six-four chord should be regarded *not* as a tonic insofar as its *function* is concerned, but as a *dominant* with two simultaneous nonchord tones—a sixth and fourth above the root—which just happen to spell a tonic chord before they resolve.

Illustration 8.13

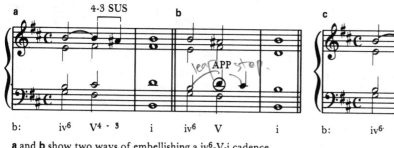
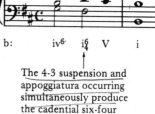

a

4-3 SUS

b

c

4 - 3

6 - 5

b: iv6   V4 - 3   i   iv6   V   i

b: iv6   i$^6_4$ V   i

a and **b** show two ways of embellishing a iv6-V-i cadence. If both embellishments are used *together*, **c** results.

The 4-3 suspension and appoggiatura occurring simultaneously produce the cadential six-four chord.

For this reason, it is possible to regard the harmonic motion to a cadential six-four chord as if it were simply a motion to a dominant. The dominant triad that normally follows may then be considered a harmonic repetition.

Illustration 8.14

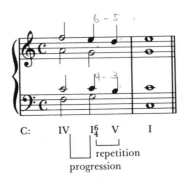

NOTE: In both **a** and **b**, the bass in the passing six-four chord resembles a passing tone.

2. The Passing Six-Four Chord

Somewhat less common than the cadential six-four chord, the passing six-four chord derives its name from the fact that the bass (the fifth) is approached and left by step, in the manner of a passing tone. This stepwise motion *through* the bass sometimes appears in contrary motion in an upper voice. (This is found in choral styles more often than in instrumental music.) The chord is usually a dominant (V_4^6), sometimes a tonic (I_4^6). It is normally *weaker metrically* than the preceding and following chords.

Illustration 8.15

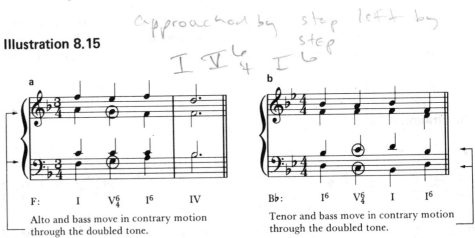

Alto and bass move in contrary motion through the doubled tone.

Tenor and bass move in contrary motion through the doubled tone.

NOTE: In both **a** and **b**, the bass in the passing six-four chord resembles a passing tone.

3. The Pedal Six-Four Chord

This chord, also called an *embellishing* or *neighboring* six-four, usually occurs between two root-position tonic triads. The bass line remains stationary, in the manner of a pedal point. Two of the other voices usually move upward and downward by step in the manner of upper neighbors. Like the passing six-four, the pedal six-four chord is normally *weaker metrically* than the preceding and following chords. A good example is the opening measure of "Silent Night."

Example 8.7   Franz Grüber: "Silent Night"

Soprano and alto move in the
manner of upper neighbors.

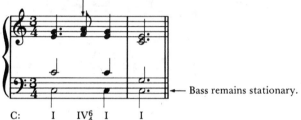

Bass remains stationary.

C: I   IV$^6_4$ I   I

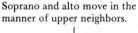

4. The Arpeggiated Six-Four Chord

The arpeggiated six-four chord appears when a triad is arpeggiated in the bass, producing root-position, first-inversion, and second-inversion triads in the process.

Illustration 8.16

a: i   i^6 i$^6_4$ i

Although it is most often a tonic, the arpeggiated six-four chord occasionally appears as a dominant as well. Both the arpeggiated six-four and the pedal six-four chords are found less often in the music of Bach, Handel, and other composers of the Baroque era than in the music of the Classical and Romantic composers (late eighteenth and nineteenth centuries).

FOR PRACTICE MATERIAL AND ASSIGNMENTS, TURN TO PAGE 204.

C. Principles of Harmonization

The ability to harmonize a melody convincingly is a valuable skill that can be required of the musician from time to time. Apart from this practical value, it provides an opportunity to apply the principles of functional tonality in a creative and personal way. The following procedure will prove useful in arriving at harmonizations that are convincing and that conform to functional principles. As a means of illustrating each step, the first part of this melody will be used.

Example 8.8   English folk song

CADENCE POINTS

1. Identify the melodic cadence points. These points normally will be supported by harmonic cadences—authentic, plagal, half, or deceptive. In this melody, melodic cadences occur at m. 4 and m. 8.

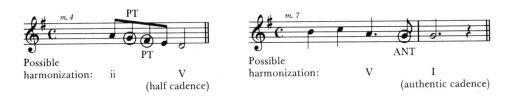

HARMONIC RHYTHM

2. Determine the harmonic rhythm most appropriate, given the tempo, meter and style. At a moderate tempo, this prevailingly quarter-note melody seems to require a chord change at least twice per measure, possibly more often at certain points.

EMBELLISHING TONES

3. Determine which of the melody tones are *obviously* embellishing. These are likely to be those that fall between downbeats or are otherwise metrically weak. In addition to the embellishing tones already identified at the cadence points, two other possibilities exist.

4. Look for obvious melodic arpeggiations. The chord outlined is almost certainly the best choice for a *single* supporting harmony. In this melody, *partial* arpeggiations occur in m. 1 and m. 2. They may or may not be supported by a single harmony.

CHORDAL OUTLINING

5. Make a list of chord possibilities for all other appropriate melodic pitches. By regarding each melody tone as a potential root, third, or fifth of a triad, you should be able to list three possibilities for each melody tone—four possibilities where a dominant seventh or supertonic seventh chord are possible.

CHORD INVENTORY

6. Select a series of harmonies based on all previous considerations. Try to choose a succession that contains mostly harmonic progressions. Keep retrogressions to a minimum. Write the chords in root position under the melody tones.

CHORD SELECTION

First phrase of melody

G: I   IV   iii   vi   IV   vii°   I   vi   V   I   ii   V
              R   P   P   P   P   P   P   P

P = Progression
R = Retrogression

NOTE: Motion *from* the tonic is not classified or calculated in this illustration. *Any* chord may follow the tonic.

7. Create a more melodic bass line. In many works, the second most important melody is the bass line. If you have used many descending-fifth root movements in your harmonization (i.e., progressions), you will probably find that the bass line sounds a bit angular. You can create a

MELODIC BASS LINE

more melodic bass through the use of inversion and through the addition of passing tones. Remember, however, that second inversion should be restricted to the four uses described earlier in this chapter. As a final step, part-write the harmonization in a four-voice style, if appropriate, or arrange a suitable piano accompaniment. This may be a simple block chord accompaniment or a more elaborate arpeggiated figure of some type. A four-part realization follows.

Illustration 8.17

G: I   I⁶   ii⁶   iii   vi   IV   vii°⁶   I   vi   V⁶   I   ii⁶   V

FOR PRACTICE MATERIAL AND ASSIGNMENTS, TURN TO PAGE 205.

PRACTICE MATERIAL AND ASSIGNMENTS FOR PART A

A. 1. Part-write in four voices a chord that will create the specified harmonic motion from each of the following chords: P = Progression; R = Retrogression; S = Same function (Repetition). Use root position except where the second chord is a diminished triad. Provide harmonic analysis.
   2. Practice playing each succession at the keyboard.

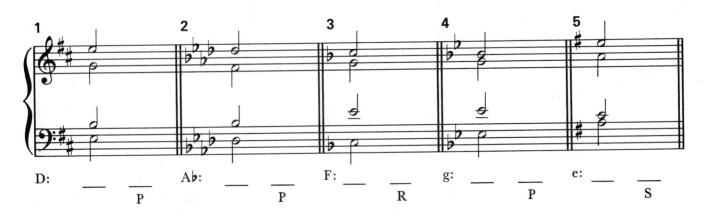

D: ___ ___   Ab: ___ ___   F: ___ ___   g: ___ ___   e: ___ ___
        P   P   R   P   S

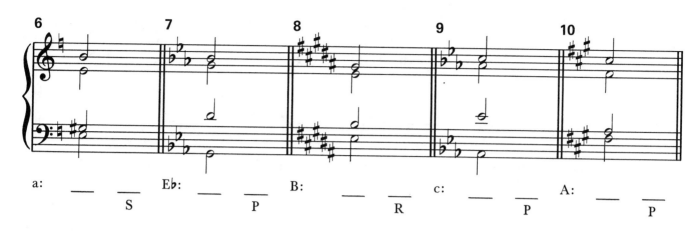

a: ___ ___   Eb: ___ ___   B: ___ ___   c: ___ ___   A: ___ ___
       S   P   R   P   P

B. Provide harmonic analysis of the following. Then identify the motion between the harmonies in this manner: P = Progression; R = Retrogression; S = Same function (Repetition).

1 Mozart: *Piano Sonata, K. 284* (III)*

Key D: ___ I ___ VI ___ II ___ V7 ___ I ___ IV ___ P app/V

Harmonic motion: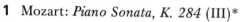

*This movement is contained in its entirety in *Anthology for Musical Analysis,* fourth edition, by Charles Burkhart (Holt, Rinehart and Winston, 1986).

2 J. S. Bach: "Du Friedensfürst, Herr Jesu Christ"

Key ___: ___ ___ ___ ___ V^6_5 ___ ___ ii^6_5 ___ ___

Harmonic motion: ___ ___ ___ ___ ___ ___ ___

C. Write a root-position supertonic seventh chord and dominant seventh chord in each of the specified keys. Add sharps or flats to the chords as necessary.

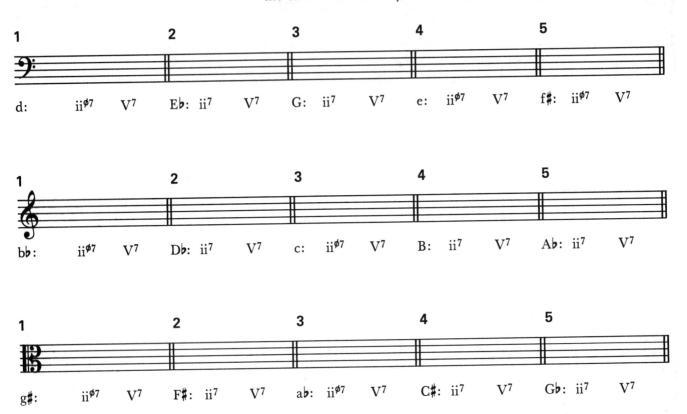

d: ii$^{\varnothing 7}$ V^7 E♭: ii^7 V^7 G: ii^7 V^7 e: ii$^{\varnothing 7}$ V^7 f♯: ii$^{\varnothing 7}$ V^7

b♭: ii$^{\varnothing 7}$ V^7 D♭: ii^7 V^7 c: ii$^{\varnothing 7}$ V^7 B: ii^7 V^7 A♭: ii^7 V^7

g♯: ii$^{\varnothing 7}$ V^7 F♯: ii^7 V^7 a♭: ii$^{\varnothing 7}$ V^7 C♯: ii^7 V^7 G♭: ii^7 V^7

PRACTICE MATERIAL AND ASSIGNMENTS FOR PART B

Complete the following exercises in four voices, part-writing and resolving the six-four chord in an appropriate manner. Then identify the type of six-four chord employed. Practice playing each completed exercise at the keyboard.

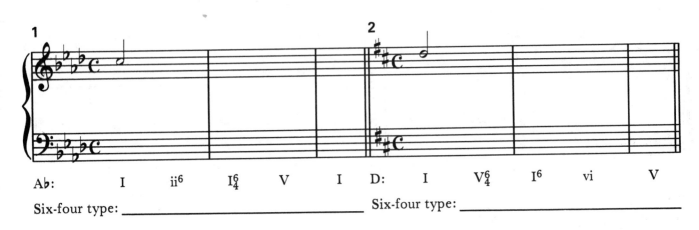

A♭:   I   ii^6 I$^6_4$ V   I   D: I   V$^6_4$ I^6 vi   V

Six-four type: _____   Six-four type: _____

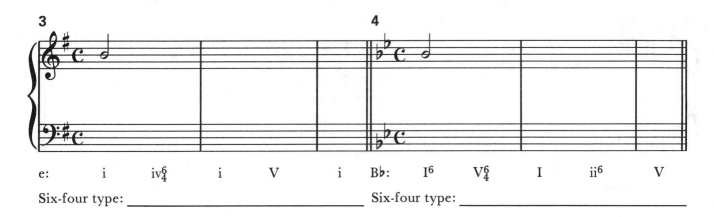

3

e: i   iv$^6_4$ i   V   i

Six-four type: _____

4

B♭:   I^6 V$^6_4$ I   ii^6 V

Six-four type: _____

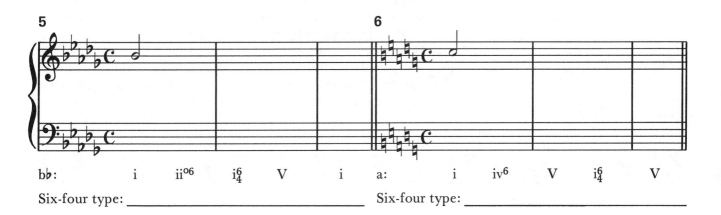

5

b♭:   i   ii^{o6} i$^6_4$ V   i

Six-four type: _____

6

a: i   iv^6 V   i$^6_4$ V

Six-four type: _____

PRACTICE MATERIAL AND ASSIGNMENTS FOR PART C

A. Given the melody and chords, notate the implied bass line lightly in pencil. Then create more stepwise motion in the bass. (Do not *overload* the bass with nonchord tones.) To this two-voice framework, add the inner voices, using appropriate part-writing procedures.

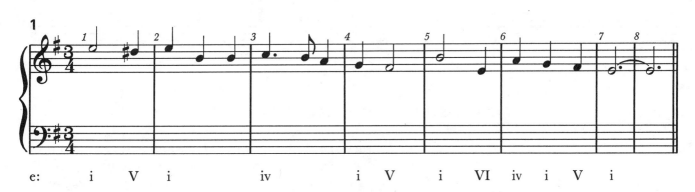

1

e: i   V   i   iv   i   V   i   VI   iv   i   V   i

F: I   vi   iii   IV   V   I   vi   V   I   vi   IV   V   I

B. 1. Using the procedure outlined in Part C of this chapter, harmonize the following melodies, writing out the chords in simplest position beneath each appropriate melody note.
2. On separate manuscript paper, copy the melody and add a bass line on a second staff. Use inversions and embellishing tones to give the bass line a more melodic character. Then part-write your harmonization in four voices.

SUGGESTIONS FOR AURAL DRILL

A. Your instructor will choose, at random, four-part realizations of Exercise A on text page 202 or Exercise A on Workbook page 70. He or she will first play the tonic triad, then the chord succession. You are to identify the succession, using Roman numeral symbols.

B. Your instructor will choose chord successions from Exercise B on Workbook page 71 and play each succession three times. Before playing the succession, he or she will tell you how many chords there are to be; you are to write down a number for each chord. For example, if there will be seven chords in the succession, you should write: 1. 2. 3. 4. 5. 6. 7.

Listen carefully for the first two playings. On the third, circle the number of the chord you hear to be the tonic. Then indicate by Roman numeral symbols the final chord (optional: *two* chords) of the succession.

C. Your instructor will play four-part realizations for several of the exercises on text pages 204-205 or Workbook page 74, Exercise C. He or she will give you the beginning soprano and bass notes. You are to notate the outer voices along with a Roman numeral harmonic analysis. (Suggested number of playings: 4)

TEST YOUR COMPREHENSION OF CHAPTER EIGHT

A. Classify each of the following two-chord successions in this manner: P = Progression; R = Retrogression; S = Repetition (Same function).

B. Write in four voices the chord that will create the indicated type of harmonic motion. Observe all part-writing procedures.

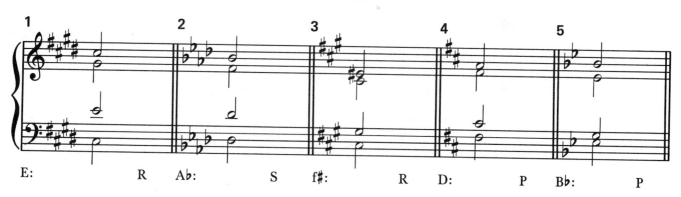

C. Write root-position ii⁷ and V⁷ chords in the keys indicated.

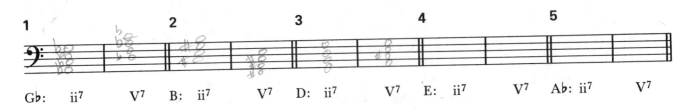

G♭:   ii⁷   V⁷   B: ii⁷   V⁷   D: ii⁷   V⁷   E: ii⁷   V⁷   A♭: ii⁷   V⁷

D. Part-write the requested type of six-four chord.

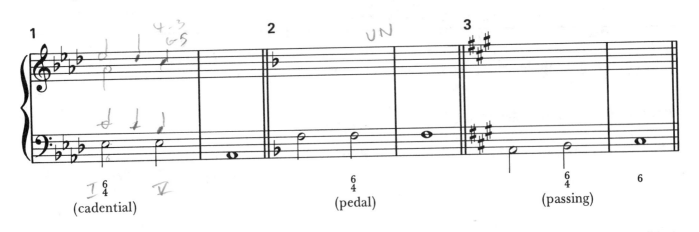

(cadential)   (pedal)   (passing)

E. Resolve the following minor-key triads to an appropriate chord.

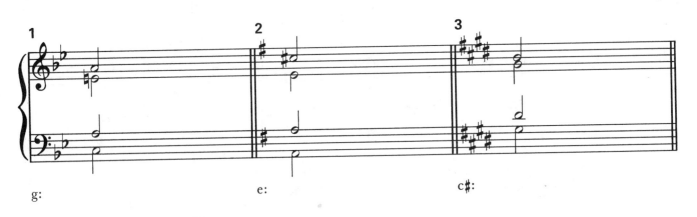

g: e: c♯:

Answers appear on page 367.

CHAPTER NINE

FORM AND DRAMATIC SHAPE IN MUSIC

TERMS TO KNOW

chordal   monophonic

dramatic peak   polyphonic

dramatic shape   texture

homophonic

A. The Creation of Musical Form

At the most basic level, musical form is determined by the similarity and contrast of musical material. This similarity and contrast, in turn, are the result of the interaction of the various musical elements. In some cases, a single element is more important than all the others in defining the form. This is the case in the following example, where the most important element of formal definition is the perfect authentic cadence in m. 8.

SIMILARITY AND CONTRAST

Example 9.1 Schubert: *German Dance, D. 975*

As far as the actual musical material is concerned, the two sections are quite similar. True, the melody is different in the second half, but even so, it is closely related to the melodic material of the first half. Notice that it is built entirely from the musical figure of m. 7. Nor is there a *tonal* contrast between the two sections, since both are entirely in D major. Nor is there a change in the melodic and rhythmic activity of the two hands. In both sections, a melodic line in the highest voice is supported by a consistent accompanimental pattern. While there *is* a change in articulation and dynamic level (note the second-beat accents and the *mf* marking in the second section), the contrast is not striking.

**SYMBOLIZING
SECTIONAL
RELATIONSHIPS**

Using letters, the form of this piece should be designated A | B.* (Uppercase letters are used to designate *section* relationships while lower-case letters are used for phrase relationships.) The letter B does not necessarily suggest strong contrast—it only indicates that the second section is not a repetition or varied repetition of the first; in that case, the designations A | A or A | A' (read "A prime") would be more appropriate. The vertical line separating the two letters signifies a strong cadential separation between the sections.

More often than not, a number of elements together create the form of a piece. Generally, the more elements that contribute to the similarity or contrast in a musical work, the more clearly defined is the form.

B. Texture

An important element in the creation of musical form is *texture*. Texture refers generally to the manner in which the melodic and harmonic dimensions in a composition fit together and relate to each other. The most common terms used to describe this element are:

1. *Monophonic:* a single musical line, unaccompanied by other musical sounds.
2. *Homophonic:* a texture in which one line is the most important, with the other lines in a clearly supporting role. This can take the form of a single-line melody with an accompaniment pattern as in Example 9.1, or several rhythmically similar lines in combination, as are found in many four-voice chorale harmonizations. When all voices move with precisely the same rhythms, the texture is sometimes described as *chordal.*
3. *Polyphonic:* a texture consisting of two or more independent melodic lines. In a polyphonic texture, two or more lines are melodically distinct and compete more or less equally for attention. Some chorale harmonizations, particularly those of J. S. Bach, are in this sense more polyphonic than homophonic. Compare the following:

---

*Repeat signs do not affect the formal designation of a piece.

Example 9.2

(a) J. S. Bach: "Christus, der uns selig macht"

more homophonic

(b) J. S. Bach: "Wenn wir höchsten nöten sein"

more polyphonic

In addition to these terms, two other adjectives are commonly used in describing texture.

1. *Full:* usually a texture of many different parts spaced rather closely together
2. *Thin:* usually a texture consisting of relatively few individual parts spaced rather widely

Texture *alone* can contribute significantly to our overall perception of form. More often, however, a change in texture will be accompanied by a change in melodic and rhythmic structure, harmony and tonality, or dynamics and manner of articulation.

C. Dramatic Shape

An additional aspect of form is *dramatic shape.* This may be described as the psychological or emotional contour of a work—its impact on the listener as it unfolds. Dramatic shape is created through musical tension and relaxation.

While any number of shapes are possible, the ones that seem to produce the most satisfying effect are those that build to a high point—*a dramatic peak*—at the midpoint or beyond.

Illustration 9.1

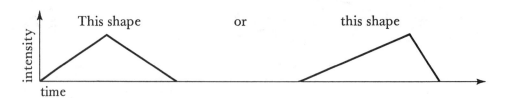

have been used successfully more often than

Of course, in an extended work, the movement toward the dramatic peak does not necessarily occur as a single, uninterrupted build-up. More often, it comprises a series of peaks and valleys, just as a melody does not normally rise to its high point in a continuous, uninterrupted flow.

There are many ways of achieving musical intensification.

MEANS OF INTENSIFICATION

1. *Dynamics:* This is the most familiar means, and it usually takes the form of a *crescendo,* although a suddenly louder passage can effect an *abrupt* intensification. *Crescendos* are usually combined with one or more other techniques to achieve their desired effect.

2. *Rhythm:* A gradual heightening of rhythmic activity, often through the use of progressively shorter note values or through the successive compression of a musical event into smaller and smaller units, can generate musical intensity. Observe how the shortening of the idea in the following example heightens the forward propulsion of the passage.

Example 9.3 Haydn: *String Quartet, Op. 77, No. 2, H. III:82* (I)

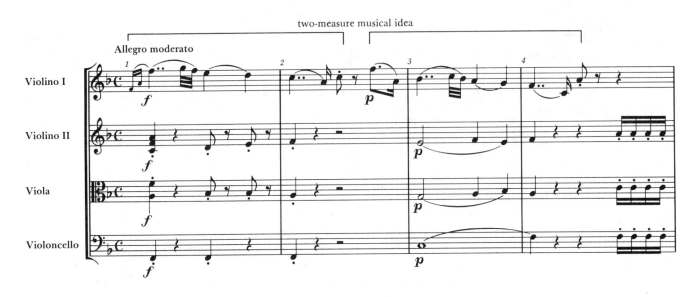

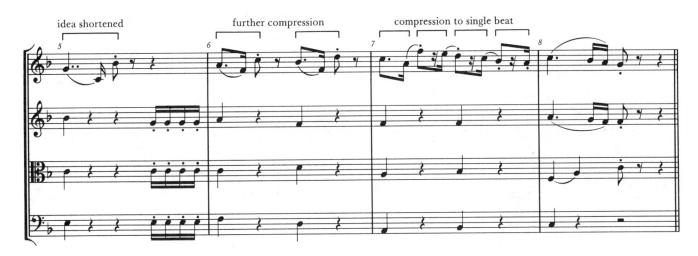

3. *Texture:* A gradual thickening or animation of the texture can be achieved by the addition of instruments or through the introduction of more musical lines.

4. *Register:* Often, higher pitches are used to generate feelings of tension; low pitches are used to create feelings of relaxation. Therefore, a gradually rising melodic line often intensifies the music. In the next example, this technique is combined with a *crescendo*, increased rhythmic activity, and a textural thickening to produce a two-measure intensification that culminates in m. 6.

Example 9.4   Beethoven: *Piano Sonata, Op. 10, No. 1* (II)

5. *Harmonic rhythm:* A regular rate of chord change lends a certain feeling of stability to the music, whereas changing patterns can create a sense of restlessness and unpredictability, which, in turn, can heighten musical intensity. Even more pronounced can be the effect of a steady increase in the rate of chord change. The following example combines an accelerated harmonic rhythm with an upward pitch movement, *crescendo,* textural thickening, and rhythmic animation.

Example 9.5   Beethoven: *Piano Sonata, Op. 53* (I)

I   V$^4_2$ I   V$^4_2$
rate of harmonic change increases

6. *Repetition:* A pattern (melodic, harmonic, or rhythmic) repeated several times in succession, or a pitch repetition can be a useful means of building intensity, because the expectation for change becomes greater with each repetition. (Expectation leads to tension.) Sequences and pedal points often provide this sort of effect.

FOR CLASS DISCUSSION

Play the following excerpt or listen to a recording of it several times. How many different techniques does the composer use to create musical intensity?

Example 9.6 Chopin: *Prelude, Op. 28, No. 21*

D. Methods of Analysis

A thoroughgoing analysis of any piece of music requires a consideration of the various musical elements singly and in interaction. Two general approaches, somewhat the reverse of each other, but both valid, can be used. Each involves an investigation of the elements of music, which may be classified under four broad headings—formal structure, melodic/rhythmic structure, harmonic/tonal structure, and texture/articulation/dynamics.

1. The Inductive Approach

As the name implies, this approach begins with the small and works toward the large—from specific to general. An inductive analysis might begin with a consideration of each element separately, then consider their interaction, and finally arrive at a conclusion regarding the formal structure and dramatic shape.

2. The Deductive Approach

This approach begins with the most general of observations—the overall musical form—and proceeds then to discover how the various musical elements, separately and in combination, work together to create the form.

The major difference in the two approaches resides in the point at which the form is identified: In the inductive approach, it is the last step in the analysis, whereas in the deductive approach, it is the first step. In most cases, the overall form is sufficiently clear that the deductive approach can be used. In those cases where there is some question as to the location or the relative strength of the important formal divisions, the inductive approach can be helpful.

Following is an analysis of a short, rather simple work. Although future analyses will be more complex (because the works themselves will be more complex), this analysis may serve as a model for later ones.

Beethoven: *Dance*

Analysis
Beethoven: *Dance*

FORMAL STRUCTURE

- Two-part; symmetrical (both halves equal in length)
- Designation: A I B
- Primary element of form definition: cadence at m. 8 (the strongest of the piece aside from the final cadence)
- Contrast between sections: The two halves generally are similar in character. One important element of contrast is mentioned under Texture/Articulation/Dynamics.

MELODIC/RHYTHMIC STRUCTURE

Although both halves comprise an eight-measure period of two phrases, the periods are different in character.

First Half	Second Half
arching contour and wide range	more stationary contour and more restricted range
some rhythmic variety, although not pronounced	less rhythmic variety (constant eighth notes)
strong tonic-dominant axis (see melodic reduction)	less of a tonic-dominant axis but more obvious step progressions (see melodic reduction)
contains triadic outlining	does not contain triadic outlining
entirely diatonic	some chromaticism (note also the resolution of all tendency tones)

MELODIC REDUCTION

Illustration 9.2

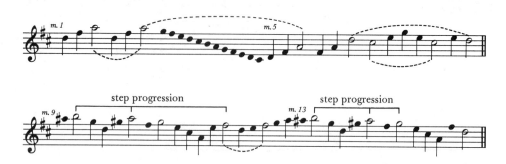

HARMONIC/TONAL STRUCTURE

- No tonal contrast (both sections are in D)
- No pronounced harmonic differences

However, the harmonic *rhythm* is considerably faster in the B section. Compare:

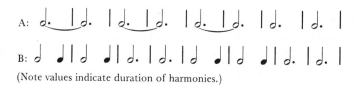

(Note values indicate duration of harmonies.)

TEXTURE/ARTICULATION/DYNAMICS

- Texture homophonic in both halves

    However, there *is* a marked change in the left-hand accompaniment pattern, from an eighth-note arpeggiation to a two-note chordal pattern, emphasized by rests on the first beat of each measure. At the same time, the register in the left-hand part shifts upward.

- No pronounced articulative or dynamic changes

SUMMARY STATEMENT

This piece comprises two halves, equal in length and similar in general character. The form is defined primarily by the cadential punctuation of m. 8 and also by changes in melodic character and in the nature of the left-hand accompaniment. Other factors play no significant form-defining role.

PRACTICE MATERIAL AND ASSIGNMENTS

A. Detail the creation of musical intensity in the following excerpts.
Do not concern yourself with the analysis of specific harmonies,
but focus instead on the *rate* of harmonic change.

1 Beethoven: *Piano Sonata, Op. 13* (II)*

*This movement is contained in its entirety in *The Norton Scores, Vol. II,* third edition, by Roger
Kamien (W. W. Norton & Company, Inc., 1977).

2 Beethoven: *String Quartet, Op. 59, No. 2* (IV)

B. Using the analysis in this chapter as a model, explain how each of the musical elements contributes to the creation of the following two-part forms.

1 Beethoven: *Minuet*

2 Schubert: *German Dance*

CHAPTER TEN
DIATONIC SEVENTH CHORDS I

In Chapter Eight, brief mention was made of two types of seventh chords —the dominant seventh and the supertonic seventh. When a seventh is placed above the root of *any* triad, a seventh chord is obtained.

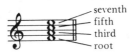

All seventh chords function identically to their triadic counterparts, with the exception that a seventh chord rarely appears as the *final* chord of a cadence. This is because the seventh creates a dissonance against the root that demands a resolution.

A. Diatonic Seventh Chords

In the following illustration, a seventh chord is constructed on each degree of the major scale.

Illustration 10.1

SEVENTH CHORD TYPES   The symbols under each chord in Illustration 10.1 indicate the triad type and the interval formed by the root and seventh, in the following manner.

Illustration 10.2

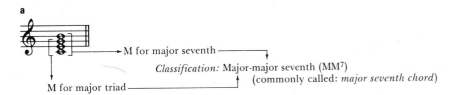

Illustration 10.2b

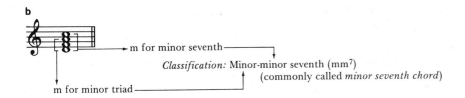

Functional symbols (Roman numerals) are applied to seventh chords in the same way as they are for triads.

SYMBOLS FOR
SEVENTH
CHORDS

1. An upper-case Roman numeral indicates a major triad as the basis; a lower-case Roman numeral indicates a minor triad basis.
2. A $^+$ or $^{\circ}$ after the Roman numeral indicates an augmented or diminished triad, respectively, as the basis.
3. A superscript seven (^{7}) alone indicates a *diatonic* seventh above the chord root—that is, a pitch that is unaltered from its natural appearance in the scale.

The functional symbols for the diatonic seventh chords of major keys are shown below.

Illustration 10.3

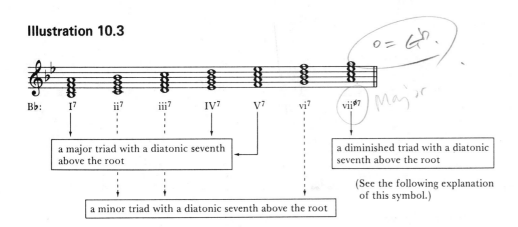

Note the symbol for the diminished-minor seventh chord (on scale degree seven). This chord, also referred to as the *half-diminished seventh,* appears diatonically on the leading tone in major keys. The symbol $^{\emptyset7}$ is conventionally used to distinguish it from the diminished-diminished seventh chord (simply called "diminished seventh") that appears diatonically on the leading tone in minor keys.

THE $^{\emptyset7}$
AND $^{\circ7}$

Illustration 10.4

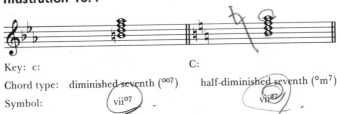

Key: c: C:

Chord type: diminished seventh (^{oo7})   half-diminished seventh ($^{o}m^7$)

Symbol: vii^{o7} vii^{ø7}

The most commonly encountered seventh chords in minor keys are those of the harmonic minor scale, but with two exceptions.

SEVENTH CHORDS IN MINOR KEYS

1. The seventh chord built on the tonic is rare.
2. The seventh chord built on the mediant is usually a major seventh chord.

Illustration 10.5

C minor

Chord type:	$^{o}m^7$	MM^7	mm^7	Mm^7	MM^7	^{oo7}
Symbol:	ii^{ø7}	III^7	iv^7	V^7	VI^7	vii^{o7}

The sixth or seventh scale degree is present in *every* diatonic seventh chord. Since these degrees are variable in the melodic minor scale, they create two different seventh chord types *for each scale degree*. These differences are automatically reflected in the chord symbols by observing the points previously mentioned.

Illustration 10.6

Melodic minor

ascending   descending

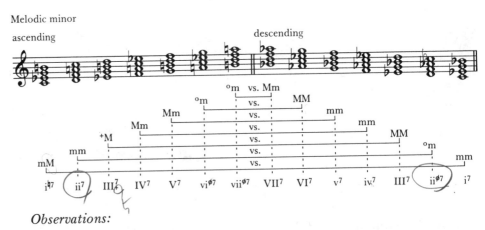

Observations:

1. To distinguish between the two seventh chord types possible on the tonic, the symbol i^7 is used for the minor-minor seventh, which is the more common. Nevertheless, seventh chords on the tonic are the least common of all seventh chords, since the tonic, more than any other chord, is one of stability and repose.

2. The use of an upper-case Roman numeral VII will always imply that the root is the *natural* minor scale degree (a whole step below the tonic).

The most common diatonic seventh chords are given below in general order of frequency, along with their most usual function.

FREQUENCY OF SEVENTH CHORDS

BEADGC F

Illustration 10.7

Seventh chord type	Appears most often as:	Referred to as:
major-minor seventh	V⁷ in major and minor	dominant seventh
minor-minor seventh	ii⁷, iii⁷, vi⁷ in major iv⁷ in minor	minor seventh
diminished-diminished seventh	vii°⁷ in minor	diminished seventh
diminished-minor seventh	vii⌀⁷ major ii⌀⁷ in minor	half-diminished seventh
major-major seventh	IV⁷ in major VI⁷, III⁷ in minor	major seventh

Even though it appears commonly on only one scale degree, the major-minor seventh chord is the most common type. The minor-minor seventh chord, although it may appear on one of several scale degrees, is most often found as a supertonic.

FOR PRACTICE MATERIAL AND ASSIGNMENTS, TURN TO PAGE 233.

B. Seventh Chords of Dominant Function

Throughout the Renaissance, seventh chords had appeared as by-products of linear motion, the seventh treated as a nonchord tone and resolved downward by step in almost all cases.

PERSPECTIVE

Example 10.1 Arcadelt: "O felici occhi miei"

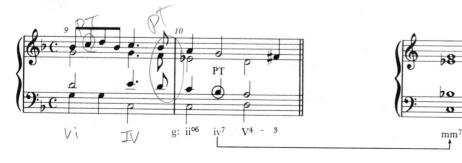

Claudio Monteverdi (1567-1643) was one of the first composers to use the seventh chord in a way that suggests he considered the seventh as a member of the chord. In the following example, notice the dramatic leap from the seventh, with no subsequent resolution.

Example 10.2   Monteverdi: "Ma che temi" from *Orfeo*

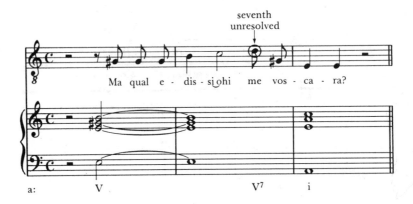

The V⁷, together with the vii°⁷ and vii⁰⁷, form a group of *functionally related* chords—seventh chords of dominant function. All three tend very strongly toward the tonic, even more so than the pure triads from which they are formed. Monteverdi's unusual treatment of the seventh in the preceding example notwithstanding, most composers in the seventeenth, eighteenth, and nineteenth centuries continued to resolve it as if it were a non-chord tone. In many cases, it is possible to analyze a chord containing a seventh in *either* of two ways: as a seventh chord or as a triad with an embellishing tone (PT, SUS, etc.). In seventh chords of dominant function:

RESOLUTION

1. The seventh is normally resolved downward by step.
2. The leading tone is normally resolved to the tonic, especially when it is in an outer voice.

Illustration 10.8

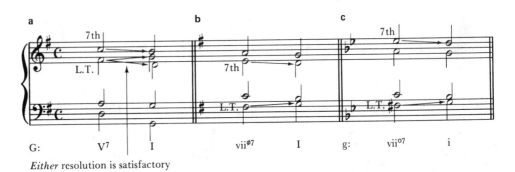

Either resolution is satisfactory

Notice in **a** that the leading tone may resolve *either* to the tonic or to the fifth of the tonic chord. This is because it is in an inner voice. However, when the leading tone is in the soprano, its most satisfactory resolution is to the tonic. In the case of the dominant seventh chord, this means that either the V⁷ or the I (i) *must be incomplete.* In either case, it is the chord fifth that is omitted.

Illustration 10.9

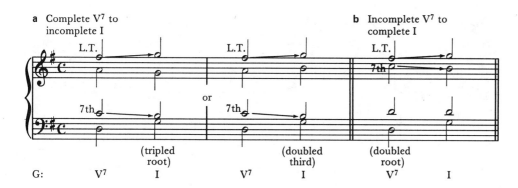

NOTE: Resolution of a *complete* V⁷, with the leading tone in the soprano, to a *complete* tonic results in voice-leading problems.

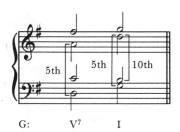

Too large an interval between alto and tenor and consecutive fifths between alto and bass.

Seventh chords of dominant function may be found in any position. Notice that they have one more inversional possibility than pure triads—third inversion.

Illustration 10.10

a Dominant seventh chord: F major (or F minor)

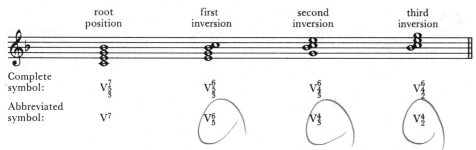

b Leading tone seventh chord: F major

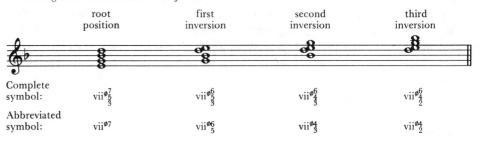

	root position	first inversion	second inversion	third inversion
Complete symbol:	vii⌀$^7_5_3$	vii⌀$^6_5_3$	vii⌀$^6_4_3$	vii⌀$^6_4_2$
Abbreviated symbol:	vii⌀^{7}	vii⌀$^6_5$	vii⌀$^4_3$	vii⌀$^4_2$

c Leading tone seventh chord: F minor

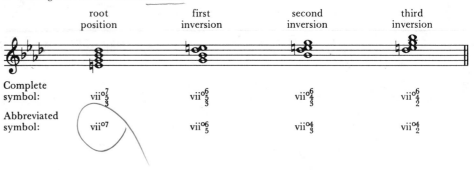

	root position	first inversion	second inversion	third inversion
Complete symbol:	vii°$^7_5_3$	vii°$^6_5_3$	vii°$^6_4_3$	vii°$^6_4_2$
Abbreviated symbol:	vii°^{7}	vii°$^6_5$	vii°$^4_3$	vii°$^4_2$

The resolution of inverted seventh chords is similar to that of root-position seventh chords, except that inversions of the dominant seventh (V^6_5, V^4_3, and V^4_2) rarely require the omission of any chord tone from either the dominant seventh chord or from the tonic.

Illustration 10.11

a Inversions of the V^7 resolved

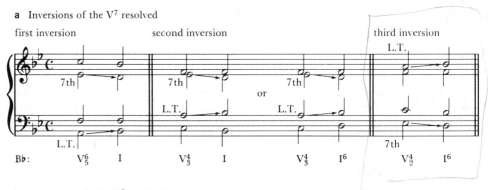

b Inversions of the vii°^{7} resolved

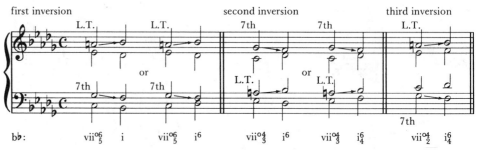

Observations:

1. When the leading tone is in the bass, the resolution of the seventh chord is to a root-position tonic triad, since the leading tone requires resolution to the tonic.
2. When the seventh of the seventh chord is in the bass, its resolution is downward by step to an inversion of the tonic.
3. When neither the seventh nor the leading tone is in the bass, this voice may resolve stepwise downward or upward.
4. *All* voices move by step except those in which a common tone is retained.

Distinct similarities exist among the V_3^4, the V_4^6 (passing six-four), and the vii^{o6}. In the most common context, the bass in each of these chords resembles a passing tone. Not only are they similar in function and sound, but they also are distinguished from each other by only a single chord tone.

SIMILARITIES AMONG THE V_3^4, V_4^6, AND vii^{o6}

Illustration 10.12

$E\flat$:   I V_4^6 I^6 I V_3^4 I^6 I vii^{o6} I^6

FOR CLASS DISCUSSION

Study the following excerpts and discuss the types of seventh chords used, doublings and omissions of chord tones, inversions, and the resolution of the chord seventh and leading tone.

Example 10.3

(a) J. S. Bach: "Gott lebet noch"

F:

*These harmonies, which are not diatonic in the key, are of a type discussed in Chapter Thirteen. Disregard them for now.

(b) Kuhlau: *Sonatina, Op. 55, No. 4* (II)

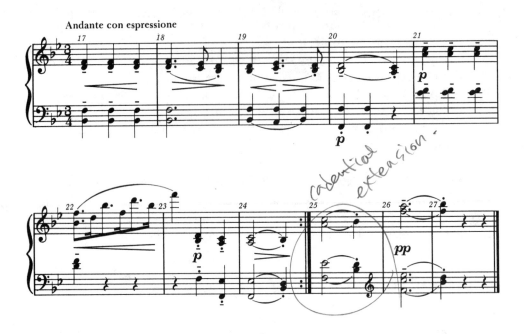

(c) Haydn: *String Quartet, Op. 17, No. 5, H. III:29* (III)

LESS COMMON PRACTICES   Occasionally, the dominant seventh chord moves deceptively to the submediant rather than to the tonic. No new part-writing procedures are involved in this resolution.

Illustration 10.13

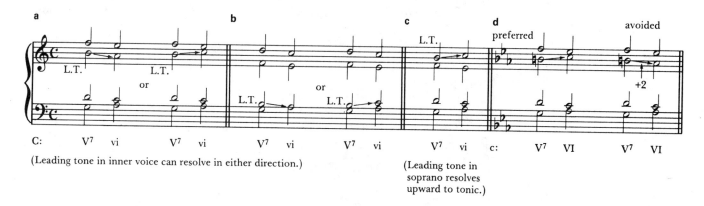

(Leading tone in inner voice can resolve in either direction.)

(Leading tone in
soprano resolves
upward to tonic.)

NOTE: In minor, moving the leading tone downward to the root of the VI creates an augmented second.

On rare occasions, a seventh chord is followed by a chord that does not contain the note representing the normal downward resolution of the seventh. In most of these cases, the seventh is a common tone between the two chords and it is retained in the same voice.

RETENTION OF THE SEVENTH

Illustration 10.14

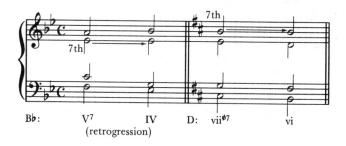

Sometimes the downward resolution of the seventh is simply delayed. Notice how, in the following illustration, the seventh is retained as part of the chord at *1* and then resolved at *2*.

DELAYED RESOLUTION OF THE SEVENTH

Illustration 10.15

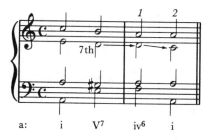

Following are some examples of each of these less common procedures. Observe how, in most cases, the seventh can be analyzed optionally as some type of nonchord tone. This, of course, reflects the linear, nonharmonic origin of the chord.

Example 10.4
(a)   Mozart: *Piano Sonata, K. 332* (I)*

*This movement is contained in its entirety in *Analytical Anthology of Music,* by this author (Alfred A. Knopf, Inc., 1984).

(b)   Beethoven: *Piano Sonata, Op. 10, No. 1* (I)*

*This movement is contained in its entirety in *Music Literature: Volume I,* by Gordon Hardy and Arnold Fish (Harper & Row Publishers, Inc., 1963).

(c)   Beethoven: *Piano Sonata, Op. 10, No. 1* (III)*

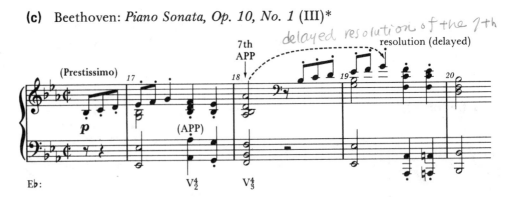

*This movement is contained in its entirety in *Analytical Anthology of Music,* by this author (Alfred A. Knopf, Inc., 1984).

FOR PRACTICE MATERIAL AND ASSIGNMENTS, TURN TO PAGE 234.

PRACTICE MATERIAL AND ASSIGNMENTS FOR PART A

A. Using the symbols MM, Mm, mm, and so on, classify each of the following seventh chords. Then practice singing each upward and downward from the lowest pitch.

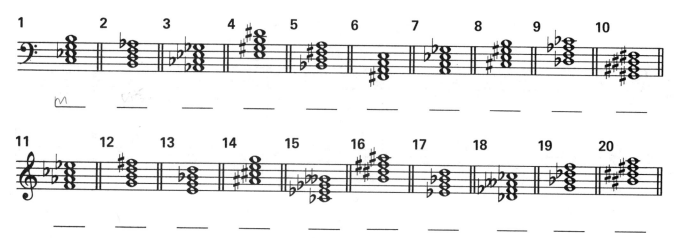

B. Spell the indicated seventh chord in root position in each of the requested keys. Be sure to add all necessary sharps or flats.

1 A♭: vii⌀7   2 G: vi⁷   3 b: V⁷   4 F: IV⁷   5 g: vii°⁷

6 a: VI⁷   7 E: ii⁷   8 f♯: ii⌀7   9 E♭: iii⁷   10 G♭: ii⁷

C. Provide the correct Roman numeral analysis for each chord in the keys indicated.

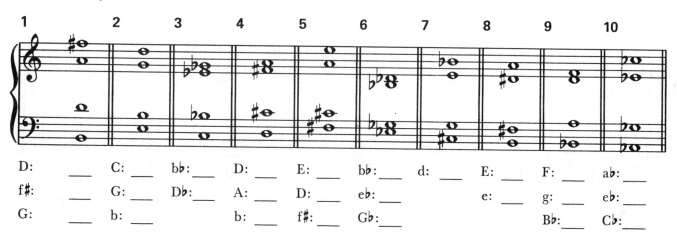

D: ___	C: ___	b♭: ___	D: ___	E: ___	b♭: ___	d: ___	E: ___	F: ___	a♭: ___
f♯: ___	G: ___	D♭: ___	A: ___	D: ___	e♭: ___		e: ___	g: ___	e♭: ___
G: ___	b: ___		b: ___	f♯: ___	G♭: ___			B♭: ___	C♭: ___

PRACTICE MATERIAL AND ASSIGNMENTS FOR PART B

A. Resolve each of the following seventh chords as indicated. Also, identify the seventh chord by function, using Roman numerals and superscripts to show inversions. Practice playing each at the keyboard.

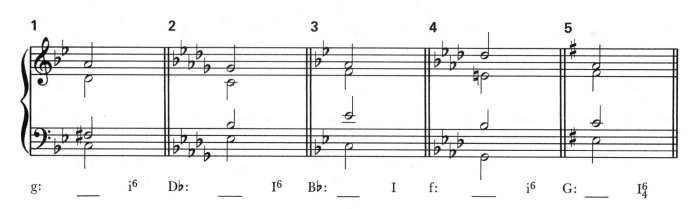

B. Correct the part-writing errors in the following two-chord successions. Then provide Roman numeral analysis.

C. Realize the following figured bass lines in a four-part chorale style. Then provide Roman numeral analysis. Practice playing each at the keyboard. Try to sing each line in turn as you play all four parts.

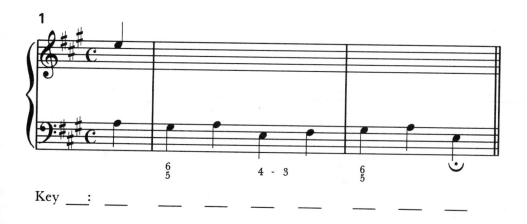

Key ___: ___ ___ ___ ___ ___

2

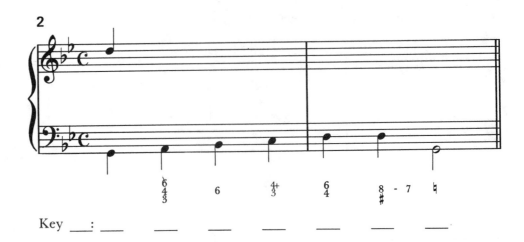

Key ___ : ___   ___   ___   ___   ___   ___

3

Key ___ :   ___   ___   ___   ___   ___   ___   ___   ___

D. Provide harmonic analysis of the following excerpts. Circle and label all nonchord tones. Indicate the inversions of all seventh chords and name the type of figure the seventh of the chord most closely resembles (passing tone, suspension, and so on). Draw a line connecting the seventh of the chord to its resolution.

1 J. S. Bach: "Nun danket alle Gott"

A: ___   ___   ___   ___   ___   ___

2 Haydn: *String Quartet, Op. 9, No. 4, H. III:22* (Menuet)

3 Mozart: *Rondo, K. 485*

4 Beethoven: *Piano Sonata, Op. 10, No. 1* (I)

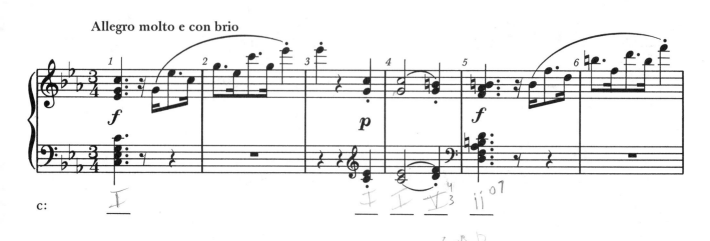

SUGGESTIONS FOR AURAL DRILL

A. Your instructor will play various types of seventh chords in root position. You are to identify the type (mm⁷, Mm⁷, °m⁷, and so on).

B. Practice singing the various types of seventh chord from the root upward and downward, in this manner: 1-3-5-7-5-3-1.

C. Your instructor will play a tonic chord (major or minor) followed by a diatonic seventh chord in that key. You are to identify by Roman numeral symbol the seventh chord played.

D. Your instructor will write a tonic chord (in root position, first inversion, or second inversion) on the chalkboard and will then play this chord, preceding it with a seventh chord of dominant function. You are to notate the seventh chord, with correct soprano and bass pitches. Arrange the inner voices so that they move smoothly to the inner voices of the given chord. Sources for this exercise may be drawn from text pages 234-235 (Exersises A and B).

E. Your instructor will play a four-voice passage. Given the first note in the soprano and bass, you are to notate the outer voices and provide Roman numerals for each chord. Material for this exercise may be drawn from text pages 204-205 and 235-236, and Workbook pages 74-75 (Exercise C), and page 84 (numbers 4 and 5 of Exercise C), or from the *371 Harmonized Chorales and 69 Chorale Melodies* by Bach-Riemenschneider.

CHAPTER ELEVEN
DIATONIC SEVENTH CHORDS II

Diatonic seventh chords other than those built on the dominant or leading tone are the subject of this chapter. These seventh chords are usually of three types: major, minor, and half-diminished.*

Illustration 11.1

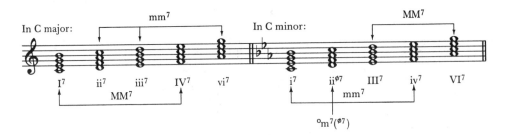

A. Common Practices

No new voice-leading principles govern the use of nondominant seventh chords. The presence of four chord members eliminates the need for doubling in most four-voice situations. The seventh, which normally resolves downward by step, is often prepared in the same voice in the preceding chord, fulfilling the function of a suspension.

*Alternate seventh chord types in minor keys are discussed on page 244.

Example 11.1 Handel: "I know that my Redeemer liveth," No. 43 from
Messiah

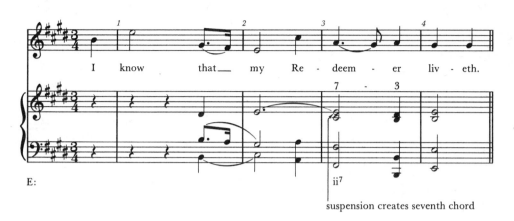

suspension creates seventh chord

Most nondominant seventh chords appear in root position more often than in inversion. In fact, the sole exception is the supertonic, which appears most often in first inversion.

FIRST-INVERSION SUPERTONIC

Example 11.2 J. S. Bach: "Alle Menschen mussen sterben"

Second- and third-inversion nondominant seventh chords are uncommon. As with first inversion, the supertonic is the chord that appears most often in these positions. In third inversion, the seventh in the bass usually fulfills the function of a suspension or passing tone.

SECOND- AND THIRD-INVERSION SUPERTONIC

Example 11.3 Mozart: *Symphony, K. 550 (I)**

preparation

g: ii∅⁴₂   V⁶₅

"elongated" suspension   resolution

*This movement is contained in its entirety (in piano reduction) in *Examples for the Study of Musical Style,* by William R. Ward (Wm. C. Brown Company Publishers, 1970). The full orchestral score is contained in *The Norton Scores, Vol. I,* third edition, by Roger Kamien (W. W. Norton & Company, Inc., 1977).

PRE-DOMINANT SEVENTH CHORDS

The most common nondominant seventh chords are the pre-dominants—the supertonic and the subdominant. Both of these chords resolve most naturally to the dominant, perhaps by way of a cadential six-four chord. Aside from the different root movements, there is little difference in the voice leading. In fact, when the supertonic seventh chord appears in first inversion, *only a single pitch is different* between it and the subdominant seventh. Their sound, appearance, and function are similar.

Illustration 11.3

In major:

a Subdominant seventh   **b** Supertonic seventh

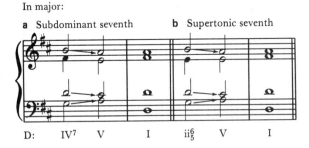

D: IV⁷   V   I   ii⁶₅   V   I

In minor:

a Subdominant seventh   **b** Supertonic seventh

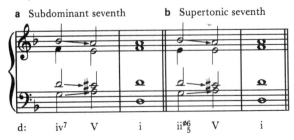

d: iv⁷   V   i   ii∅⁶₅   V   i

Black notes indicate the single pitch difference between **a** and **b** and arrows point out identical voice movements.

Some care must be taken, however, in resolving the IV⁷ directly to V, in order to avoid consecutive fifths when the seventh of the chord is in a higher voice than the third.

Illustration 11.4

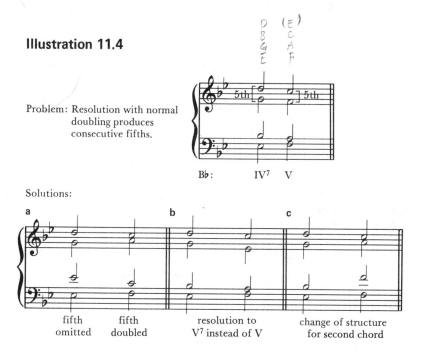

Problem: Resolution with normal doubling produces consecutive fifths.

Bb: IV⁷   V

Solutions:

a   b   c

fifth   fifth   resolution to   change of structure
omitted   doubled   V⁷ instead of V   for second chord

In the next example, Bach avoids the problem through an optional doubling.

Example 11.4 J. S. Bach: "Ich bin's, ich sollte büssen," No. 16 from *St. Matthew Passion, BWV 244*

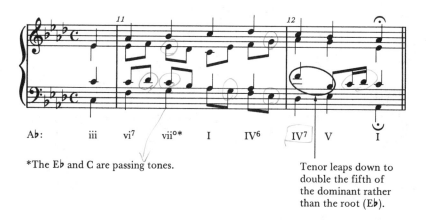

Ab: iii   vi⁷   vii°*   I   IV⁶   IV⁷   V   I

*The Eb and C are passing tones.

Tenor leaps down to double the fifth of the dominant rather than the root (Eb).

Seventh chords are particularly common in sequential passages. The seventh itself often occurs in a *chain suspension*—a series of suspensions in which each resolution becomes the preparation for a new suspension. The following example illustrates not only seventh chords in chain suspensions, but also a typical eighteenth-century harmonic formula, the descending circle of fifths.

SEQUENCES AND CHAIN SUSPENSIONS

Example 11.5 Vivaldi-J. S. Bach: *Organ Concerto in D Minor, BWV 972* (IV)

F: vi   ii⁷   V⁷   I⁷   IV⁷   vii⁰⁷

Broken lines or slurs connect suspension preparations and dissonances. Arrows indicate suspension resolutions.

<table>
<tr><td>THE SEVENTH
AS A
NONCHORD
TONE</td><td>Frequently, seventh chords can be analyzed just as appropriately as triads with nonchord tones. The most important consideration in this regard would appear to be the duration of the seventh. As a general rule, if the seventh lasts for more than one beat, the chord can be analyzed appropriately as a seventh chord, although matters of style and tempo obviously also play a part.</td></tr>
</table>

Example 11.6 J. S. Bach: "Jesu, der du meine Seele"

g: i   i⁶   V   i⁶   vii⁰⁶   i   ii⁰⁶₅   V   i

In the preceding example, the chord at *a* is not analyzed as a seventh chord while the chord at *b* is. The primary reason is the duration of the seventh.

FOR PRACTICE MATERIAL AND ASSIGNMENTS, TURN TO PAGE 250.

B. Less Common Practices

<table>
<tr><td>ALTERNATIVE
SEVENTH
CHORDS
IN MINOR</td><td>In Chapter Ten, it was shown that the variable sixth and seventh scale degrees create two types of seventh chord on each and every degree of the minor scale. We have already considered the more common seventh chords in each of these pairs. Of the alternative seventh chords, the IV⁷ and vi⁰⁷ occur perhaps the most frequently.</td></tr>
</table>

Illustration 11.5

c: IV⁷   vi⁰⁷

(Black note = variable sixth degree)

These alternative forms are usually followed by a chord of dominant function. In fact, *like their triadic counterparts,* they are almost always generated by a melodic movement from the raised sixth degree to the raised seventh degree. More often than not, this movement occurs in the bass.

Example 11.7 J. S. Bach: "Warum betrubst du dich, mein Herz"

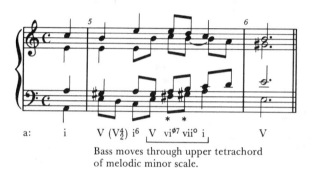

a: i   V (V⁴₂) i⁶ ⌐V vi⁰⁷ vii° i⌐   V

Bass moves through upper tetrachord
of melodic minor scale.

*raised sixth and seventh degrees

The IV⁷ in a minor key is the sole instance of a major-minor seventh chord that does *not* have a dominant function. This chord typically appears in first inversion and resolves to a first-inversion dominant or dominant seventh, as shown below.

Example 11.8 J. S. Bach: "Jesu, meines Herzens Freud'"

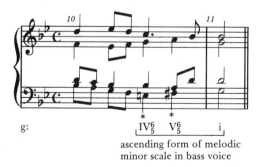

g: ⌐IV⁶₅ V⁶₅   i⌐

ascending form of melodic
minor scale in bass voice

*raised sixth and seventh degrees

One other alternative seventh chord besides the IV⁷ and vi^{ø7} involves the raised sixth degree—the ii⁷. However, it is rarely used because the linear tendencies of both the raised sixth degree and the chord seventh are toward the leading tone.

Illustration 11.6

Proper resolution of these pitches results in a doubled leading tone.

INCOMPLETE SEVENTH CHORDS

When nondominant seventh chords appear in succession, they are frequently incomplete, especially in strict four-voice styles, where it is desirable to avoid the consecutive fifths that may otherwise occur. The preferred note to omit is the fifth unless this chord member forms an augmented or diminished interval with another chord member. In that case, the third is omitted instead.

Example 11.9 J. S. Bach: "O Ewigkeit, du Donnerwort"

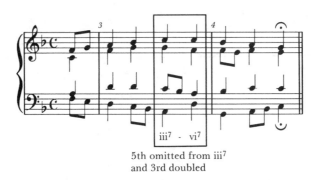

iii⁷ - vi⁷

5th omitted from iii⁷
and 3rd doubled

Notice how *complete* seventh chords in Example 11.9 would have created consecutive fifths.

Illustration 11.7

Observe the consistent omission of the fifth in the harpsichord part in the following chain of seventh chords.

Example 11.10 Purcell: *Ode for St. Cecilia's Day**

a: iv⁷   VII⁷ III⁷   VI⁷   ii⁷   V⁷   i

*This movement is contained in its entirety in *Analytical Anthology of Music*, by this author (Alfred A. Knopf, Inc., 1984).

C. Harmonizing a Melody Using Nondominant Seventh Chords

Because the seventh of a chord normally resolves downward by step, a melody note should be regarded as a potential chord seventh *only* if it is followed by a pitch that is a step lower.

Illustration 11.8

*Only these tones may be regarded as potential chord sevenths.

However, just because a melody tone *can* be regarded as a seventh, this does not mean that it *should* be so regarded. A given melody tone can function as the root, third, or fifth of a chord as well. On the other hand, even if the melody tone cannot function as a seventh, it is possible that an *inner* voice may fulfill that role. Observe in the following harmonization of the melody of Illustration 11.8 that three pitches *not* identified as potential sevenths are nevertheless harmonized with seventh chords, the seventh appearing in one of the other voices.

Illustration 11.9

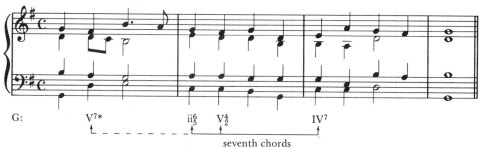

G: V⁷*   ii⁶₅ V⁴₂   IV⁷

seventh chords

*Or, alternately, a V with PT in alto.

As in melody harmonization with pure triads, the principles of functional tonality should be applied. Refer back to page 200 for a review of melody harmonization procedures.

INTERCHANGEABILITY OF CHORDS

Just as seventh chords of dominant function are, to some extent, interchangeable, certain nondominant seventh chords may often be substituted for each other. Because they are related by both function and common tones, the supertonic and subdominant seventh chords (the *pre-dominant* sevenths) form such a pair.

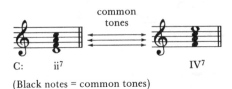

(Black notes = common tones)

Often the choice of chord is dependent on the melodic line. If one of the *three common tones* appears in the melody, *either* chord may be appropriate. On the other hand, the appearance of one of the *non*common tones in the melody dictates the use of one chord over the other.

Illustration 11.11

FOR PRACTICE MATERIAL AND ASSIGNMENTS, TURN TO PAGE 252.

SUMMARY

The following chart is a general summary of the eighteenth-century use of nondominant seventh chords.

Chord	Symbol		Type		Position found in:				Frequency	Most common chord of resolution	
	in major	in minor	in major	in minor	root	1st inv.	2nd inv.	3rd inv.		in major	in minor
Tonic	I^7	i^7	MM^7	mm^7	most common	rare	rare	rare	rare	IV	iv
Supertonic	ii^7	$ii^{\varnothing 7}$	mm^7	$^{\circ}m^7$	occasional	often	rare	occasional	very common	V or I^6_4	V or i^6_4
Mediant	iii^7	III^7	mm^7	MM^7	most common	rare	rare	rare	rare	vi or IV	VI
Subdominant	IV^7	iv^7	MM^7	mm^7	often in major; less so in minor	often in minor; less so in major	rare	occasional	less common than supertonic but more common than the others	V	V
Submediant	vi^7	VI^7	mm^7	MM^7	often	rare	rare	rare	less common than subdominant; more common than tonic or mediant	ii or IV	V

PRACTICE MATERIAL AND ASSIGNMENTS FOR PART A

A. Write the requested seventh chord type above each of the given roots. Notate for four voices in the structure specified.

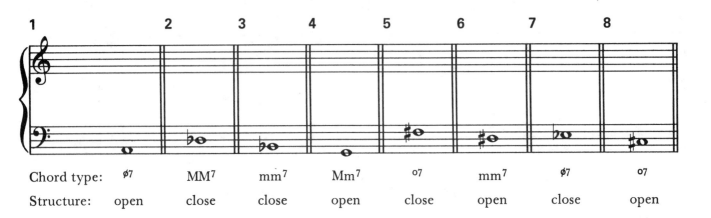

	1	2	3	4	5	6	7	8
Chord type:	⌀7	MM7	mm7	Mm7	o7	mm7	⌀7	o7
Structure:	open	close	close	open	close	open	close	open

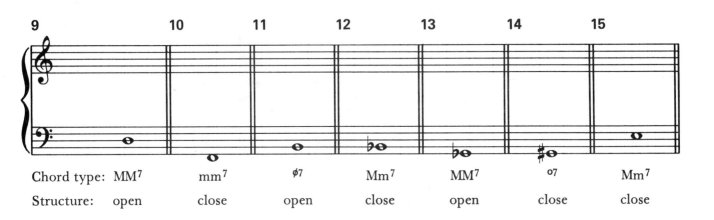

	9	10	11	12	13	14	15
Chord type:	MM7	mm7	⌀7	Mm7	MM7	o7	Mm7
Structure:	open	close	open	close	open	close	close

B. Provide harmonic analysis of the following chorale excerpts. Notate the seventh chords on the staff below the chorale, and indicate the nature of the seventh (suspension, passing tone, and so on).

1 J. S. Bach: "O wie selig seid ihr doch, ihr Frommen"

2 J. S. Bach: "Werde munter, mein Gemüte"

C. Analyze the following passage in the same manner as the analysis on page 244.

   1. Provide harmonic analysis, identifying all seventh chords.

   2. Connect all suspended sevenths and their preparations with broken slurs.

   3. Show all suspension resolutions by arrows, as on page 244.

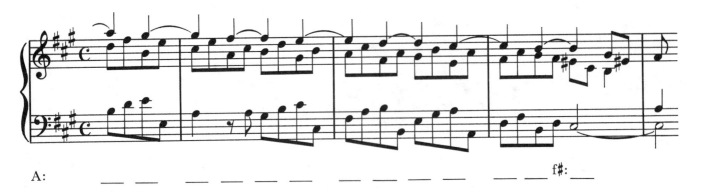

A: ___ ___ ___ ___ ___ ___ ___ ___ f#: ___

PRACTICE MATERIAL AND ASSIGNMENTS FOR PARTS B AND C

A. 1. Resolve the following seventh chords in the most characteristic manner—that is, to the most common chord of resolution, using the smoothest possible voice leading. Your primary consideration should be the stepwise resolution of the seventh. This may require an inversion for the chord of resolution, or an optional doubling. Provide a harmonic analysis in the key indicated.

2. Practice playing the two-chord successions and singing them upward and downward from the lowest tone.

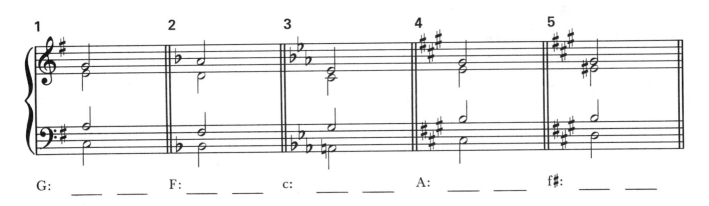

G: ___   F: ___   c: ___   A: ___   f#: ___

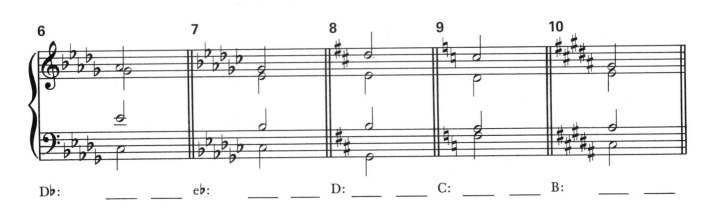

Db: ___   eb: ___   D: ___   C: ___   B: ___

B. Identify the keys in which each of the following seventh chords is diatonic and indicate the function of the chord in each key. For minor keys, you need consider only the seventh chords shown in Illustration 10.5 (page 224).

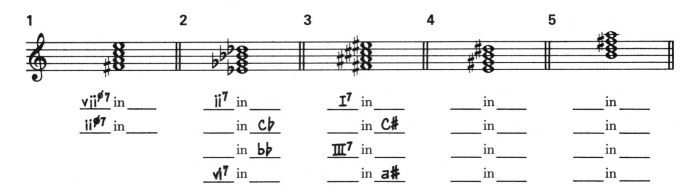

(Note clef change)

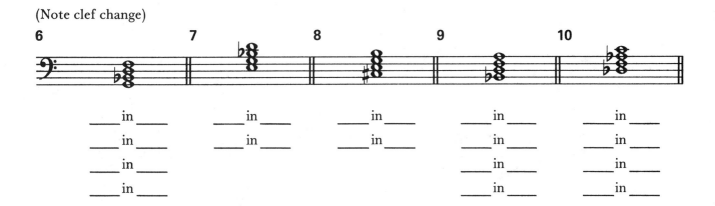

(Note clef change)

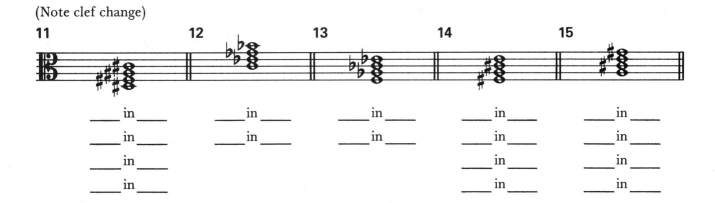

C. Harmonize the following melodies.

1. Use nondominant seventh chords at those points that seem appropriate.

2. Choose inversions that will result in a melodic bass line. Be careful in the use of second-inversion triads and the less common inversions of the various seventh chords.

3. Indicate the selected harmonies by Roman numeral (with superscripts) between the staves.

4. Write out the bass line implied by your harmonization on the blank staff. The first exercise is begun for you.

SUGGESTIONS FOR AURAL DRILL

A. Your instructor will play several seventh chords of different types, in root position or inversion. You are to identify the type of seventh chord (mm⁷, Mm⁷, and so on) and the inversion.

B. Your instructor will play a tonic chord (major or minor) followed by a diatonic seventh chord in that key. This chord may be in root position or inversion. You are to identify by Roman numeral symbol, with superscript if necessary, the seventh chord played.

C. Your instructor will play a tonic chord followed by a two-chord succession. You will be given the soprano and bass notes of the first chord. You are to notate the two-chord succession. Material for this exercise may be drawn from text pages 252 and 256 (Exercises C and D) or from the Workbook, pages 91, 92, and 93.

TEST YOUR COMPREHENSION OF CHAPTERS TEN AND ELEVEN

A. Construct the indicated seventh chords and identify their type (i.e., $^{\varnothing 7}$, mm⁷, and so on).

1	2	3	4	5

In E:
on mediant

Type: ____

In a♭:
on submediant

____

In G♭:
on dominant

____

In B:
on supertonic

____

In G:
on subdominant

____

6	7	8	9	10

In c♯:
on leading tone

Type: ____

In F:
on submediant

____

In b♭:
on supertonic

____

In e:
on leading tone

____

In D♭:
on mediant

____

B. Identify each seventh chord by Roman numeral and superscript (to show the inversion).

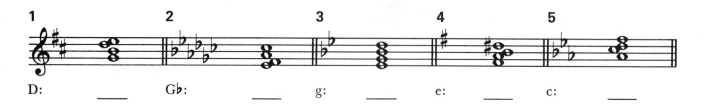

D: _____   Gb: _____   g: _____   e: _____   c: _____

C. Resolve each of the following seventh chords in the most appropriate manner. Then provide harmonic analysis.

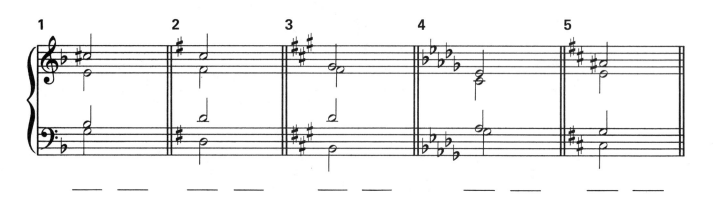

D. Realize the following figured basses and provide Roman numeral analysis.

Answers appear on page 368.

TERMS TO KNOW

chromatic tone modulation   modulation
closely related keys   pivot chord modulation
common chord   tonal shift

Modulation is the process of changing tonal centers. It is one of the most effective means of introducing contrast in music and thereby creating or defining its form. A change of key signature may or may not accompany a modulation. Two types of modulation, common in the Baroque and Classical periods, are discussed in this chapter.

MODULATION

1. pivot chord modulation
2. chromatic tone modulation

Two other types—enharmonic modulation and pivot tone modulation—became more common in the nineteenth century. These types are therefore considered in Volume Two. In the Baroque and Classical periods, the most common form of modulation was the pivot chord type.

A. Pivot Chord Modulation

A *pivot chord modulation* involves a chord that can be seen to function in both the old and new keys. This "pivot" has the effect of creating a smooth, natural-sounding transition to the new tonality. When the pivot chord is *diatonic* in both keys, it is called a *common chord.** To locate a pivot chord, if one is present, it is necessary to identify the first chord that is no longer diatonic in the original key. The chord directly preceding it is usually the pivot chord.

In the following examples, observe how the pivot chords are located and identified.

PIVOT CHORD MODULATION

LOCATING THE PIVOT CHORD

*In Volume Two, we will learn that a *pivot chord* is not always a *common chord.* For now, however, you may regard the two terms as synonymous.

Example 12.1
(a) Mozart: *Piano Sonata, K. 330* (II)

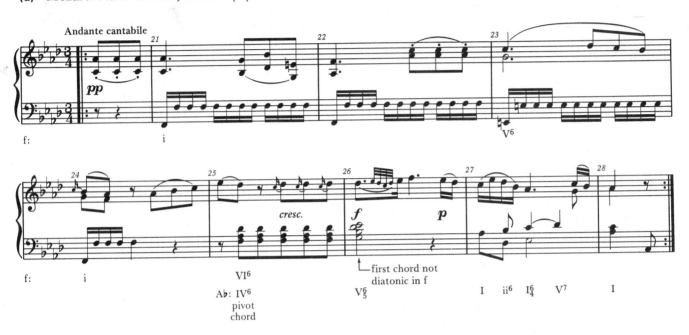

(b) Beethoven: *Piano Sonata, Op. 26* (III)*

*This movement is contained in its entirety in *Analytical Anthology of Music*, by this author (Alfred A. Knopf, Inc., 1984).

Notice in Example 12.1(b) above, that the D major triad of m. 15 is *not* designated as the pivot chord, even though it may be analyzed as the mediant (III) in B minor. In a minor key, a *second-inversion* mediant almost always functions as a cadential six-four chord in the relative major key. (In B minor, III$^6_4$ = I$^6_4$ in D major.) For this reason, the chord of m. 15 is considered as the first chord *not diatonic* in the old key (B minor). The pivot chord is located directly before it.

Occasionally, the method just described for locating the pivot chord does not yield the most convincing musical analysis. In the following example, the composer may well have considered the change in tonality to coincide with the beginning of the second section (at the double bar). This being the case, m. 17, instead of m. 19, would be considered to contain the pivot chord.

Example 12.2   Anonymous (Anna Magdalena Bach's Notebook): *Minuet, BWV Anh. 114*

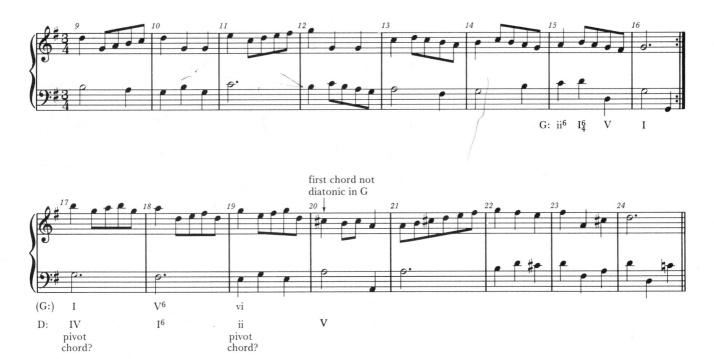

In the following example, it is the melodic embellishing tone that determines the location of the pivot chord. Notice that, although the harmony remains the same for the duration of m. 6 (an F major triad), its change of function is reflected by the appearance of B♮ on the third beat. Because of that altered tone, the F major triad sounds more like a IV in C major than a I in F major. Accordingly, the pivot chord is located in the first part of the measure, acting simultaneously as I in F major and as IV in C major.

Example 12.3 Haydn: *Piano Sonata, H. XVI:9* (II)

F: I   V⁷

(F:)   I
C: IV   IV   I⁶

TONAL
SHIFT

Tonality changes that occur *within* a phrase are sometimes distinguished from those that occur *between* phrases or sections, the former termed modulations and the latter termed tonal shifts. A *tonal shift* is an immediate and abrupt change of tonality, usually following a clear cadence in the old key. Tonal shifts often occur without the benefit of a pivot chord to soften the effect of the change. Indeed, the tonal shift is often used specifically for its abrupt effect.

CLOSELY
RELATED
KEYS

Pivot chord modulations and tonal shifts are most common between closely related keys—that is, keys with no more than one flat or one sharp difference. For a given tonality, the closely related keys consist of the relative major or minor, the dominant and *its* relative, and the subdominant and *its* relative.

Illustration 12.1

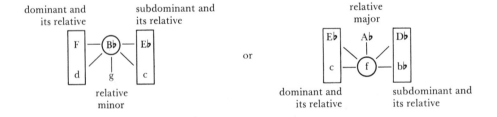

While *any* chord common to two keys may function as a pivot, the chords that most often do so are the pre-dominants in the new key. This is because key areas are most quickly and convincingly established through pre-dominant-dominant-tonic motion. The following illustration shows the pre-dominants in the keys closely related to C.

Illustration 12.2

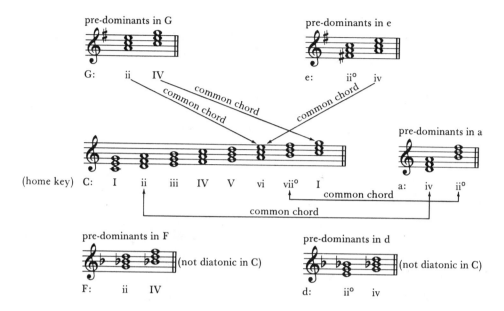

NOTE: The only two keys in which *both* pre-dominants are common chords in the home key (C) are a (the relative minor) and G (the dominant). The keys of F and d (the subdominant and its relative) contain pre-dominants that are *not* common chords in the home key.

Following are the pre-dominants in the keys closely related to A minor.

Illustration 12.3

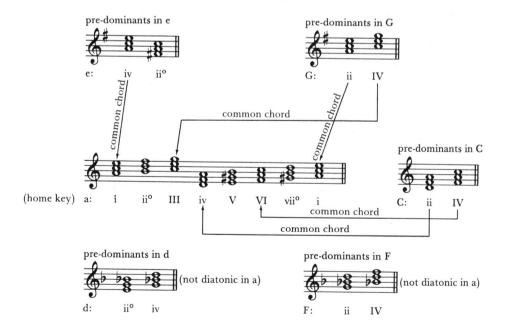

NOTE: The two keys in which *both pre-dominants* are common chords in the home key (a) are C (the relative major), and G (the relative major of the dominant). The keys of d and F (the subdominant and its relative) contain pre-dominants that are *not* common chords in the home key.

These observations seem to support the fact that, within the closely related key system, modulations to the dominant or to the relative major or minor tend to occur more often than do modulations to the subdominant or its relative key.

Illustration 12.4

More frequent modulations	Less frequent modulations
I-V, as from C major to G major (the most common modulation in a major key)	I-IV, as from C major to F major
i-III, as from A minor to C major (the most common modulation from a minor key)	I-ii, as from C major to D minor
I-vi, as from C major to A minor	i-iv, as from A minor to D minor
i-v, as from A minor to E minor	i-VI, as from A minor to F major

NOTE: Despite the fact that the modulations in the right-hand column are listed as "less frequent," *all* the modulations contained in this chart are common.

FOR CLASS DISCUSSION

Look back for a moment at the musical examples given thus far in the chapter. Which of the modulations are among the more frequent modulations listed above? What is the tonal relationship in each case? In which of these modulations does the pivot chord function as a pre-dominant in the new key?

Although the most common function of a pivot chord is as a pre-dominant, this is not *always* the case. In the following example, the pivot chord functions as VI in the new key.

Example 12.4 Mozart: *Symphony, K. 550* (III)

A change of key is most often signaled by the consistent use of a new sharp, flat, or natural. This is readily apparent in most of the foregoing examples. Notice in the following example that the *solitary* C♯ does *not* signal a modulation, whereas the *consistent* use of F♯ from m. 5 onward does.

IDENTIFYING A TONAL CHANGE

Example 12.5 Haydn: *Symphony No. 97* (III)

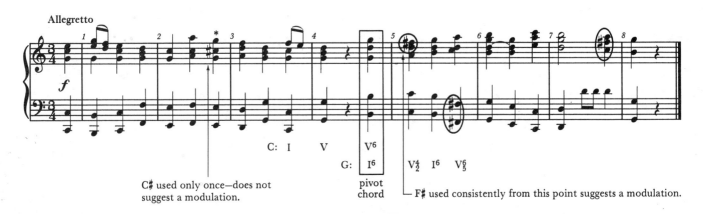

*This type of chromatic harmony is discussed in Chapter Fourteen.

FOR PRACTICE MATERIAL AND ASSIGNMENTS, TURN TO PAGE 270.

B. Chromatic Tone Modulations and Tonal Shifts

A *chromatic tone modulation* is one in which: 1) a common chord is not present; 2) a diatonic pitch moves to a chromatically altered pitch in one or more voices. Because the two keys have no chord in common (as in the pivot chord modulation), the change of key seems more abrupt.

CHROMATIC TONE MODULATION

Illustration 12.5

diatonic pitch and chromatically altered pitch

Bb: I IV

F: V I

A chromatic tone modulation which occurs abruptly, following a clear cadence, may be termed a chromatic tonal shift. The following guidelines apply to most chromatic tone modulations and chromatic tonal shifts.

CHROMATIC ALTERATIONS

1. If the altered pitch is raised by a half step (as in F-F♯ or Bb-B♮), it is quite possibly functioning as the leading tone of the new key, and the pitch to which it resolves will be the new tonic.

Illustration 12.6

diatonic   chromatic   new
pitch   alteration   tonic

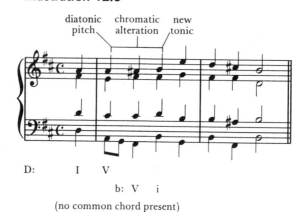

D: I V

b: V i

(no common chord present)

2. If the altered pitch is *lowered* by a half step, it is quite possibly functioning as the seventh of a V^7 in the new key, and the pitch to which it resolves will be the *third* of the new tonic chord.

Illustration 12.7

diatonic   chromatic   third of
pitch   alteration   new tonic

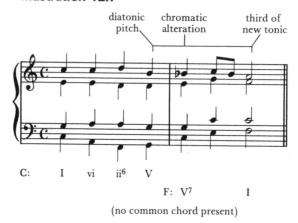

C: I vi ii⁶ V

F: V^7 I

(no common chord present)

Chromatic tone modulations are not as common as pivot chord modulations. While they *may* involve closely related keys, they often lead to more remote tonalities. Remote modulation is considered in Volume Two. Following are examples of chromatic tone modulations or tonal shifts *within* the closely related key system.

Example 12.6

(a) J. S. Bach: "Schaut, ihr Sünder"

g: i   V⁶   i   i   i   vii°⁶   i   V   iv⁶   V   B♭: I   V⁶   I   I

*The E♭ in the key signature is not included in the original version. Notice also that the key change occurs between phrases (a tonal shift) and that the chromatically altered tone (f♮) appears in a different voice than the diatonic tone (f♯).

(b) Haydn: *Piano Sonata, H. XVI:34* (I)*

*This movement is contained in its entirety in *Analytical Anthology of Music,* by this author (Alfred A. Knopf, Inc., 1984).

(c) Brahms: *Sonata No. 2 for Violin and Piano, Op. 100* (I)*

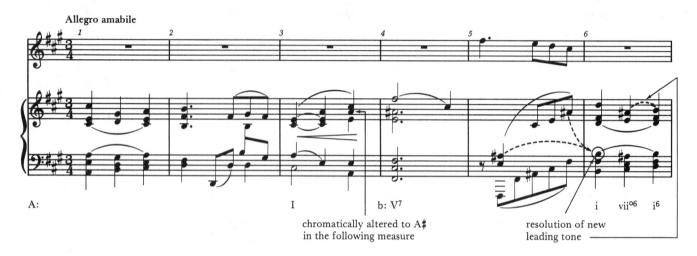

chromatically altered to A♯
in the following measure

resolution of new
leading tone

*This movement is contained in its entirety in *Anthology of Musical Structure and Style,* by Mary Wennerstrom (Prentice-Hall, Inc., 1984).

C. Melody Harmonization Using Modulations to Closely Related Keys

Following is a procedure you can use in harmonizing melodies that obviously modulate or in discovering points within a melody with no accidentals that may be harmonized in a closely related key.

1. Examine the melody for evidence of a modulation. Such evidence may be the consistent appearance of certain accidentals.
2. If you find no evidence of a modulation, examine the melody for the *possibility* of a modulation (a melodic cadence that can support a harmonic cadence in a closely related key). Remember that:

   a. The standard cadences are:

   authentic ⎫
   half ⎬ most common
   plagal
   deceptive

   b. The possible closely related keys are:

   the relative
   the dominant and its relative
   the subdominant and its relative

Some of the possible keys will be ruled out immediately by the melody notes. For the remaining possibilities, apply each of the standard cadence formulas, remembering that the two most common cadences are the authentic and the half cadences.

3. If you find a melodic cadence that can be harmonized in a closely related key, see how early in the phrase the melody will support a harmonization in this key. In other words, *how soon does the melody
become diatonic in the new key?*

4. If there is a point in the phrase that *clearly* must be harmonized in the
old key, consider the possibility of a pivot chord immediately following that point. If you find no possibility for a pivot chord, the modulation must be a chromatic one.

5. Apply the harmonization procedures described in Chapter Eight (see
page 200).

This process is illustrated below, using a slightly modified version of the
chorale "Jesu, deine Liebeswunden."

The key signature, the accidental G♯s, and the melodic cadences of the first
and last phrases clearly suggest A minor as the home tonality. The closely
related keys, then, are:

Apply the five steps listed above.

1. Evidence of a modulation exists in the second and third phrases in the
consistent use of G♮s.

2. Cadence possibilities for the second phrase:

a. Keys ruled out by the melody note F♮ are G and E minor.

b. The authentic and half cadences possible in the remaining closely
related keys (C, F, and D minor) are:

Authentic cadence: C major

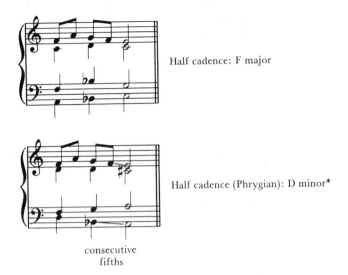

Half cadence: F major

Half cadence (Phrygian): D minor*

consecutive
fifths

NOTE: This cadence produces consecutive fifths.

    c. Since the Phrygian cadence in D minor produces unavoidable consecutive fifths, we will eliminate this key from consideration (although the iv could be in root position instead of first inversion—iv-V).

3. The entire phrase is diatonic in both C and F.
4. Because the entire phrase is diatonic in both C and F, it can be harmonized in its entirety in one of those keys. The final chord of the first phrase, most likely an A minor triad, can be considered as a pivot to *either* key.

A different set of possibilities is presented by the third phrase. With the use of B♮s, the keys of F and D minor are no longer suggested. On the other hand, with no F present *in any form,* the phrase might be harmonized in either G or E minor. C major also is a possibility. The possible cadences in these keys are shown below.

Illustration 12.8

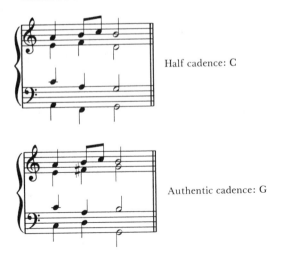

Half cadence: C

Authentic cadence: G

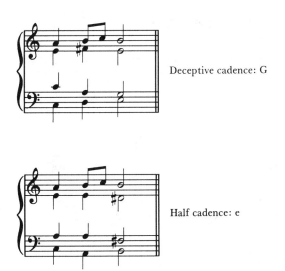

Deceptive cadence: G

Half cadence: e

Again, the entire phrase may be harmonized in any of these keys, using the procedures already outlined. The final choice of keys may be determined by trying out the various possibilities to see which one sounds the best. Since C is the only key that presents a possibility for *both* the second and third phrases, it may be the best choice. A possible harmonization is shown below.

Illustration 12.9

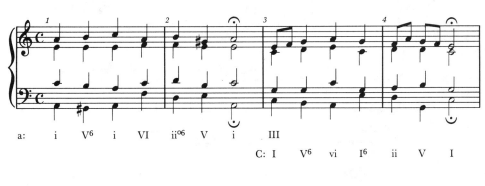

a: i V⁶ i VI ii°⁶ V i III

C: I V⁶ vi I⁶ ii V I

V iii vi vi⁴₂ IV vii°⁶ V vi

a: i V⁶ i VI ii°⁶ V i

FOR PRACTICE MATERIAL AND ASSIGNMENTS, TURN TO PAGE 272.

PRACTICE MATERIAL AND ASSIGNMENTS FOR PART A

A. List the five closely related keys to each of the following.

1 Eb _____ _____ _____ _____ _____

2 f# _____ _____ _____ _____ _____

3 Gb _____ _____ _____ _____ _____

4 B _____ _____ _____ _____ _____

5 d# _____ _____ _____ _____ _____

6 A _____ _____ _____ _____ _____

7 E _____ _____ _____ _____ _____

8 g _____ _____ _____ _____ _____

9 Ab _____ _____ _____ _____ _____

10 b _____ _____ _____ _____ _____

B. List four keys in which each of the following chords is diatonic and indicate the chord's function in each of those keys.

Example: c#   B: ii   c#: i   g#: iv   A: iii

1 F# _____ _____ _____ _____

2 c _____ _____ _____ _____

3 B _____ _____ _____ _____

4 g _____ _____ _____ _____

5 eb _____ _____ _____ _____

6 Bb _____ _____ _____ _____

7 d _____ _____ _____ _____

8 a _____ _____ _____ _____

9 E _____ _____ _____ _____

10 Ab _____ _____ _____ _____

C. Complete the following four-part passages, modulating by pivot chord to the specified key. Use a pivot chord that functions as a pre-dominant in the new key. Provide a complete harmonic analysis, including the dual harmonic function of the pivot.

1

Bb to F: ___ ___ ___ ___ ___ ___ ___ ___

2

f to Ab: ___ ___ ___ ___ ___ ___ ___

3

D to b: ___ ___ ___ ___ ___ ___ ___

4

Ab to c: ___ ___ ___ ___ ___ ___

PRACTICE MATERIAL AND ASSIGNMENTS FOR PARTS B AND C

A. Provide a complete harmonic analysis of the following excerpts. Indicate whether the modulation is of the pivot chord or chromatic tone type. For all pivot chord modulations, identify the common chord and indicate its dual harmonic function.

1 Beethoven: *Symphony No. 7, Op. 92* (II)

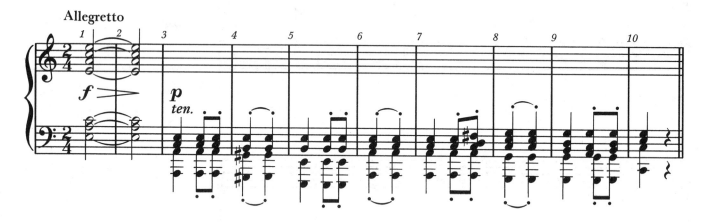

2 Beethoven: *Piano Sonata, Op. 90* (I)*

*This movement is contained in its entirety in *Examples for the Study of Musical Style,* by William R. Ward (Wm. C. Brown Company Publishers, 1970).

3 Brahms: *Waltz, Op. 39, No. 15*

4 Handel: *Suite No. 9* from *Pièces pour le Clavecin, HWV 442* (Preludio)*

*This movement is contained in its entirety in *Music for Analysis,* second edition, by Benjamin, Horvit and Nelson (Houghton Mifflin Company, 1984).

B. Realize the following figured bass lines for four voices. Provide harmonic analysis, identifying the type of modulation in each.

C. Harmonize the following melodies, including at least one modulation in each.

1. Place the harmonies in simple position on the staff beneath the melody.
2. Create a more melodic bass line through the use of inversions.

3. On separate manuscript paper, part-write the harmonization for four voices.
4. Identify the modulation(s) you have used as pivot chord or chromatic tone types.

SUGGESTIONS FOR AURAL DRILL

Your instructor will play a four-voice passage that involves a modulation. Given the first note in the soprano and bass, you are to notate the outer voices and provide Roman numerals for each chord. Include the dual harmonic analysis for the pivot chord if a pivot chord is present. Material for this exercise may be drawn from text pages 274, 277, and 278, or Workbook page 95. (*Note to instructor:* You may wish to play only the two measures prior to and following the point of modulation.)

TEST YOUR COMPREHENSION OF CHAPTER TWELVE

A. Place the letter corresponding to the correct answer in the blank.

1. The five closely related keys to G major are _____.

   a. e, d, b, C, a
   b. a, c, D, b, e
   c. D, b, C, F, e
   d. C, a, b, D, e

2. The five closely related keys to F minor are _____.

   a. c, E♭, A♭, D♭, F
   b. E♭, A♭, c, b♭, D♭
   c. g, c, A♭, E♭, D♭
   d. A♭, E♭, D♭, c, e♭

B. Indicate the keys in which the following chords may function as pre-dominants.

   1. c♯m⁷   Keys:

   2. e   Keys:

   3. E♭   Keys:

   4. g   Keys:

   5. F   Keys:

C. Identify each modulation as a pivot chord or chromatic tone type.
   Then name the old and the new keys.

1

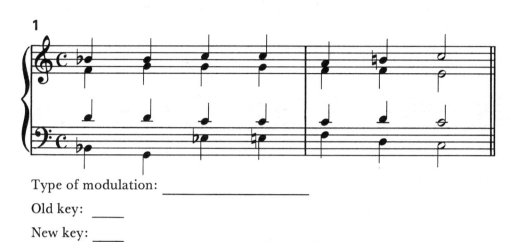

Type of modulation: _____

Old key: _____

New key: _____

2

Type of modulation: _pivot_

Old key: D^b

New key: b^b

3

Type of modulation: _pivot_ vi / ii

Old key: A

New key: E

D. In the modulating bass lines that follow, identify the pivot chord and indicate by Roman numeral its dual harmonic function. Be sure to indicate the old and new keys along with the Roman numerals.

1

2

3

4

5

Answers appear on page 369.

CHAPTER THIRTEEN

THE BINARY PRINCIPLE; SECONDARY FUNCTION

TERMS TO KNOW

Corelli clash
secondary dominant
secondary leading-tone chord

simple binary form
tonicization

Note to the Instructor: Instructors who wish to present binary form and secondary function as completely separate topics may do so by beginning with Part B (Secondary Function) and following with Part C (Part Writing and Harmonization). Part A (Simple Binary Forms) can then be undertaken separately.

A. Simple Binary Forms

Of the various musical forms employed in the Baroque era, one of the most popular was the *binary,* or two-part, structure. Binary forms can be designated A | B. In most examples of the form from the Baroque era, both sections are repeated. While the second section may differ from the first tonally and/or thematically, the contrast is generally not pronounced. Rather, a unified mood prevails, and the single most important element in defining the form is the clear cadential punctuation that separates the two sections.

GENERAL DESCRIPTION

HARMONIC TONAL PLANS

Three harmonic/tonal plans found frequently in binary forms are:

Illustration 13.1

a

Section:	A		B	
Cadence:		Half or Authentic		Authentic
Tonality:	I ——————— I		I ——————— I ———	
	i ——————— i		i ——————— i	

b

Section:	A		B	
Cadence:		Authentic		Authentic
Tonality:	I ——————— V		V ——————— I ———	
	i ——————— v or III		v (III) ——————— i	

c

Section:	A		B	
Cadence:		Authentic		Authentic
Tonality:	I ——————— V		Various keys ——— I ———	
	i ——————— v or III		Various keys ——— i	

The first of these plans is tonally the simplest. The second involves a move to a new tonal center by the end of the first part and a reversal of this tonal movement in the second part. It reflects a stage of development that led to the third type. In this type, further tonal changes follow the initial move to a new key.

Analysis
Corelli: *Sonata, Op. 5, No. 7* (Sarabande)

Arcangelo Corelli (1653-1713) was a highly skilled violinist who wrote principally for that instrument. His favorite genre was the *trio sonata,* a multimovement work featuring two violins in a polyphonic interplay over a figured bass line that was realized by a harpsichordist (or organist) and a bass-register melody instrument. Many of the movements are in binary form. Corelli also wrote numerous *solo* sonatas, which comprise a *single* violin part over a figured bass. An example follows. The large notes are those which Corelli actually notated. The small notes are one possible realization of the figured bass line.

Example 13.1 Corelli: *Sonata, Op. 5, No. 7* (Sarabande)

FORMAL STRUCTURE

This movement is in two parts:

||: A
  (mm. 1-8)   :||: B
                  (mm. 9-16)   :||

Each principal section is composed of two four-measure phrases.

Illustration 13.2

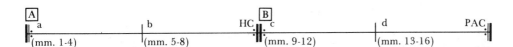

The elements that serve most strongly to create this binary form are the cadences—the strong half cadence of m. 8 and the perfect authentic cadence of m. 16. (Notice that the divisive effect of the perfect authentic cadence of m. 4 is undermined by its weak metric placement and its relatively early appearance in the music.) Although the contrast between the two sections is not pronounced, the material of the two halves is sufficiently different that the form may be described by the symbol A | B. (A | A' would signify essentially the same musical material in both parts.)

MELODIC/RHYTHMIC STRUCTURE

PITCH BASIS   The melodic pitches of the first half constitute the harmonic minor scale on D.

Illustration 13.3

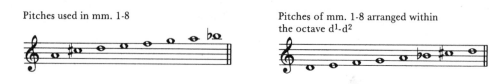

Pitches used in mm. 1-8

Pitches of mm. 1-8 arranged within the octave d¹-d²

While the first half of the movement is completely diatonic, chromatic alterations appear in the second half. These are the result of chromatic harmonies discussed in more detail in Part B of this chapter. By m. 14, the pitch material is once again diatonic.

RANGE AND CONTOUR   The melodic range is relatively narrow, moving largely within the octave from dominant to dominant (a¹ to a²). The four phrases of this movement contain no melodic repetition, and each phrase has its own unique contour, illustrated in exaggerated form below.

Illustration 13.4

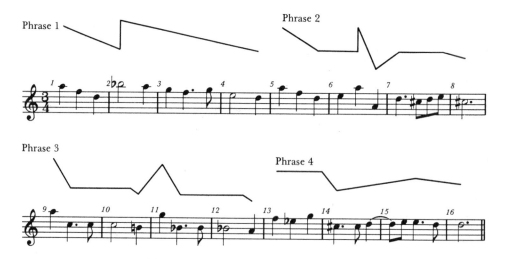

RHYTHMIC CHARACTER   Despite their differing contours, the element of contrast among the phrases is not very pronounced, owing to their rhythmic similarity. Eleven of the sixteen measures consist of the following rhythms.

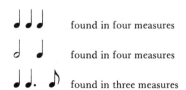

♩ ♩ ♩   found in four measures

𝅗𝅥 ♩   found in four measures

♩ ♩. ♪   found in three measures

The material of mm. 9-10 appears in sequence at mm. 11-12. The only **SEQUENCE** sequence of the movement (see Chapter Five), it is real, as opposed to tonal, since the intervallic relationships are precisely maintained.

Illustration 13.5

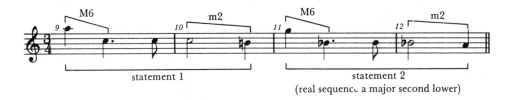

statement 1   statement 2
(real sequence a major second lower)

The outer lines of this movement have a sense of logic and direction, owing **LARGE-SCALE** in part to the large-scale melodic motion. **MELODIC MOTION**

Illustration 13.6

bass (*mm. 5-8*)

melody (*mm. 1-4*)

melody (*mm. 5-8*)

Notice the *simultaneous* step progressions in the second half of the excerpt.

Illustration 13.7

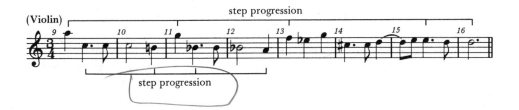

HARMONIC/TONAL STRUCTURE

MODAL KEY SIGNATURE   Although this movement is in D minor, a key signature of no flats or sharps is used. Signatures of one less flat or sharp than the number actually required, not uncommon in the Baroque era, are a vestige of the Church modes. Recall that the white-key scale on D constitutes the Dorian mode. The habitual raising of the seventh degree (to C♯) and lowering of the sixth degree (to B♭) in performance was partially responsible for the conversion of the Dorian mode to minor. Here, Corelli follows tradition by adding the B♭ as an accidental instead of including it in the key signature.

The tonal plan of the A section is similar to the first of those shown in Illustration 13.1, ending with a half cadence *in the principal tonality*. However, the B section more closely resembles the third tonal plan, since the music actually makes reference (albeit very brief) to *two* different keys within a four-measure span before returning to the home key. These measures are discussed in detail in Part B of this chapter.

THE CORELLI CLASH   A striking dissonance, the minor ninth, appears at the very end of m. 15. It is caused by the simultaneous appearance of the leading tone in the tenor (the C♯) and the anticipation of the final tonic in the melody (the D). This dissonance is so common in Corelli's cadences that it has been dubbed the "Corelli clash."

Illustration 13.8

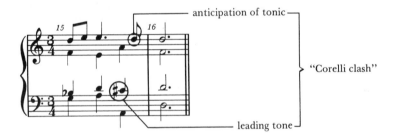

TEXTURE/ARTICULATION/DYNAMICS

Since texture is uniform throughout this movement and neither dynamic nor articulation markings are present, these factors may be disregarded in consideration of the form.

B. Secondary Function

Measures 9-16 of Corelli's Sarabande from *Sonata, Op. 5, No. 7*, in D minor, are reproduced in the illustration that follows. While the chords of mm. 9-12 are not diatonic in the principal key of D minor, they do not seem to establish a *new* tonal center. Note that the chord at point *X* could be analyzed as a V⁷ *if the key were G;* likewise, the chord at point *Y* could be analyzed as a V⁷ *if the key were F.* Observe the way these relationships are symbolized *in the key of D minor.*

Illustration 13.9

Explanation: The chord
is a V⁷ in G. G is IV in
D minor.

Explanation: The chord
is a V⁷ in F. F is III in
D minor.

*This chromatic harmony is a type not discussed in this volume. You may disregard it for now.

TONICIZATION

The chords on the *first* beats of mm. 9 and 11, in first inversion and lacking the added seventh, may be analyzed as V⁶/IV (read "V⁶ of IV") and V⁶/III (read "V⁶ of III") respectively. All of these chords are examples of *secondary function*—chords that *momentarily* function as dominants, dominant sevenths, leading-tone triads or leading-tone seventh chords with respect to a temporary, or secondary, tonic. In mm. 10 and 12, the G and F major triads respectively have been *tonicized*—temporarily given the properties of a tonic—because they are preceded by their own dominants and dominant seventh chords. However, neither the G nor the F chord assumes the role of tonic for more than a few beats and, therefore, the reference to a new tonal center is too brief to be considered a modulation.

How long must a tonicization last before it may be viewed as a modulation? There is no precise answer to this question, and opinions concerning a given passage may vary with the listeners. As a general rule, an isolated secondary dominant does not sufficiently establish a new tonal center, even when followed by a cadence. Usually, a progressional pattern of several chords, punctuated by a cadence, is necessary to create the feeling of a tonal change. For our present purposes, however, we may view tonicizations as merely very short modulations and modulations as extended tonicizations. The difference is one of degree rather than kind.

Secondary dominant and dominant seventh chords to all possible diatonic triads—that is, *those which are major or minor*—are shown below for the keys of C major and C minor. Sevenths are shown in parentheses as black notes.

TONICIZATION OR MODULATION?

V/ AND V⁷/

Illustration 13.10

C major

C minor

Observations:

1. A secondary dominant or dominant seventh chord *always* has its root a perfect fifth above (or a perfect fourth below) the chord it tonicizes.
2. A secondary dominant is *always* a major triad; a secondary dominant seventh chord is *always* a Mm^7 chord.

   NOTE: If either of the two foregoing conditions does not exist, the chord in question is not a secondary dominant or dominant seventh.

3. The vii° and ii°, because they are diminished triads, *cannot be tonicized* unless first altered to become major or minor triads.
4. In a major key, the tonic triad does not require an alteration to become a secondary dominant since it is *already* a major triad and since its root lies a perfect fifth above the subdominant. Typically, however, when composers wish to tonicize the subdominant, they add a minor seventh above the tonic. The resulting V^7/IV has a stronger tonicizing effect. Note that this added seventh will be a chromatically altered tone within the key.

Illustration 13.11

a Tonicizing effect on IV is minimal

b Tonicizing effect is much stronger due to added seventh above tonic

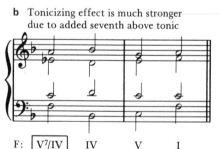

5. Two triads in minor—the III and the VII—require no alteration to act as secondary dominants. Of the two, the VII is the more common secondary dominant, acting as V/III. This is because minor-key passages so frequently make allusions to the relative major key.

Example 13.2   Handel: *Suite No. 4* from *Pièces pour le Clavecin, HWV 429* (Sarabande)

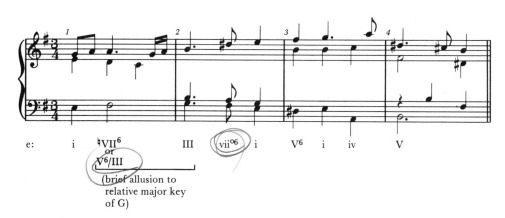

Secondary leading-tone triads and seventh chords (sevenths shown in parentheses as black notes) to all possible diatonic triads—*those which are major or minor*—are shown below for the keys of C major and C minor.

vii°/
AND
vii°7/

Illustration 13.12

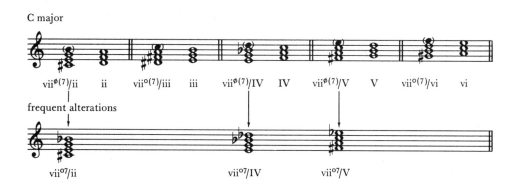

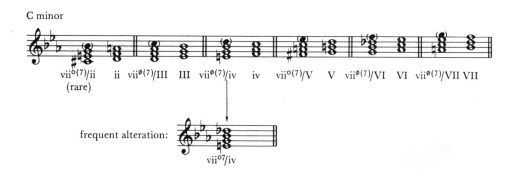

Observations:

1. A secondary leading-tone triad or seventh chord *always* has its root a minor second below the chord it tonicizes.
2. A secondary leading-tone triad is *always* diminished while a secondary leading-tone seventh may be either diminished (^{o7}) or half-diminished ($^{\varnothing7}$).

NOTE: If the foregoing conditions do not exist, the chord in question is not a secondary leading-tone triad or seventh.

**°7
VERSUS
ø7**

The ^{o7} is the more common of the two leading-tone seventh chords. It is *almost always* used when the tonicized chord is minor and it is frequently the choice even when the tonicized chord is major (notice the frequent alterations indicated in the preceding illustration). The $^{\varnothing7}$ is *rarely, if ever,* used to tonicize a *minor* triad.

**SECONDARY
DOMINANTS
IN SUCCESSION**

A secondary dominant (or dominant seventh chord) may be followed by *another* secondary dominant. This most often occurs in descending circle-of-fifths progressions, in which each chord is transformed, in turn, into a secondary dominant or dominant seventh chord by having its third raised.

Illustration 13.13

(Black notes indicate "secondary leading tones" to root of next chord)

This is essentially what takes place in the Corelli Sarabande. If we regard the chord of m. 12 as a *temporary tonic,* the functional analysis of mm. 9-12 would become:

Illustration 13.14

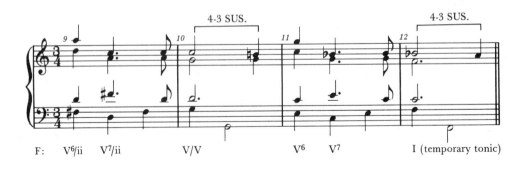

FOR PRACTICE MATERIAL AND ASSIGNMENTS, TURN TO PAGE 293.

C. Part Writing and Harmonization Using Secondary Function

All considerations that apply to the dominant, dominant seventh chord, leading-tone triad, and leading-tone seventh chord apply equally to their secondary counterparts.

VOICE LEADING

1. Just as the chord third of the dominant is not doubled (because it is the leading tone of the key), the chord third of a *secondary* dominant should not be doubled (because it is the leading tone in a *secondary* key).
2. The seventh of a *secondary* dominant seventh chord should resolve downward by step, just as does the seventh of a *primary* dominant seventh chord.
3. The appearance and treatment of secondary functions in inversion are identical to those of primary functions.
4. It is sometimes necessary to use less common doublings in order to resolve the altered tones in a secondary function.
5. While altered tones are normally resolved in the direction of their inflection, this may result in an undesired doubling. For example:

g: V^6_3/V V

Here, the downward resolution of the chord seventh and resolution of the altered tone E♮ in the direction of its inflection results in a *doubled leading tone*. Therefore, the best guideline to part-writing secondary functions is this: Part-write as though the music were in the key of the tonicized chord. For example, part-write a V^7/V in g as though it were a V^7-I in D.

One final observation regarding voice leading: Just as the leading-tone triad usually appears in first inversion, so does the *secondary* leading-tone triad.

Illustration 13.15

E♭:   ii vii^{o6}/vi vi⁶ vii^{o6}/V V⁶   I

Although part-writing procedures were broadened somewhat in the late eighteenth and the nineteenth centuries, particularly in instrumental music, composers continued to observe the general principles, as the following examples show.

Example 13.3

(a) Mozart: *Piano Sonata, K. 284* (I)

NOTE: The addition of the seventh to the tonic (D) creates a tonicizing effect on G (IV). Observe the stepwise resolution of the seventh.

(b) Beethoven: *Piano Sonatina, Op. 49, No. 2* (II)

NOTE: The secondary leading-tone triad is in first inversion; the secondary leading tone is resolved.

(c) Schubert: *Symphony No. 8* (I) (piano reduction)

NOTE: The secondary leading tone is not doubled, and it is resolved (to the "secondary tonic" A). The seventh is resolved downward by step.

In harmonizing a melodic line, a secondary dominant relationship can be established between any two chords whose roots are in a descending perfect-fifth relationship, so long as the second of these chords is a major or minor triad and so long as the pitch in the melody permits it.

MELODY HARMONIZATION

Illustration 13.16 *Morris Dance* (English)

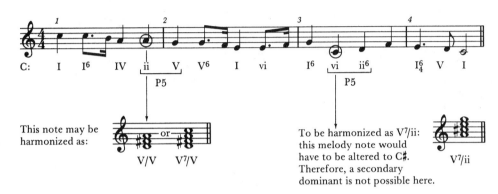

In the same manner, when two chords are in ascending second root relationship, the first can be converted to a secondary leading-tone triad or seventh chord by altering it so that it forms a diminished triad or diminished seventh chord a *half step below* the second chord.

Illustration 13.17

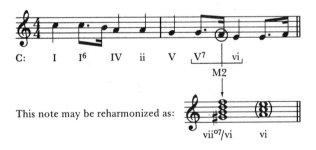

By applying these techniques to the folk song below, we can produce a more chromatic harmonization.

Illustration 13.18 *Prayer of Thanksgiving* (Dutch)

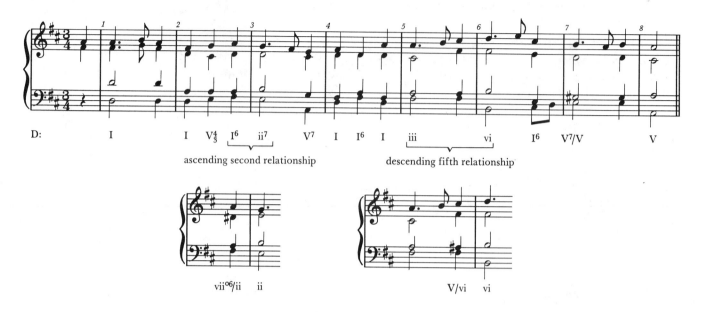

When an altered tone appears in a *nonmodulating* melodic line, it is helpful to realize that:

1. A chromatically raised pitch is usually the chord third of a secondary dominant or the root of a secondary leading-tone triad.
2. A chromatically lowered pitch is usually the chord seventh of a secondary dominant seventh or the chord fifth of a secondary leading-tone triad or seventh.

Both situations are illustrated in the following example.

Example 13.3 J. S. Bach: *French Suite No. 6, BWV 817* (Polonaise)*

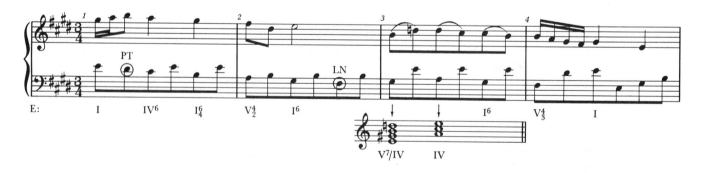

*This movement is contained in its entirety in *Analytical Anthology of Music,* by this author (Alfred A. Knopf, Inc., 1984).

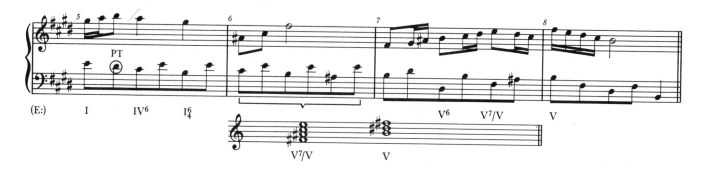

NOTE: It is also possible to view mm. 6-8 as a modulation to the dominant. Observe the consistent use of A♯ and the cadence on B in m. 8.

FOR PRACTICE MATERIAL AND ASSIGNMENTS, TURN TO PAGE 298.

PRACTICE MATERIAL AND ASSIGNMENTS FOR PARTS A AND B

A. Name the keys in which each of the following chords functions as indicated.

1

vii°⁷/vi: _____
vii°⁷/iii: _____
vii°⁷/V: _____

2

V/ii: _____
V/iv: _____
V/vi: _____

3

V⁷/IV: _____
V⁷/VI: _____
V⁷/iii: _____

4

vii°/ii: _____
vii°/IV: _____
vii°/V: _____

5

vii°⁷/vi: _____
vii°⁷/IV: _____
vii°⁷/III: _____

6

V⁷/VII: _____
V⁷/iii: _____
V⁷/ii: _____

7

vii°⁷/ii: _____
vii°⁷/vi: _____
vii°⁷/iv: _____

8

V⁷/V: _____
V⁷/VI: _____
V⁷/III: _____

9

vii°⁷/V: _____
vii°⁷/iv: _____
vii°⁷/vi: _____

10

vii°⁷/III: _____
vii°⁷/V: _____
vii°⁷/IV: _____

B. Provide a harmonic analysis of the following excerpts. In certain cases, you may have to decide whether a particular group of measures is a tonicization or a modulation. In these cases, consider the tempo, the length of the passage, and the presence or absence of strong cadences. Where a tonicization appears *after* a modulation has occurred, analyze the tonicization *in the new key*.

1 Beethoven: *Piano Sonata, Op. 2, No. 1* (IV)

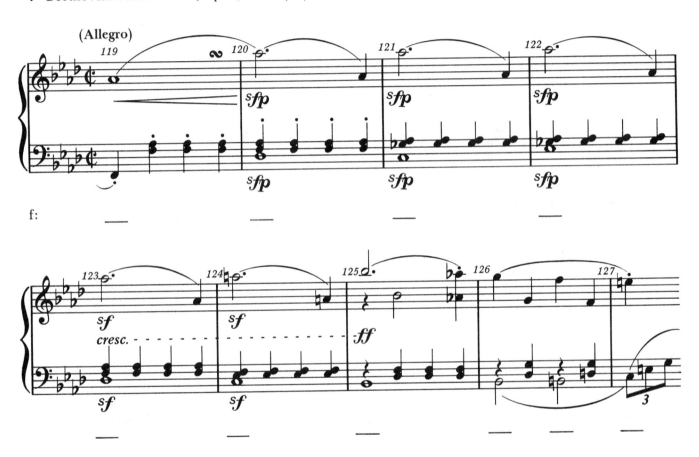

2 J. S. Bach: *The Well-Tempered Clavier, Book I* (Prelude No. 1, *BWV 846*)*

*This movement is contained in its entirety in *Anthology for Musical Analysis,* fourth edition, by Charles Burkhart (Holt, Rinehart and Winston, Inc., 1986).

3 Schumann: *Carnaval, Op. 9* (No. 4, "Valse noble")*

*This movement is contained in its entirety in *Anthology of Musical Structure and Style,* by Mary Wennerstrom (Prentice-Hall, Inc., 1984).

D. Using the diagram on page 281 as a model, show the formal structure of the following movement. Use upper-case letters to designate the principal sections and lower-case letters to designate phrase relationships. Answer the specific questions posed. It is best to answer these questions *in order.* You may also find it helpful to answer some or all of them before constructing your formal diagram.

Corelli: *Trio Sonata, Op. 4, No. 3* (Sarabande)

FORMAL STRUCTURE

Provide a formal diagram as described in the general instructions.

MELODIC/RHYTHMIC STRUCTURE

1. Compare the first and second violin parts with respect to range and activity. Are they fairly equal in this respect, or is one part more "melodic" than the other?

2. Two motives help to unify this movement. One, a rhythmic motive, is present in the upper parts; the other, a melodic motive, is present in the bass line. Identify them.

HARMONIC/TONAL STRUCTURE

1. What is the principal tonality of the movement? Is it reflected by the key signature? Explain.
2. Locate the first reference to a new tonality and identify it as a modulation or tonicization. What is the new tonal center that is suggested?
3. Explain the striking dissonance that occurs in m. 7. Two more such dissonances occur in the movement. Locate them.
4. Identify the tonal areas present in the second half of the movement and describe their relationship to the principal tonality.
5. Which of the harmonic/tonal plans outlined on page 280 does this movement most closely resemble?

PRACTICE MATERIAL AND ASSIGNMENTS FOR PART C

A. Add the key signature and then write and resolve the following secondary functions in four voices. Practice each at the keyboard.

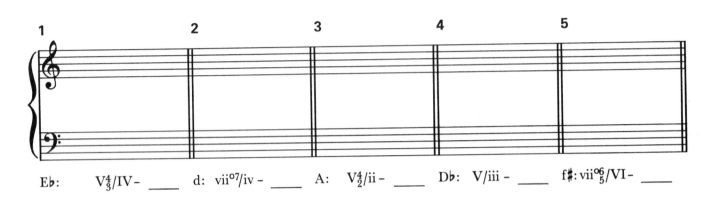

Eb: V_3^4/IV – ____   d: $vii°7/iv$ – ____   A: V_2^4/ii – ____   Db: V/iii – ____   f#: $vii°_5^6/VI$ – ____

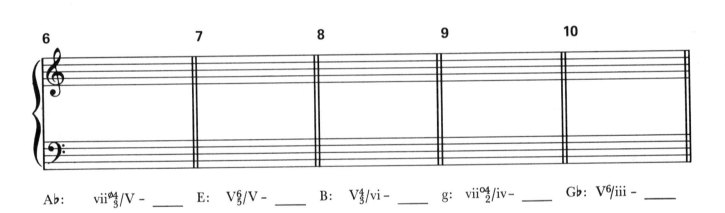

Ab: $vii°_3^4/V$ – ____   E: V_5^6/V – ____   B: V_3^4/vi – ____   g: $vii°_2^4/iv$ – ____   Gb: V^6/iii – ____

B. Add three voices to the following figured bass lines. Then provide harmonic analysis.

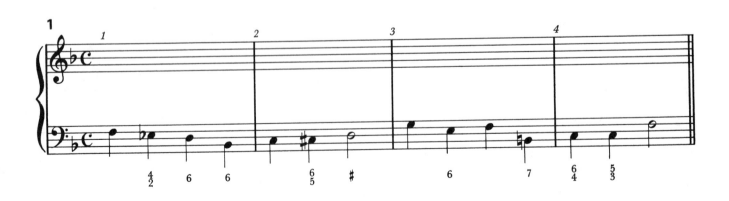

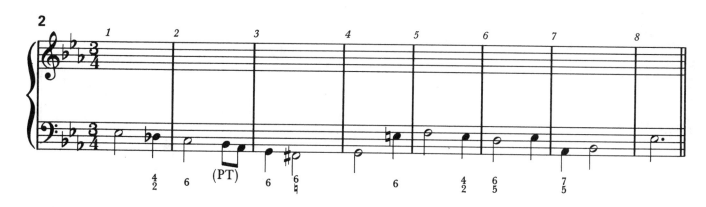

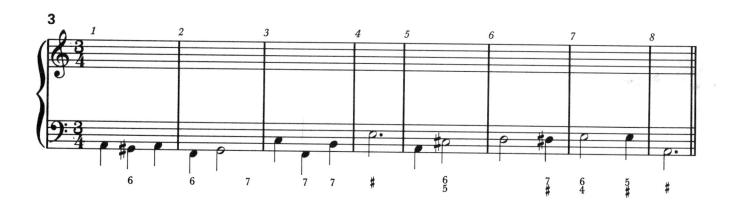

SUGGESTIONS FOR AURAL DRILL

A. Your instructor will choose at random from the following set of three-chord successions. In each case, the first chord is the tonic. You are to identify the function of the following two chords.

B. Your instructor will play a short, four-voice passage. Given the first note in the soprano and bass, you are to notate the outer voices and provide Roman numerals for each chord. Material for this exercise may be drawn from text pages 298-299, or Workbook pages 110-111. Additional material may be drawn from the *371 Harmonized Chorales and 69 Chorale Melodies* by Bach-Riemenschneider: Chorales 6 (mm. 1-2), 8 (mm. 1-2), 12 (mm. 5-7), 102 (mm. 1-4), or 106 (mm. 1-2). (*Note to instructor:* For material drawn from the text, you may wish to play only two-measure excerpts.)

CHAPTER FOURTEEN

ROUNDED BINARY AND TERNARY FORMS

TERMS TO KNOW

rounded binary form   ternary form

A. Rounded Binary Form

A variant of the binary principle that gained popularity in the later Baroque era and persisted well into the Classical period was the *rounded binary form.* As the name implies, this structure contains an element of repetition, often a shortened return of the opening material, which "rounds off" the form: A I BA'. Although tonally and thematically there may be *three* parts to the rounded binary form, it has only *two* principal sections. Usually, this is because the strongest cadence (apart from the final one) occurs at the end of the A section. The inconclusive and/or metrically weak cadence between the B and A' causes these two parts to be perceived as a single unit.

GENERAL DESCRIPTION

Illustration 14.1

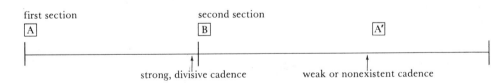

In the typical rounded binary form, the B material does not display marked contrast to that of the A section and is, in fact, often related to it. The A section may or may not modulate to a related key. If it does, the B material usually works its way back to the original key, coming to a half cadence immediately before the return of the opening material.

Christoph Willibald Gluck (1714-1787) was a German-born, Italian-trained composer of operas in the early Classical period. His operatic scenes are composed of instrumental overtures, preludes, arias, and dances, which separate portions of dialogue presented in choruses, arias, and recitatives. Some of these individual selections are in rounded binary form.

Example 14.1 Gluck: *Orphée et Euridice* (Ballet)

The form of this movement may be diagrammed this way.

Illustration 14.2

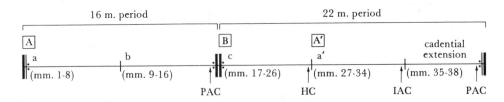

Observations:

1. The B material (mm. 17-26) is different from the opening material. However, the *general melodic character* is similar, owing in part to the dotted rhythm ♩. ♪♪ that is prominent in both sections.

2. A second element of contrast is the tonality. The move to the dominant (E major) occurs in the A section at m. 9, through a pivot chord modulation. This key remains in effect until the return of the original tonality at m. 21.

3. The B and A′, punctuated by a half cadence, are perceived as a single unit, which is clearly separated from the A section by the more strongly divisive perfect authentic cadence at m. 16.

4. Measures 27-34 are a shortened and varied return of the original material. Measures 5-12 of the original material are omitted from this repetition, and mm. 13-16 are transposed to remain in the tonic. To this repetition, a four-measure cadential extension, typical in the Classical style, is appended.

B. Ternary Form

GENERAL DESCRIPTION

The ternary principle—statement-digression-restatement—has a long history and can be found in music dating back to the Middle Ages. However, it was not until the Baroque era and later periods that ternary forms came into widespread use. Whereas the rounded binary form is composed of two principal sections (A|BA′), the ternary structure consists of three distinct sections that are often self-complete—A|B|A.

Following are some typical features of ternary form.

1. The B material often presents a stronger contrast than is typical in the rounded binary form.

2. The initial A section usually ends in the tonic key.

3. The B section is usually in a key different from that of the A section. Furthermore, it tends to begin and end in that key—that is, *it is tonally stable.*

4. The B section is usually more clearly separated cadentially from the final section than is the case in the rounded binary form.

5. The final section is often a complete restatement of the original material.

Many examples of ternary form do not display all of these characteristics. Perhaps the most decisive single factor is the strength of the cadence preceding the return of the original material. If it can be appropriately analyzed as a *conclusive* cadence in the key of the middle section, the form is probably ternary. However, even if the cadence cannot be so analyzed, one or more of the other characteristics may be sufficiently pronounced to create a ternary division.

Robert Schumann (1810-1856) was one of the most important nineteenth-century composers of piano music and song. Many of his works are in ternary form, their strongly contrasting sections perhaps reflecting the manic-depressive psychosis that afflicted him and that eventually led to his death. The following piece is from a set of thirteen short piano works selected by Schumann from a group of about thirty that he composed in 1838. The name means "Scenes from Childhood."

Example 14.2 Schumann: *Kinderscenen, Op. 15* (No. 6, "An Important Event")

The form of this short piece is shown below. Notice that only the middle section is repeated.

Illustration 14.3

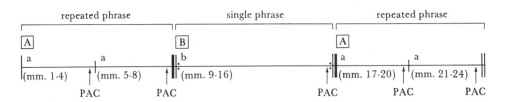

FOR CLASS DISCUSSION

1. In what ways does the B section contrast to the A section?
2. With five *perfect authentic cadences, why do we perceive the work to be in only* three *principal parts?*
3. This short piece is filled with examples of secondary function. Locate and identify them.

If you have carefully considered the foregoing questions, you have probably determined that this work is a rather clear example of ternary form (as opposed to binary or rounded binary). Other examples may be less obvious and, as is often the case, there may be room for differing points of view.

Example 14.3 Beethoven: *Piano Sonata, Op. 27, No. 1* (III)

This eloquent Adagio, composed by Beethoven in 1802, is perhaps best analyzed as a ternary form.

Illustration 14.4

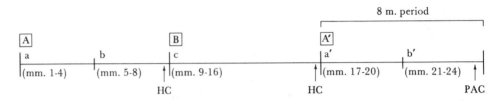

Although cadential separation between the sections was cited earlier as perhaps the most important single factor in creating a three-part division, the cadences here (both half cadences) are not strongly devisive. The element that creates *this* ternary form is contrast—tonal, melodic, and textural.

Observations:

1. The A and A' sections are entirely in the tonic, while the B section is entirely in the key of the dominant.
2. Little, if any, melodic or rhythmic similarity exists between the middle and outer sections.
3. The B section also presents a subtle textural contrast. The melody is in bare octaves throughout, over a repeated-chord accompaniment that is, initially at least, in a higher register than the accompaniment of the A and A' sections.
4. The final section is a complete restatement of the first section.

Ternary forms can be expanded by the addition of preludes (short introductions) and/or *codas* (short extensions at the end), or each of the three sections may be lengthened considerably. In the Classical period (c. 1750-1825) a favored form, the *compound ternary,* was embodied in the minuet-trio movement of many sonatas, symphonies, and chamber music. In the nineteenth century, composers set many solo piano works and songs in three-part forms. These manifestations of the ternary principle are examined in Volume Two.

PRACTICE MATERIAL AND ASSIGNMENTS

Provide a complete analysis of the following works. Consider each of the following.

FORMAL STRUCTURE

Be certain to explain why the piece is a rounded binary and not a ternary form, or vice versa.

MELODIC/RHYTHMIC STRUCTURE

Consider phrase-period structure, large-scale melodic motion, motivic structure, and rhythmic character.

HARMONIC/TONAL STRUCTURE

Be careful to distinguish between modulations and tonicizations.

TEXTURE/ARTICULATION/DYNAMICS

Do not neglect the important part these elements may play in creating the similarity and contrast that defines many forms.

1 J. S. Bach: *French Suite No. 6, BWV 817* (Minuet)

2 Gluck: "J'ai perdu mon Euridice," No. 43 from *Orfée et Euridice*

heur;   sort___ cru - el!___   quel - le ri - gueur!___   rien___ n'é - ga - le___ mon___ mal -

heur!   je___ suc - combe à___ ma___ dou - leur!

Now my love has gone forever.
All my days have turned to night.
From my heart, gone forever
Ev'ry ray of hope and light,
None can know my bitter plight.
My beloved, can you hear me?
Oh tell me, are you near me!
Oh tell me, Hear my voice so sad and sighing
In tears and terror, In fears and sorrow crying.

Now my love has gone forever.
All my days have turned to night.
From my heart, gone forever
Ev'ry ray of hope and light,
None can know my bitter plight.

3 Kuhlau: *Piano Sonatina, Op. 55, No. 4* (II)

4 Schumann: *Kinder Sonata No. 1, Op. 118a* (I)

CHAPTER FIFTEEN
VARIATION TECHNIQUES

VARIATION DEFINED

Variation refers generally to the modification, upon repetition, of a musical passage. The opposed principles of unity and variety, issues of perennial concern to composers, are at once embodied in the variation principle. For this reason, variation is one of the most important techniques at a composer's disposal. It can be applied to musical events as small as a motive or as large as a complete theme. Virtually *any* element of the musical fabric can be varied—the melody, the rhythm, the harmonic support, the tonality or modality, the orchestration, the register, the texture, the dynamic contour, or the articulation. It should be obvious that certain techniques already discussed can be viewed as forms of variation. Two of the oldest, for example, are *sequence* and *voice exchange*—the simultaneous exchange of musical material between two voices.

Example 15.1

(a) *Alle, psallite—Alleluya* (thirteenth-century motet—Montpellier MS H 196)

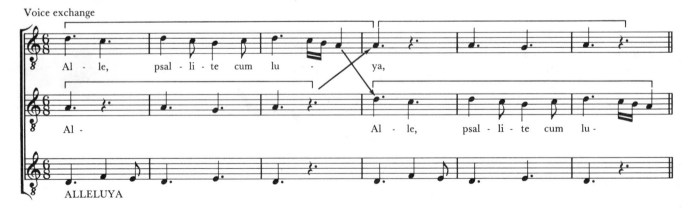

(b) *Danse Royale* (thirteenth century—Paris, Bibl. Nat. fr. 844)

Certain musical works are constructed entirely around the variation principle. These began to appear during the Renaissance,* and by late in the Baroque era, two types were common.

SECTIONAL VERSUS CONTINUOUS VARIATIONS

1. *Sectional variations* consisted of a well-defined melodic theme of substantial length—usually several phrases forming a simple or rounded binary structure. The theme was followed by a set of variations, each a self-contained unit set apart from the others by a decisive cadence.
2. *Continuous variations* featured a series of variations over a repeating bass line or harmonic progression called a *ground*. Today, the former type is usually designated a *passacaglia* and the latter a *chaconne*, but Baroque composers were somewhat indiscriminate in their use of the two terms. Grounds were generally shorter than the melodic theme of sectional variations, common lengths being four or eight measures. They were usually in moderately slow triple meter, and they appeared in either major or minor. Because of the brevity of the ground itself, the variations tended to have a less sectional feeling, and composers often enhanced the sense of continuity by providing rhythmic motion between variations.

"Ground compositions" enjoyed their widest popularity during the Baroque era. On the other hand, sectional variations remained popular throughout the Classical and Romantic periods and have persisted even into the twentieth century.

A. Sectional Variations

The movement below is from the second of two collections of harpsichord suites written by Handel and published in 1733. It consists of a theme followed by three variations. Because of the length of the theme, and because each variation ends with a perfect authentic cadence, this is an example of the sectional type of composition known as a *theme and variations*.

---

*Early precedents, such as the famous canon *Sumer is icumen in*, or Machaut's isorhythmic motets, can be found in the thirteenth and fourteenth centuries.

Example 15.2 Handel: *Suite No. 3* from *Pièces pour le Clavecin, HWV 507A* (Menuetto)

Analysis

Handel: *Suites de Pièces pour le Clavecin: Suite No. 3* (Menuetto)

The Theme

First of all, the theme of this movement is itself a rounded binary form. As in the examples of the preceding chapter, the principal means of defining the form is the strong perfect authentic cadence that separates the two parts. The melodic material of the second part, while somewhat different, is obviously derived from the first part.

Illustration 15.1

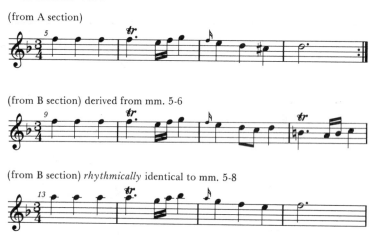

(from A section)

(from B section) derived from mm. 5-6

(from B section) *rhythmically* identical to mm. 5-8

Likewise, there is little textural contrast; both parts are *free-voiced*—that is, a fixed number of voices is not strictly maintained throughout the work—and somewhat polyphonic. Material from the first part returns in m. 19.

Exactly where should the A′ be located? The diagrams below show three possibilities.

Illustration 15.2

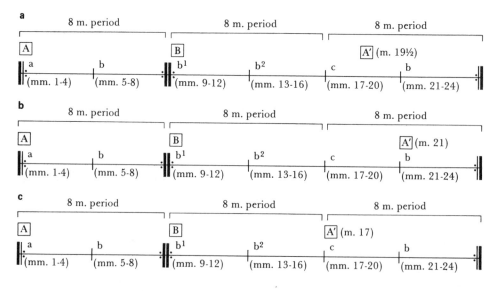

The first possibility obviously coincides with the *precise point of musical return.* (Measures 19½-24 are melodically identical to mm. 3½-8.) However, because this return occurs in the middle of a phrase, it may be appropriate to locate the return *after* this phrase, as in **b,** or at its beginning, as in **c.** Because the B material modulates (to C major in mm. 9-12 and to F major in mm. 13-16) and because m. 17 is the point at which the original tonality returns, it is perhaps most appropriate to regard this point as the A′.

The Variations

FORMAL STRUCTURE

The form of the theme—its length, its phrasing, and its rounded binary structure—is rigorously maintained in each of the variations. This is characteristic of variations in the Baroque era *and* in the ensuing Classical period. Not until the nineteenth century did composers begin to take liberties with the formal structure of the theme.

MELODIC/RHYTHMIC STRUCTURE

Variation 1

A striking element of change appearing in Variation 1 is the increase in the rhythmic animation of the melodic line, owing to the continuous, steady stream of eighth notes. Even so, the melodic line bears a rather close resemblance to the theme. Notice how the most important pitches of the theme tend to appear prominently in the florid right-hand part. We might say that the *surface* of the melodic line is changed while the structural melody remains. Likewise, the bass line remains very close to that of the theme. The first four measures of the theme and Variation 1 are compared below. Continue this comparison for the rest of the variation.

Illustration 15.3

Variation 2

Like Variation 1, this variation remains faithful to the general melodic structure of the theme in both the right- and left-hand parts. The most significant difference, of course, is that the two hands have exchanged rhythmic roles, with the running eighth notes now appearing in the bass. The first four measures of the theme and Variation 2 are compared below. Continue the comparison for the entire variation.

Illustration 15.4

Variation 3

In a way, this variation *combines* the elements of variations 1 and 2, the running eighth-note idea now appearing in *both* hands. The right-hand part is clearly similar to that of Variation 1. The left hand part is somewhat less closely related to that of Variation 2 even though the structural notes of the theme are present in *both* variations. Actually, the bass line of Variation 3 appears to have been constructed using the bass line of Variation 1 as its point of departure. The extra pitches appear to have been chosen to form a harmonious line against the soprano. The first four measures of Variation 3 are compared with those of Variation 1 below. Continue the comparison for the entire variation.

Illustration 15.5

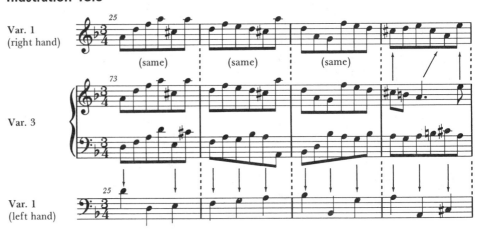

HARMONIC/TONAL STRUCTURE

Like the formal structure, the theme's tonal structure is retained in each of the variations. The individual harmonies are retained for the most part as well, with a few minor changes in each variation to accommodate the more significant melodic changes. Examine each of the variations to note the harmonic changes that occur.

TEXTURE/ARTICULATION/DYNAMICS

As in most Baroque works, articulation and dynamic markings were not specified by the composer. Texture, however, is an important element of variation. All three of the variations are two-voice textures (for the most part), contrasting in this respect with the three- and four-voice texture of the theme. As mentioned earlier, the variations are texturally distinct *from each other* by virtue of the placement of the more active line: In Variation 1, it is the upper part; in Variation 2, it is the lower part; in Variation 3, it constitutes the upper *and* lower part

In analyzing *any* set of variations, an expedient procedure is to make two lists—one of the elements that are retained in each variation (unity) and one of the elements that change (variety). A list for the Handel Menuetto follows.

Illustration 15.6

	Elements of retention	Elements of change
Var. 1	form (number of phrases and phrase lengths) structural melody bass line harmony tonality	surface melody texture
Var. 2	form structural melody structural bass line harmony tonality	surface bass line texture
Var. 3	form structural melody structural bass line harmony tonality	surface melody surface bass line texture

A chart like this provides an overview of the variation techniques employed in a given work. This particular movement typifies the Baroque approach to variation in several respects.

1. The *form* of the theme is not altered in the variations.
2. The harmonic and tonal structure of the theme remains essentially intact in the variations.
3. Melody, rhythm, and texture are the principal elements of change in the variations.

In this work, the final variation employs more elements of change than the other two, causing it to bear the least resemblance to the theme.

B. Continuous Variations

Portions of two compositions based on a ground are given below for the purpose of comparison. Example 15.3(a) is taken from a chaconne consisting of sixty-two variations, one of the largest sets Handel wrote. Example 15.3(b) is the beginning of one of Bach's better-known cantatas.

Consider the elements of retention and change that occur during each statement of the ground in both compositions. Also consider the interrelationships among the variations in Example 15.3(a).

Example 15.3

(a) Handel: *Suite No. 9* from *Pièces pour le Clavecin, HWV 442* (Chaconne)

(b) J. S. Bach: *Cantata, Jesu, der du meine Seele, BWV 78* (I)*

*This movement is contained in its entirety in *Analytical Anthology of Music,* by this author (Alfred A. Knopf, Inc., 1984).

Following are some points worth noting concerning the two excerpts.

1. Both works are constructed on a recurring bass line; Handel's is eight measures long while Bach's is four measures in length.

Illustration 15.7
(a) Handel

(b) Bach

2. Because the grounds lack the rhythmic and intervallic variety common-ly associated with melodic lines, and because they function more as supports for their respective harmonic progressions than as melodies in their own right, it is perhaps more appropriate to regard these works as chaconnes rather than passacaglias. As a point of comparison, consider how much more "melodic" is the bass line from Bach's famous *Passacaglia for Organ in C Minor*.

Illustration 15.8*

*This movement is contained in its entirety in *Analytical Anthology of Music,* by this author (Alfred A. Knopf, Inc., 1984).

3. Both compositions are in the moderate triple meter typical of ground compositions.
4. Both grounds feature a stepwise descent from tonic to dominant, Han-del's a diatonic descent and Bach's a chromatic descent.

Illustration 15.9
(a) Handel

tonic   dominant

(b) Bach

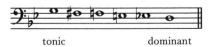

tonic   dominant

5. In the Bach excerpt, the ground appears in various registers within the texture. In the Handel excerpt, the ground remains in the bass.

6. Although both works display a greater sense of continuity than the Handel menuetto, the Bach excerpt is more continuous than the Handel chaconne for the following reasons.

   a. The ground is half as long.
   b. The ground ends on the dominant, so that the resolution of this chord is also the beginning of the next statement of the ground.
   c. The rhythmic activity of the lines "spills over" from one statement of the ground to the next more consistently and more urgently than in the Handel excerpt.

Illustration 15.10

7. Each of the variations in the Handel chaconne has been shown here for a particular reason. For example:

   a. Variation 4 is included because it is customary to think of the variation process as an *elaboration* of a theme. Here, the opposite is true. The variation actually represents a *simplification* of the theme, exposing the harmonic progression in its most basic form. Also, this variation seems to serve as a structural melody for some of the other variations.

b. Variations 24 and 25 are included because they exemplify a tendency among composers to group certain variations together through common processes. This is especially true when a composition consists of many variations on a relatively short pattern, and the need to impose a larger unity on the composition as a whole is more pronounced.

c. Variation 29 is included because of its interesting relationship to Variations 24 and 25.

Try to discover for yourself the features of the other variations which prompted their inclusion.

8. The Bach excerpt is the beginning of the chorale fantasia that opens the cantata. The movement is built around the chorale, *Jesu, der du meine Seele,* the first phrase of which appears below.

Example 15.4 J. S. Bach: "Jesu, der du meine Seele"

Each of the eight phrases of the chorale melody is treated in the same manner in this compelling movement.

a. Each chorale phrase is sung exclusively by the sopranos, doubled by the horn and by the flute at the octave.

b. With each soprano phrase, the ground appears in the bass.

c. Each phrase of the chorale text is first introduced by the lower voices in imitative fashion and set to melodic material unrelated to the chorale, after which the sopranos enter with the chorale text and melody. The movement unfolds in a series of textural "waves," cresting with each entry of the chorale phrase.

9. The chromatic form of the ground was favored among Baroque composers for the expression of grief. Bach used the same basic formula for the "Crucifixus" of his *Mass in B Minor.*

Example 15.5 J. S. Bach: "Crucifixus" from *Mass in B Minor**

*This movement appears in its entirety in *Anthology for Musical Analysis,* fourth edition, by Charles Burkhart (Holt, Rinehart and Winston, Inc., 1986).

PRACTICE MATERIAL AND ASSIGNMENTS

A. Answer the following questions concerning the work below.

1. Is this movement more in the character of a chaconne or passacaglia as the terms are defined in this chapter?
2. List the elements of retention and change in each variation.
3. Indicate which variations are related to each other and describe the relationships.
4. Explain how the gradual increase in musical intensity is created in this movement.
5. Provide a harmonic analysis of:

   a. mm. 1-4
   b. mm. 45-48

Handel: *Suite No. 7* from *Pièces pour le Clavecin, HWV 432* (Passacaille)

B. Following is a portion of a keyboard suite by François Couperin. The first couplet may be regarded as a theme followed by several variations. (Couplets 3, 4, and 6 are given.) Answer the questions posed as completely as possible.

1. First Couplet (Theme)

   a. Using letter names, describe the form. What musical elements create this form?
   b. Identify the cadences present. Which is the strongest and why?
   c. Identify by Roman numeral the chord of m. 13.
   d. Locate an example of a six-four chord and indicate its type.

2. Couplets 3, 4, and 6

   Make a chart, similar in format to that on page 323, which shows the elements retained in each variation and the elements that change. Using your chart, indicate which variation you feel differs most substantially from the theme. Which elements are are most consistently retained in the variations?

Couperin: *Les Folies françoises, ou les Dominos*

First Couplet: *La virginité*

Gracieusement

Third Couplet: *L'ardeur (sous le Domino incarnat)*

Animé

Fourth Couplet: *L'espérance*

Gayement

Sixth Couplet: *La persévérance*

Tendrement, sans lenteur

C. Select one of the themes below and construct two complete variations plus the *beginnings* of three more. Order the variations in such a way that fewer and fewer elements of the theme are retained in succeeding variations.

The first step, of course, is to select a convincing harmonization. In so doing, be sure to consider all chord possibilities, implied root relationships, and suggestions of secondary function or brief modulations.

THE PROPERTIES OF SOUND

Music is the organization of sound and silence. *Sound* is the sensation produced in the ear resulting from the fluctuations in air pressure produced by a vibrating object. These fluctuations, called *sound waves,* consist of alternating *compressions* (crowding together) and *rarefactions* (spreading apart) of the air molecules. Unless obstructed, they radiate outward from the source in all directions. The distance from one point of maximum compression or rarefaction to the next constitutes a single *cycle* of a sound wave.

Illustration A1.1

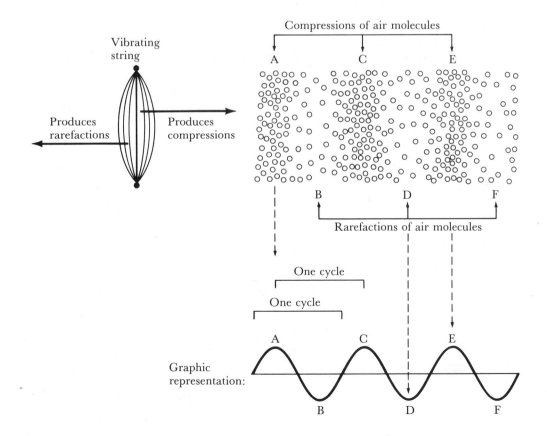

Sound has three physical properties that we perceive as sensory characteristics. They are:

Physical property	Sensory characteristic
frequency	pitch
amplitude	loudness
harmonic content	color (timbre)

FREQUENCY AND PITCH

Frequency is the rate at which a periodic (regularly recurring) vibration pattern repeats itself, measured in *cycles per second* (also called "Hertz"). A *continuing* periodic vibration results in a *musical tone*—a sound of definite pitch. The higher the frequency of a musical tone, the higher we perceive the pitch to be. So-called "tuning A" —the standard orchestral tuning pitch—has a frequency of 440 Hertz, while middle C on the piano keyboard has a frequency of 261.63 Hertz. The ear perceives every doubling of frequency as a pitch rise of an octave. Therefore, the A one octave below "tuning A" is 220 Hertz, while the A an octave below *that* pitch is 110 Hertz. The A two octaves below *this* pitch—the lowest A on the piano, is, at 27.5 Hertz, slightly above the *threshold of pitch discrimination*. This frequency, nominally 15 Hertz, is the point below which we hear the beating of the air compressions rather than a steady musical tone.

AMPLITUDE AND LOUDNESS

The *strength* of an object's vibration (as opposed to its *rate* of vibration) determines a sound wave's *amplitude*—the measure of the difference in air pressure between compressions and rarefactions. The greater the difference in pressure, the higher the amplitude and the louder the perceived sound.

Illustration A1.2

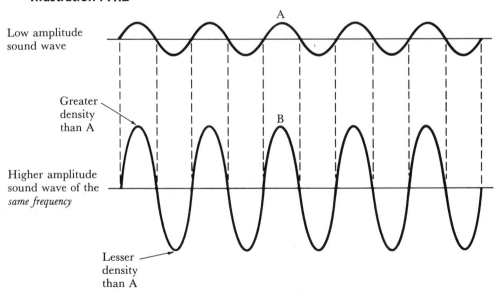

Low amplitude sound wave

Greater density than A

Higher amplitude sound wave of the *same frequency*

Lesser density than A

NOTE: Cycle lengths of the two waveforms correspond. Waveform B and waveform A will have an identical pitch, but waveform B will sound louder than waveform A.

**THE HARMONIC
SERIES
AND TIMBRE**

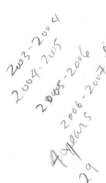

Strings, pipes, and other objects tend to vibrate in segments of their length as well as in their entirety. These different modes of vibration, which occur simultaneously, produce frequency components called *harmonics.* The frequency produced by an object vibrating in its total length is called the *fundamental.* It is usually the loudest of the pitches produced. Harmonics are exact whole-number multiples of the fundamental frequency. They "color" the sound of the fundamental, imparting a characteristic tone color, or *timbre.* The example here shows how the vibrations of a string at its entire length, one-third its length, and one-fourth its length exist simultaneously.

If vibration mode A produces a fundamental (first harmonic) of (110 Hertz), then vibration mode B produces the first *overtone,* or *second* harmonic (220 Hertz—twice the frequency of the fundamental) and vibration mode C produces the second overtone, or *third* harmonic (330 Hertz—three times the frequency of the fundamental).

Illustration A1.3

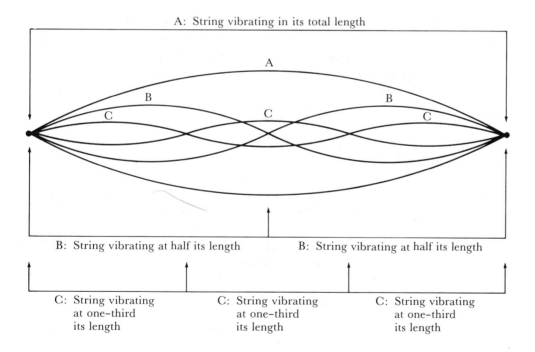

A: String vibrating in its total length

B: String vibrating at half its length   B: String vibrating at half its length

C: String vibrating
at one-third
its length

C: String vibrating
at one-third
its length

C: String vibrating
at one-third
its length

Although this process continues, producing harmonics four times the fundamental, five times the fundamental and so on, the higher harmonics decrease rapidly in amplitude, to the point at which they have little or no effect on the sound. The complex of harmonics present in most musical tones, called the *harmonic series,* or *overtone series,* is shown in the following illustration, above a fundamental of 𝄢.

HARMONIC SERIES

Illustration A1.4

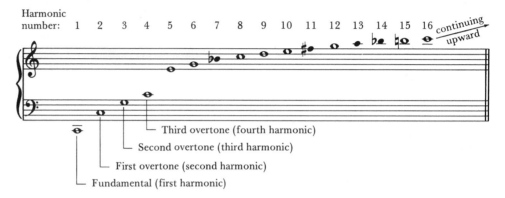

Harmonic number: 1 2 3 4 5 6 7 8 9 10 11 12 13 14 15 16 continuing upward

Third overtone (fourth harmonic)
Second overtone (third harmonic)
First overtone (second harmonic)
Fundamental (first harmonic)

NOTE: The frequency ratio between any two tones in this complex is identical to the ratio of their harmonic numbers. Black notes indicate pitches that can be only approximately designated by our notation system.

CONSONANCE VERSUS DISSONANCE

Unlike the foregoing properties of sound, consonance and dissonance are not *purely physical* attributes. From an acoustic point of view, the more harmonious the relationship of two tones—that is, *the simpler their frequency ratio*—the more consonant their resulting sound. This is because, in the simpler frequency ratios, the compressions and rarefactions of the air molecules coincide more often.

Illustration A1.5

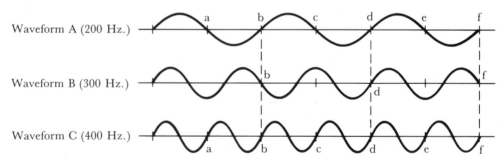

Waveform A (200 Hz.)
Waveform B (300 Hz.)
Waveform C (400 Hz.)

NOTE:

Waveforms A and C (a 2:1 ratio) have *six points of correspondence* (labeled a-f).

Waveforms A and B (a 3:2 ratio) have only *three points of correspondence* (labeled b, d, and f).

The simplest of ratios is that formed by the first two members of the harmonic series—the fundamental and first overtone. This produces the most consonant sound combination—the *octave*. So consonant is this sound that it may at times be mistaken for a single pitch. It is because of this that pitches an octave apart are given the same letter name and the octave is the standard distance within which the musical space is further divided.

Our method of dividing the octave into twelve half steps having identical frequency ratios is a relatively recent one, which did not gain widespread acceptance until the nineteenth century. *Equal temperament,* as it is called, is actually an "out-of-tune" tuning. That is to say, each half step is slightly smaller than its acoustically pure size. An "acoustically pure" interval is one that displays the simplest possible frequency ratio. The members of the harmonic series display acoustically pure relationships. For example, the octave has a frequency ratio of 2:1, the perfect fifth a ratio of 3:2, the perfect fourth a ratio of 4:3 and so on.*

Illustration A1.6

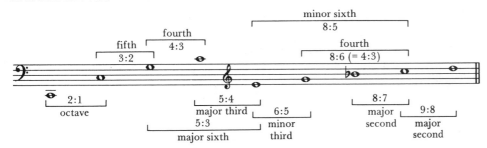

The frequency ratio of the acoustically pure half step is 16:15—the ratio between the sixteenth and fifteenth harmonics. If, however, twelve of these half steps were stacked above one another, they would span an interval *one quarter tone* (half of a half step) *larger than an octave.* It is because of this discrepancy that each half step is made slightly smaller in equal temperament. As a result, the only acoustically pure interval is the octave, while all the others deviate in varying degrees from their simplest ratios.

Because we are accustomed to these intervals, normally the discrepancies are not obvious to us. However, when an instrumentalist, such as a violinist, plays with an instrument of fixed pitch such as the piano, the violinist will find that he or she must make constant pitch adjustments in order to play "in tune" with the piano. These and other tuning problems in ensemble playing often result from this inherent discrepancy.

*Note that the frequency ratios are the same as the harmonic number ratios.

APPENDIX TWO
A METHOD FOR
INTERVAL SPELLING

A simple method for spelling intervals involves the use of reference intervals, which can be found readily and can be used as points of departure for spelling intervals that are close to them in size. Natural reference points are, of course, the unison and octave. Also useful are the perfect fourth and perfect fifth, since they are approximately halfway between the unison and octave in size.

> *NOTE:* Any interval that encompasses five letter names constitutes a *perfect* fifth unless the two notes are B and F, in which case they constitute a *diminished* fifth. To maintain a perfect fifth relationship between two such tones (other than B and F), apply the same accidental before each pitch.

Illustration A2.1

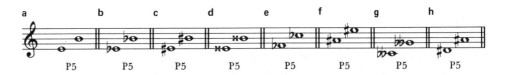

All of these intervals are perfect. Notice that *the same type of accidental* precedes both notes of the interval. However:

To make this interval perfect, it must be enlarged by a half step in one of two ways.

B and F are the only two letter names a fifth apart that are not perfect. This is because they form the only fifth that contains both half steps of the C major scale—E-F and B-C. As a result, the fifth formed is smaller by one half step than all the others.

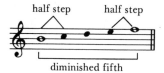

NOTE: Any interval that encompasses four letter names constitutes a *perfect* fourth unless the two notes are F and B, in which case they constitute an *augmented fourth*. To maintain a perfect fourth relationship between two such tones (other than F and B), apply the same accidental before each pitch. For example:

Illustration A2.2

All these intervals are perfect. Notice that *the same type of accidental* precedes both notes of the interval. However:

To make this interval perfect, it must be made smaller by a half step in one of two ways.

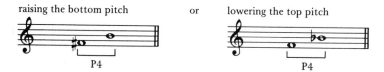

F and B are the only two letter names a fourth apart that are not perfect. This is because they form the only fourth that contains neither half step of the C major scale—B-C or E-F. As a result, the fourth formed is larger by one half step than all the others. With the unison, octave, perfect fourth, and perfect fifth as reference intervals, it is possible to spell quickly all the other intervals using the chart given on page 58. For example, to spell a major sixth above D♭, use the closest reference interval—the perfect fifth, which, above D♭ would be A♭. (Count up to the fifth letter name and add the same accidental.) Then add a major second.

Illustration A2.3

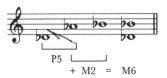

Similarly, to find a major third below A♭, count downward four letter names to E♭ (using the same accidental), which is a perfect fourth. Since the major third is a half step smaller than the perfect fourth, move upward by a minor second.

Illustration A2.4

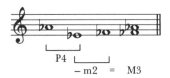

NOTE: You must move upward to F♭, *not* E♮, since the interval formed by A♭ down to E♮ still involves *four* letter names and is, therefore, a *fourth* rather than a *third.*

TERMS RELATING TO TEMPO, EXPRESSION AND PERFORMANCE

Terms Relating to Tempo

Accelerando: becoming faster

Adagio: slow, leisurely

Ad libitum: at liberty to vary from strict tempo

Allargando: growing broader

Allegretto: moderately fast (a tempo between *andante* and *allegro*)

Allegro: rapid tempo (literally, "cheerful")

Andante: moderately slow (between *adagio* and *moderato*)

Andantino: moderately slow

Animando: with growing animation

A tempo: at the (basic) tempo

Doppio movimento: twice as fast

Langsam: slow

Larghetto: slightly faster than *largo*

Largo: very slow, broad

Lento (lent): slow (between *largo* and *adagio*)

Moderato: at moderate speed

Presto: very quick (faster than *allegro*)

Rallentando: becoming slower

Ritardando: becoming slower

Ritenuto: immediately slower

Rubato: flexible tempo, through slight quickening and lessening of pace

Stringendo: quickening

Tempo primo: at the original tempo

Vivace: quick, lively

Vivo: lively

Common Expressive Markings and Other Terms Relating to Manner of Performance

Agitato: agitated, excited

Animato: animated

À piacere: execution left to performer's discretion

Appassionato: impassioned

Assai: very (used with other terms, as in *allegro assai*)

Attacca: continue without pause

Cantabile: in a singing style

Colla parte: the accompanist is to follow the soloist in tempo

Come prima: as at first

Con brio: with spirit

Dolce: sweetly

Espressivo: expressively

Grave: slow, serious

Grazioso: graceful

Legato: smoothly connected

Lunga: long, sustained

Maestoso: majestic

Marcato: with marked emphasis

Meno: less (used with other terms, as in *meno mosso*)

Molto: much (used with other terms, as in *molto meno mosso*)

Morendo: dying away

Mosso: rapid

Obbligato: a part that cannot be omitted

Ossia: alternate passage

Perdendosi: gradually dying away

Pesante: heavy

Più: more (used with other terms, as in *più mosso*)

Plus: more

Poco: little (used with other terms, as in *poco accelerando*)

Poco a poco: little by little

Quasi niente: almost nothing

Retenu: hold back

Scherzando: playful

Semplice: in a simple manner

Sempre: always

Senza: without (used with other terms, as in *senza vibrato*)

Sforzando: sudden emphasis

Sfumato: fading away

Simile: in a similar manner

Smorzando: dying away

Sonore: full, sonorous

Sostenuto: sustained

Sotto voce: subdued, in an undertone

Staccato: detached, disconnected

Subito: suddenly

Tacet: silent

Tenuto: sustained

Tranquillo: quiet, calm

Très: very (used with others terms, as in *très vif*)

Troppo: too much

Tutti: all (instruments)

Vif: lively

Not all instruments are pitched *in concert*—that is, not all of them produce a *sounding* pitch that corresponds identically (allowing for octave transpositions) to the *written* pitch played. Those which do are *concert pitch instruments*. Those which do not are *transposing instruments*.

> *NOTE:* The name of the key in which an instrument is pitched is the note that will sound when that instrument plays a *written C.*

The B♭ clarinet will produce a sounding B♭ when a written C is played. In other words, the B♭ clarinet *sounds a major second lower than written.* To produce a sounding C, the clarinet must play a written D. Therefore, B♭ clarinet parts must be *written a major second higher than the intended sound.*

Following are the ranges and transpositions of the more common instruments. Black notes are the safe, practical range for nonprofessional players, while white notes show the extended range available to more advanced players. In most cases, the upward range can be further extended by highly accomplished players.

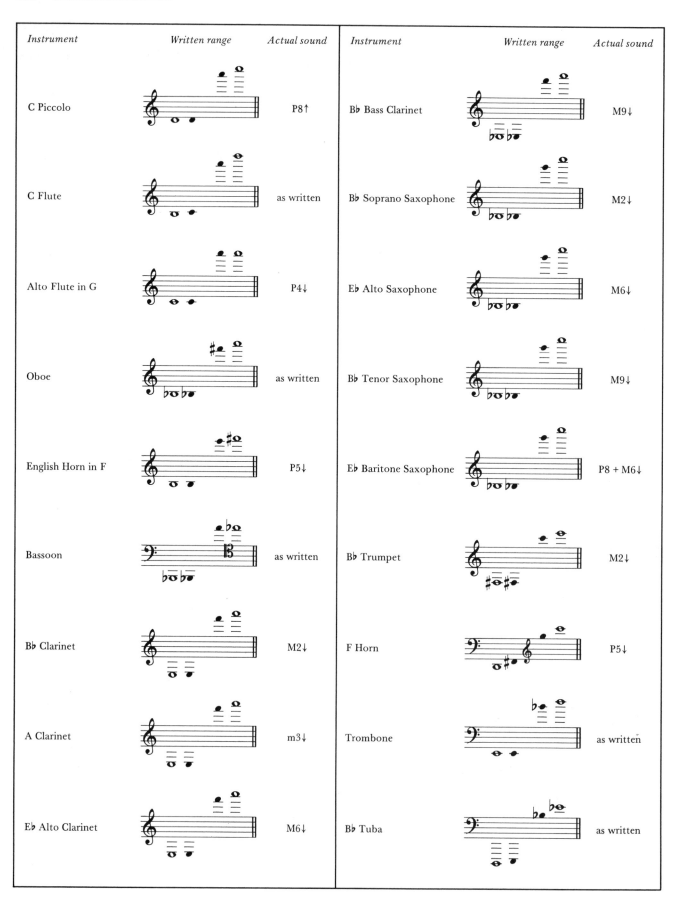

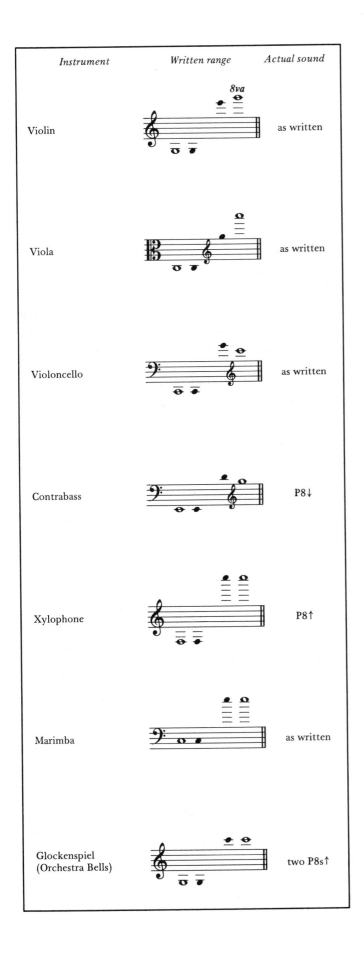

GLOSSARY

Accent: Emphasis placed on a particular note through metric placement, dynamic level, articulation, duration, or register.

Accidental: A sign placed before a note to indicate a temporary raising or lowering of its pitch or a cancellation of a previous accidental.

Agogic accent: Emphasis placed on a particular note by virtue of its longer duration than the surrounding notes.

Amplitude: A measure of the difference in air pressure between compressions and rarefactions, a difference which the ear perceives as loudness.

Antecedent: In a period, the first of the phrases, ending without a sense of completion and requiring a consequent phrase to bring about a resolution.

Anticipation: An embellishing tone usually found at cadences, in which one voice, usually the soprano, resolves to its cadence pitch ahead of the other voices.

Appoggiatura: An embellishing tone approached by leap and resolved to a metrically weaker pitch by step, usually in the opposite direction of the leap.

Arpeggiated six-four chord: A second-inversion triad, most often a tonic, that results when the chord is outlined by the lowest voice of the texture.

Articulation: An aspect of musical performance involving the manner in which a sound is initiated or the way sounds are connected or separated.

Asymmetric meter: A meter in which the pulses of the measure are not grouped in equal units of two or three, but are grouped in units of five ($\frac{5}{8}$), seven ($\frac{7}{4}$), and so on.

Augmentation dot: A sign that, placed after a note or rest, extends its duration by one-half the undotted value.

Authentic cadence: The harmonic formula V-I (or V-i in minor keys) that serves as a point of punctuation and repose at the end of a musical thought.

Bar line: A vertical line that extends from the top to the bottom of the staff and separates the measures.

Bass: 1) A voice type with an approximate range from E to c^1; 2) The term normally used to refer to the lowest voice of a multiple-voice texture.

Beat: A durational unit synonymous with pulse in simple meters, but comprising three pulses in compound meters.

Binary form: *See* simple binary form.

Borrowed division: The use of a simple division of the beat in a compound meter, or the reverse—a compound division of the beat in a simple meter.

Breve: The longest single note value in current use, equivalent to two whole notes.

Cadence: A point of melodic and/or harmonic repose, often created through a slowing or pause in motion and serving as a punctuation between phrases.

Cadential elision: A process in which the end of one phrase and the beginning of the next phrase coincide, thereby avoiding a cadential separation between the two.

Cadential extension: The lengthening of a musical phrase upon repetition through a restatement or expansion of its cadence.

Cadential six-four chord: A metrically strong second-inversion tonic triad preceding the dominant at a cadence, and in fact best analyzed as a dominant with nonchord tones a fourth and sixth above the bass.

Chaconne: A series of continuous variations in which the theme is a repeated harmonic pattern, usually four to eight measures in length.

Chain suspension: A series of suspension figures in which the resolution of one suspension becomes the preparation for the next.

Changing tone: A two-note embellishing tone involving the pitches a step above and below a more important tone and its repetition.

Chorale: A hymn tune that originated in the Lutheran Church during the sixteenth century, comprising several stanzas of verse sung to the same music.

Chord: A single musical sound comprising three or more different pitches (not counting octave duplications).

Chordal: A type of texture in which all parts move with the same rhythms, producing a succession of harmonies.

Chord spacing: *See* spacing.

Chromatic: A term referring to music or intervals not confined to the pitch material of a given scale or mode.

Chromatic alteration: The raising or lowering of a pitch by one or two half steps through the prefixing of an accidental.

Chromatic scale: The scale formed by all twelve pitches of the octave, arranged in ascending or descending order.

Chromatic tendency tone: A chromatically altered pitch with a strong inclination to resolve by half step. Chromatically raised pitches usually tend upward while chromatically lowered pitches tend downward.

Chromatic tone modulation: A change of tonal center in which a diatonic pitch and its chromatic alteration in the following chord signal the modulation.

Church modes: *See* modes.

Clef: A sign placed at the left side of a staff to indicate which lines and spaces represent the various pitches.

Close structure: A type of chord spacing in which the soprano, alto, and tenor voices are as close together as possible.

Closely related keys: The five tonalities that differ from a given tonality by no more than one flat or sharp—hence, the relative major or minor, the dominant and its relative key, and the subdominant and its relative key.

Cofinal: A secondary focal pitch in the Church modes, next to the final in importance. It is often called the reciting tone.

Common chord: A pivot chord that is diatonic in both the old and the new keys.

Compound interval: An interval exceeding the octave in size.

Compound meter: A meter in which the primary division of the beat is into three parts.

Compression: In the cycle of a sound wave, the point at which the air pressure is higher than it would normally be in the absence of a sound wave.

Conclusive cadence: A cadence that sounds relatively final, ending on a tonic harmony, with the melody usually ending on the tonic pitch or, sometimes, on a member of the tonic triad.

Conjunct motion: Melodic motion involving stepwise intervals.

Consecutive fifths, octaves, or unisons: A succession of perfect fifths, perfect octaves, or perfect unisons between the same two voices.

Consequent: The final phrase of a period, which, due to its more conclusive cadence, provides a greater sense of completion than the antecedent phrase(s).

Continuo: The name given to the figured bass line in baroque-era compositions or the group of instruments that plays the figured bass (usually a keyboard instrument and a melodic bass instrument, such as the viola da gamba).

Contrary motion: The movement by two voices from one tone to the next in the opposite direction.

Contrasting period: Phrases in antecedent-consequent relationship which are composed of different material and differ in general character.

Corelli clash: A particularly striking dissonance used frequently at cadences by Corelli (somewhat less often by other baroque-era composers), in which the leading tone (often the resolution of a 4-3 suspension) occurs simultaneously with an anticipation of the tonic in another voice.

Counterpoint: Music consisting of two or more melodic lines heard simultaneously but displaying a certain degree of independence (of contour and rhythm).

Cross relation: The occurrence of a pitch and its chromatically altered form on successive beats but in different voices of the texture.

Cross rhythm: The simultaneous occurrence of two or more conflicting rhythms, one of which typically involves a borrowed division of the beat.

Cycle: A term used to identify one complete occurrence of a compression and rarefaction of the air molecules in a sound wave.

Deceptive cadence: A two-chord formula punctuating a musical thought, in which the dominant triad moves to any chord but the tonic. The chord most frequently substituted for the expected tonic triad is the submediant.

Delayed resolution: A stepwise downward movement of a chordal seventh that takes place only after a pitch or group of pitches intervene, postponing the resolution for a period of time.

Diatonic: A term referring to music or intervals confined to the pitch material of a given scale or mode.

Diminished seventh chord: The chord formed by the addition of a diminished seventh above the root of a diminished triad. It most often occurs on the leading tone of a minor key (vii^{o7}).

Direct fifths, direct octaves: The approach to a perfect fifth or perfect octave by two voices in similar motion.

Disjunct motion: Melodic motion involving intervals larger than a whole step.

Dominant: The functional name given to the fifth degree of a major or minor scale, or to the triad formed on this pitch.

Dominant seventh chord: The seventh-chord type formed on the dominant scale degree, consisting of a major triad with a minor seventh above its root. Because this type of seventh chord appears diatonically only on the dominant, it is simply called the dominant seventh.

Double flat: A sign that, placed before a note, lowers its pitch by two half steps.

Double period: Four phrases, in which the final phrase ends more conclusively than the preceding three phrases. The phrases may be similar (called a parallel double period) or dissimilar (called a contrasting double period).

Double sharp: A sign that, placed before a note, raises its pitch by two half steps.

Dramatic peak: Usually a point of maximum intensity that is often the focal point of a composition. It is often the point to which the music builds and from which it subsides to come to a close.

Dramatic shape: The psychological or emotional form of a work, as determined by its impact on the listener.

Duple meter: A meter in which the beats are grouped two to a measure.

Dynamic accent: Emphasis placed on a particular note by virtue of its performance at a louder level or with a more emphatic articulation than the surrounding notes.

Dynamics: Markings used to indicate the relative levels of loudness or softness of a musical passage.

Embellishing tone: A pitch that serves as a connection between or decoration of the more important pitches of a melodic line.

Enharmonic: A term referring to different spellings of the same pitch or interval.

Enharmonic intervals: Two intervals sounding alike but having different numerical designations and qualities, such as E♭-G♭ (a minor third) and E♭-F♯ (an augmented second).

Enharmonic keys: Two keys having the same pitch material and tonic but employing different spellings of one or more pitches, such as G♭ and F♯.

Escape tone: An embellishing tone approached by step and left by leap.

Figure: A group of pitches, usually from three to eight, bound together in a distinctive rhythmic pattern.

Figured bass: A notational method in general use for keyboard instruments during the seventeenth and eighteenth centuries. Numbers beneath the pitches of the bass line indicate the intervals to be added above the line, and thus indicate the harmonies as well.

Final: The central tone of a mode, usually the tone upon which melodies in the mode end.

First inversion: Any arrangement of the tones of a triad or seventh chord in which the third of the chord appears as the lowest pitch.

Flat: A sign which, placed before a note, lowers its pitch by one half step.

Free-voice texture: A musical texture in which the number of voices varies.

Frequency: The rate of a periodic vibration, usually expressed as a number of cycles per second, which directly affects our perception of pitch.

Functional tonality: A term describing the system by which the chords of a major or minor key are related to each other and to the tonic.

Fundamental: The lowest (and, usually the loudest) tone in a harmonic series, produced by a body (a string or air column, for example) vibrating in its entirety.

Grand staff: The combined treble and bass clef staves, on which keyboard music is notated.

Ground: A short, repeated bass line, usually four to eight measures in length. Grounds form the basis of many baroque variations, notably the passacaglia and chaconne.

Half cadence: Most commonly, a harmonic cadence ending on the dominant triad.

Half-diminished seventh chord: The chord formed by the addition of a minor seventh above the root of a diminished triad. This chord appears diatonically on the leading tone of a major key (vii^{ø7}) and on the supertonic of a minor key (ii^{ø7}).

Half step: The smallest interval normally used in Western music and the smallest interval on the piano.

Harmonic: 1) A term generally used to refer to the effect of several musical lines in combination; 2) In acoustics, the frequency components in a periodic waveform that exist in integral (whole number) multiples of the fundamental frequency.

Harmonic minor scale: The natural minor scale with the seventh degree raised by one half step. It is the form most often found to be the harmonic basis of melodies in minor keys.

Harmonic repetition: The successive sounding of the same chord or of two chords that are functionally similar, such as a subdominant and a supertonic, both of which are pre-dominants.

Harmonic rhythm: The series of durational patterns formed by the chord changes in a piece of music.

Harmonic series: In a complex waveform, the spectrum of frequencies that are whole-number multiples of the fundamental frequency. This series of frequency components is responsible for giving a sound its timbre or tone quality.

Harmony: The effect produced by the simultaneous sounding of several discrete pitches.

Hemiola: A particular type of 3:2 rhythmic ratio involving successive or simultaneous divisions of the quantity six in two ways—as two groups of three units and as three groups of two units.

Hertz: A unit designating one cycle per second of a periodic waveform.

Homophonic: A texture in which one line is the most important and the others have a clearly supporting role.

Imperfect authentic cadence: A V-I harmonic pattern lacking either the tonic in the soprano on the final chord or the descending fifth motion in the bass.

Inconclusive cadence: A cadence that sounds less final than a conclusive cadence, usually ending on a pitch and/or chord other than the tonic and requiring an eventual resolution to the tonic.

Interval: The musical distance between two pitches.

Inversion: 1) Octave transposition of one of the pitches of an interval so that the lower pitch becomes the higher pitch and vice versa; 2) Any position of a triad or seventh chord in which the root is not the lowest voice.

Key signature: An inventory of the flats or sharps used consistently within a composition or within a section of a composition, grouped together and placed immediately after the clef sign at the beginning of each staff.

Large-scale arpeggiation: Broken triad formations created by nonadjacent pitches, normally structural tones, occurring over a relatively long time span within a melody.

Leading tone: The functional name given to the major or minor scale degree one half step below the tonic, or to the triad formed on this pitch.

Ledger lines: Short horizontal lines representing an extension of the staff, drawn through the stems of notes too high or low to be placed directly on the staff.

Legato: A manner of performance in which the notes are connected together, with little separation between them.

Loco: A direction used to cancel the effect of an ottava sign.

Major scale: A seven-tone scale with the interval pattern of whole step, whole step, half step, whole step, whole step, whole step, half step.

Major seventh chord: The chord formed by the addition of a major seventh above the root of a major triad. It is most often found on the sub-dominant of a major key (IV⁷) and on the submediant and mediant (VI⁷ and III⁷) of a minor key.

Measure: One complete cycle of the accentual pattern in a given meter.

Mediant: The functional name given to the third degree of a major or minor scale, or to the triad formed on this pitch.

Melodic minor scale: The natural minor scale with the sixth and seventh degrees raised by one half step in ascent. In descending passages, the sixth and seventh degrees usually are those of the natural minor scale. It is the form most often found to be the basis of minor-key melodies.

Melody: A succession of pitches of varying durations, organized so as to constitute a musical idea or a succession of ideas.

Meter: A regularly recurring pattern of strong and weak pulses that forms the background on which the many rhythms of a piece of music are imposed.

Metric: An adjective referring to music organized in measures, that is, according to an underlying pattern of strong and weak pulses.

Minor scale: One of three seven-tone scale forms (natural, harmonic or melodic), whose lowest five tones exhibit the interval pattern of whole step, half step, whole step, whole step.

Minor seventh chord: The chord formed by the addition of a minor seventh above the root of a minor triad. It is most often found on the supertonic of a major key (ii⁷) and on the subdominant of a minor key (iv⁷).

Modes: A set of scales that formed the basis of much medieval and Renaissance music, predating the major and minor scales.

Modified sequence: A sequence in which some small change occurs (other than the change of interval quality that constitutes a tonal sequence).

Modulation: The process of changing tonal centers.

Monophonic: A texture consisting of a single musical line, which may be stated by one or more instruments or voices.

Motive (motif): A short melodic/rhythmic gesture that appears often enough during a composition to serve a unifying function.

Natural: A sign placed before a note to cancel the effect of any sharp or flat previously in effect and to restore the pitch to its unaltered state.

Natural minor scale: A seven-tone scale with the interval pattern of whole step, half step, whole step, whole step, half step, whole step, whole step.

Neighbor tone: An embellishing tone occurring stepwise between a more important pitch and its repetition.

Neumes: Symbols indicating general upward and downward vocal inflections. They were an early form of pitch notation.

Nonchord tone: The term used to describe embellishing tones when they occur in a harmonic context and are not part of the prevailing chord.

Oblique motion: The movement by one voice from one tone to a different tone while a second voice remains on the same tone.

Octave: A term referring to the interval spanned by twelve half steps, from a given pitch to the next higher or lower pitch of the same letter name. The frequency ratio between two such pitches is 2:1.

Open structure: A type of chord spacing in which the soprano, alto, and tenor voices are not as close together as possible.

Ottava sign: A symbol (8va) that, placed above a pitch, directs that it be performed an octave higher than written.

Overtone: Any of the harmonics occurring above the fundamental frequency.

Parallel major and minor: A major and minor scale pair sharing the same tonic.

Parallel motion: The movement by two voices from one tone to the next in the same direction and by the same number of steps.

Parallel period: Phrases in antecedent-consequent relationship, the last beginning with the same or similar material as the first but ending more conclusively.

Passacaglia: A continuous variation form over a repeated melody, which first most often appears in the bass but which is not restricted to the bass.

Passing six-four chord: A second-inversion triad, usually a dominant or tonic, in which the motion of the individual voices through the doubled chord tone (the fifth) resembles that of a passing tone. The resulting chord becomes, in effect, a passing chord.

Passing tone: An embellishing tone occurring stepwise between two more important tones of different pitch.

Pedal point: A pitch that is sustained or repeated while the other voices of the texture change pitch, creating dissonances against it.

Pedal six-four chord: A second-inversion triad, usually a subdominant or tonic, in which the bass line remains stationary prior to and following the chord itself, resembling a pedal point.

Perfect authentic cadence: A V-I harmonic pattern in which the tonic appears in the soprano on the final chord *and* the bass motion is a descending fifth from chord root to chord root.

Period: Two phrases, sometimes three, that are perceived as a unit because the final phrase ends more conclusively than the preceding phrase(s), thereby providing a greater sense of completion.

Periodic: In acoustics, a repeating waveform. Fixed musical tones are generated by periodic waveforms.

Phrase: A melodic unit, typically four to eight measures in length, which expresses a more or less complete musical thought.

Phrase compression: A technique employed upon repetition of a phrase, in which some portion is omitted or the phrase is otherwise shortened.

Phrase extension: A means of expanding a phrase upon repetition by adding material to its beginning, middle, or end.

Phrase member: Melodic units larger than a figure or motive that, in combination, form a phrase.

Phrygian cadence: A particular type of half cadence, found only in minor, comprising the chords iv^6-V.

Pitch: The sensation of highness or lowness attributed to a musical tone, which is the result of the frequency of a periodic waveform.

Pivot-chord modulation: A change of tonal center in which one chord, functioning in both the old and new keys, acts as a link between them.

Plagal cadence: The two-chord formula IV-I (or iv-i in minor keys) concluding a musical thought.

Polyphonic: A texture consisting of two or more independent melodic lines.

Pre-dominant: Chords that normally proceed directly to the dominant—the subdominant and the supertonic.

Pre-dominant seventh chords: The seventh chords that most often lead to a dominant-functioning chord. These are the supertonic seventh and the subdominant seventh.

Progression: The strongest type of harmonic motion, in which each chord moves to the next closest chord to the tonic, as measured in descending-fifth root movements. Harmonic progression generates a satisfying feeling of forward momentum.

Prolongation: The elaboration and extension of a structural tone through supporting and embellishing tones.

Pulse: A regularly recurring stress through which the durational values of a work are measured. In simple meters, the term pulse is usually synonymous with beat. In compound meters, three pulses usually equal one beat.

Range: The distance spanned by the highest and lowest pitches of a melodic line.

Rarefaction: The point in the cycle of a sound wave where the air pressure is less than the normal air pressure (the air pressure in the absence of the sound wave).

Real sequence: An intervallically exact transposition of a musical idea by the same instrument or voice in immediate or close succession.

Reciting tone: *See* cofinal.

Relative major and minor: A major and minor scale pair sharing the same key signature.

Repeated phrases: Two phrases in immediate succession, the second an exact repetition of the first.

Repetition: A type of harmonic motion in which a chord is repeated or moves to another chord of the same classification (i.e., pre-dominant to pre-dominant).

Resolution: The motion from a tone or chord to another tone or chord of greater stability.

Retardation: An upward-resolving suspension.

Retrogression: A type of harmonic motion in which each chord moves to a new chord farther removed from the tonic as measured in ascending-fifth root movements, such as a supertonic to a submediant.

Rhythm: A term referring generally to the temporal aspects of music—the duration of the sounds and silences.

Root: In a triad, or seventh chord, the note above which the other notes can be arranged as a stack of thirds.

Root position: Any arrangement of the tones of a chord in which the root appears as the lowest pitch.

Rounded binary form: A two-part form in which the second part is "rounded off" by a return, usually partial, of the opening material and tonality.

Scale: An inventory of the pitches that form the basis of a musical composition, arranged in ascending or descending order.

Secondary dominant, secondary leading tone chords: Chords that momentarily function as dominants, dominant sevenths, leading tone triads, or leading tone seventh chords with respect to a temporary (secondary) tonic.

Second inversion: Any arrangement of the tones of a triad or seventh chord in which the fifth of the chord appears as the lowest pitch.

Sequence: The immediate or nearly immediate repetition of a melodic figure by the same voice or instrument but at a different pitch level.

Seventh chord: A four-note chord formed when a seventh above the chord root is added to a triad.

Sharp: A sign that, placed before a note, raises its pitch by one half step.

Similar motion: The movement by two voices from one tone to the next in the same direction but by a different number of steps.

Simple binary form: A musical form, especially common during the baroque era, that consists of two principal parts distinguished primarily by the clear cadence that separates them. Although the two parts are generally similar in character, the form is usually designated by the letters A|B.

Simple interval: An interval whose span is an octave or less.

Simple meter: A meter in which the primary division of the beat is into two parts.

Six-four chord: A second-inversion triad.

Slur: A curved line placed above or below two or more notes that are to be performed in a legato (smoothly connected) fashion.

Soprano: 1) A voice type with an approximate range from c^1 to g^2; 2) The term normally used to refer to the highest voice of a multiple-voice texture.

Sound wave: A series of air pressure variations caused by a vibrating object which, through impact upon the ear drum, are transmitted to the brain and interpreted as sound.

Spacing: The manner of distributing the notes of a chord among the various voices of the texture.

Staff: A set of five horizontal lines, on and between which musical notes are written. In conjunction with a clef sign, it indicates the pitches of the notes appearing on it.

Step progression: The stepwise connection of important (usually nonadjacent) pitches in a melody that contribute to its sense of overall direction.

Structural tones: The most important pitches in a melody, that serve as focal points toward, from, or around which the other pitches move.

Subdominant: The functional name given to the fourth degree of a major or minor scale, or to the triad formed on this pitch.

Submediant: The functional name given to the sixth degree of a major or minor scale, or to the triad formed on this pitch.

Supertonic: The functional name given to the second degree of a major or minor scale, or to the triad formed on this pitch.

Supporting tone: A tone generally longer and metrically stronger than an embellishing tone but secondary in importance to a structural tone.

Suspension: The dissonance created when one voice in a texture of two or more voices is delayed in its downward stepwise motion from one tone to the next.

Syncopation: The shift in accentuation to a normally unaccented portion of a beat or measure.

Tempo: The speed of the beat.

Tendency tones: The least stable tones of a scale, each usually separated by a half step from a member of the tonic triad and displaying a strong inclination to resolve to that pitch. *See also* chromatic tendency tone.

Ternary form: A form consisting of three clearly distinct parts, each usually self-contained. The final part is usually a restatement of the first, and the second part displays stronger contrast than is typical of a binary form.

Tetrachord: Any four consecutive pitches of a scale.

Texture: The "fabric" of a musical work or passage, determined by the number of instrumental or vocal parts present and the manner in which these parts fit together. *See* homophonic, monophonic, and polyphonic.

Theme: A musical idea, usually a melody, that forms the basis or starting point for a musical work or some part thereof.

Third inversion: An arrangement of the notes of a seventh chord in which the seventh of the chord appears as the lowest-sounding pitch.

Tie: A curved line connecting two adjacent notes of the same pitch, binding them into a single sound equal to their combined durations.

Timbre: A term referring to the quality of a musical tone (tone color), which is determined by overtone content.

Tonal: A term used to describe music in which a particular pitch is endowed with a feeling of greater importance and finality than the other pitches.

Tonal accent: Emphasis on a particular pitch by its placement in a register higher or lower than the surrounding pitches.

Tonal sequence: A sequence in which the quality of certain intervals is changed, usually to remain diatonic in the key of the original statement.

Tonal shift: An immediate and abrupt change of tonality, usually following a clear cadence in the original key and often without the benefit of a pivot chord.

Tonic: The first and most stable pitch of a given major or minor scale and the pitch for which the scale is named.

Tonicization: A process whereby a chord other than the tonic is caused to sound temporarily like a tonic by being preceded and supported by its own dominant (or dominant seventh chord) or leading tone chord.

Transposition: The process of rewriting a scale, or a passage based on a scale, at a different pitch level.

Triad: A three-note chord in which the notes can be arranged as a stack of thirds, one immediately above the other.

Triple meter: A meter in which the beats are grouped three to a measure.

Variation: An important compositional technique involving the modification, upon repetition, of a musical motive, phrase or theme.

Voice crossing: A motion between two voices in which the lower voice moves above the upper voice momentarily or, conversely, the upper voice moves below the lower voice.

Voice exchange: An early variation technique in which two voices of a texture simply trade musical material.

Voice overlap: An exceptional part-writing practice in which a voice is moved above the preceding pitch of a higher voice or below the preceding pitch of a lower voice.

Whole step: An interval comprising two half steps.

ANSWERS TO COMPREHENSION TESTS

CHAPTER ONE

A. **1** a¹ **2** D **3** g **4** B **5** e³

B.

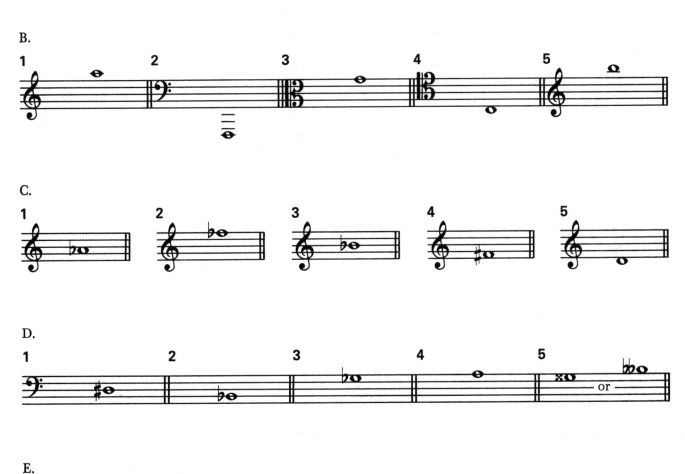

C.

D.

E.

CHAPTER TWO

A. **1** $\frac{6}{8}$ = (4) compound duple

    2 $\frac{4}{2}$ = (3) simple quadruple

    3 $\frac{3}{16}$ = (2) simple triple

    4 $\frac{9}{4}$ = (5) compound triple

    5 $\frac{7}{4}$ = (6) asymmetric

B. **1** (2) syncopation   **2** (1) borrowed division   **3** (4) hemiola   **4** (3) cross rhythm

C. **1** m. 1, beat 3: Stems for notes above the middle line should extend downward.

    2 m. 2, beat 1: For notes occupying an adjacent line and space, the higher note is always to the right.

    3 m. 2, beat 3: Ties should arc *away* from each other.

    4 m. 3, beat 3: Notes that sound together must line up vertically.

    5 m. 4, beat 1: For notes occupying an adjacent line and space, the higher note is always to the right.

    6 m. 4, beat 3: Ledger lines should be spaced evenly above the staff.

    7 m. 5, beat 1: Dots for notes appearing on lines should be placed *above* the line in the adjacent space.

D. **1** *mp* = medium soft

    2 *ff* = very loud

    3 $>$ = accent

    4 ∧ = marcato (accented with detachment between notes)

    5 = staccato (notes to be played detached)

    6 = slur (legato)

CHAPTER THREE

A. **1** Phrygian **2** harmonic minor **3** Lydian **4** Mixolydian **5** Dorian

B. **1** B and g♯ **2** D and b **3** A♭ and f **4** G♭ and e♭ **5** F and d

C. f; d♯; G; D♭; c♯

D.

E. **1** and **6** **2** and **4** **3** and **5** **7** and **10** **8** and **11** **9** and **12**

F.

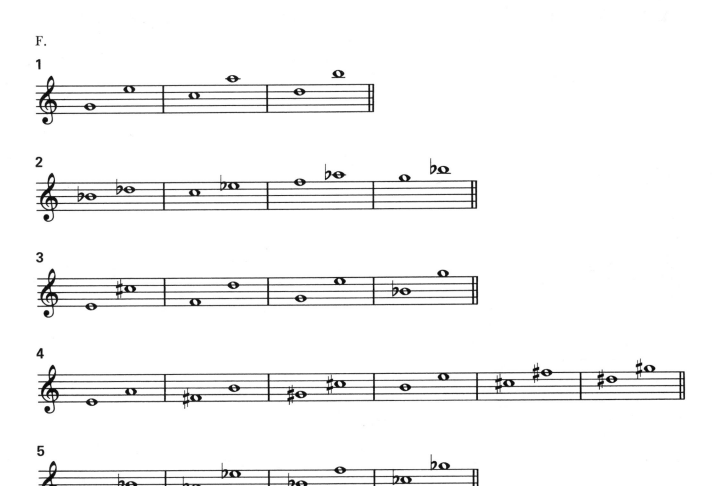

CHAPTER FOUR

A. **1** M **2** + **3** m **4** + **5** °

B.

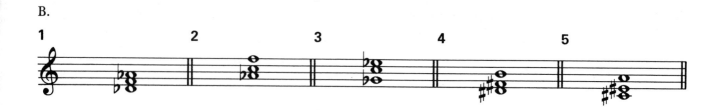

C. **1** V⁶ **2** iii **3** ii⁶ **4** vi⁶₄ **5** vii°⁶

D. **1** deceptive **2** IAC **3** half **4** plagal **5** Phrygian

E.

1 V i **2** IV V **3** iv⁶ V **4** IV I **5** iv⁶ V

CHAPTER FIVE

A.

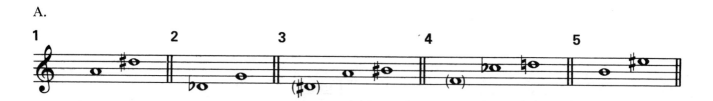

B. **1** 1. d. 2. a.
   2 1. b. 2. a.
   3 1. d. 2. b.

C. **1** (2) tonal **2** (1) real **3** (3) modified real

D. Phrase extension or phrase compression

E. **1** a. and c. **2** ♪♪♪♪ **3** a. prevailingly conjunct **4** b. repetition

CHAPTER SIX

A. Upper voice line only is given.

B.

C.

D.

CHAPTER SEVEN

A.

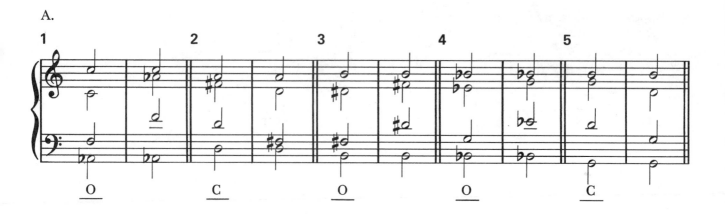

B. The only chord not doubled according to common doubling procedures is **1.**

C. Voicings may vary, depending on the choice of soprano note.

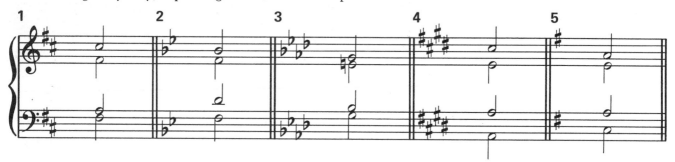

D. Answers may vary, depending on the choice of soprano note.

E. Voicings may vary, depending on the choice of soprano note.

CHAPTER EIGHT

A. **1** P **2** R **3** P **4** S **5** P

B.

E: vi   iii   A♭:   ii⁶   IV   f♯:   V   VI   D: iii   V   B♭:   IV   V

C.

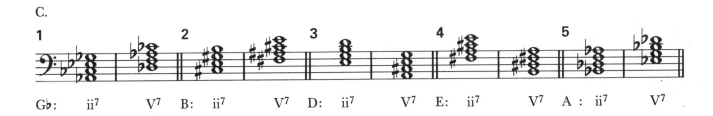

G♭:   ii⁷   V⁷   B: ii⁷   V⁷   D: ii⁷   V⁷   E: ii⁷   V⁷   A :   ii⁷   V⁷

D.

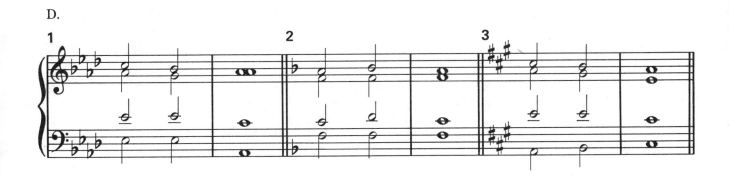

E.

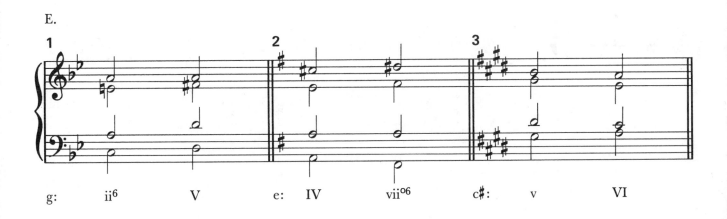

g: ii⁶   V   e: IV   vii°⁶   c♯:   v   VI

CHAPTER TEN / CHAPTER ELEVEN

A.

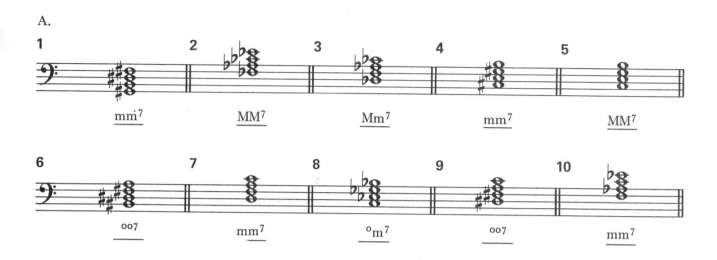

B. **1** ii$^6_5$ **2** vii$^{\emptyset 4}_2$ **3** VI^7 **4** V$^4_3$ **5** ii$^{\emptyset 4}_3$

C.

D.

CHAPTER TWELVE

A. **1** d   **2** b

B. **1** B, g♯   **2** D, b   **3** B♭   **4** F, d   **5** C

C. **1** Chromatic tone modulation from B♭ to C

   2 Pivot chord modulation from D♭ to b♭

   3 Pivot chord modulation from A to E

D. **1** Pivot chord: m. 2, beat 2; B♭: vii^{o6} g: ii^{o6}

   2 Pivot chord: m. 3, beat 2; D: vi   G: iii

   3 Pivot chord: m. 3, beat 1; C: vi   e: iv

   4 Pivot chord: m. 2, beat 2; f: i   A♭: vi

   5 Pivot chord: m. 2, beat 4; E: I^6 B: IV^6

INDEX

ABOUT THE AUTHOR

Ralph Turek received the Doctor of Musical Arts degree in Composition from the University of Cincinnati in 1975. He has received grants from the National Endowment for the Arts and the University of Maryland, and awards from ASCAP and the Union League Civic and Arts Foundation of Chicago. In 1977, he won the Music Teachers National Association Composer of the Year Award. Mr. Turek's compositions have been published by Seesaw Music and Shawnee Press, and he is the author of *Analytical Anthology of Music,* published by Alfred A. Knopf, Inc. He has taught at George Mason University in Fairfax, Virginia, and at the University of Maryland at College Park. Currently an Associate Professor of Music at The University of Akron, Mr. Turek teaches theory, composition, graduate and undergraduate analysis and music history courses, and directs the electronic music studio.